WEIRD AL

WEIRD AL

Seriously

Lily E. Hirsch

Foreword by Dr. Demento

ROWMAN & LITTLEFIELD
Lanham • Boulder • New York • London

Published by Rowman & Littlefield
An imprint of The Rowman & Littlefield Publishing Group, Inc.
4501 Forbes Boulevard, Suite 200, Lanham, Maryland 20706
www.rowman.com

6 Tinworth Street, London SE11 5AL, United Kingdom

British Library Cataloguing in Publication Information Available

Library of Congress Cataloging-in-Publication Data

Names: Hirsch, Lily E., 1979– author.
Title: Weird Al : seriously / Lily E. Hirsch.
Description: Lanham : Rowman & Littlefield Publishing Group, 2020. | Includes index. | Summary: "This is the first book to address in a serious way the impact of the music of 'Weird Al' Yankovic. Through original interviews with the man himself, Lily Hirsch addresses Yankovic's relationship to past parody songs and his unique approach to the art form, inviting music enthusiasts of all stripes to reconsider Yankovic's music"—Provided by publisher.
Identifiers: LCCN 2019038951 (print) | LCCN 2019038952 (ebook) | ISBN 9781538124994 (hardback) | ISBN 9781538125007 (epub)
Subjects: LCSH: Yankovic, Al, 1959– —Criticism and interpretation. | Humorous songs—History and criticism. | Parody in music.
Classification: LCC ML419.Y35 H57 2020 (print) | LCC ML419.Y35 (ebook) | DDC 782.42164092—dc23
LC record available at https://lccn.loc.gov/2019038951
LC ebook record available at https://lccn.loc.gov/2019038952

♾ ™ The paper used in this publication meets the minimum requirements of American National Standard for Information Sciences Permanence of Paper for Printed Library Materials, ANSI/NISO Z39.48-1992.

CONTENTS

FOREWORD

I don't get no respect.—Rodney Dangerfield

That goes double for most of the people who write and/or sing funny songs these days.

Their music is dismissed as ephemeral novelty by serious music fans and as trivial by connoisseurs of spoken comedy.

Today's teenagers—the same age group that once made songs like "Monster Mash," "The Purple People Eater," and "They're Coming to Take Me Away, Ha-Haaa!" instant million-sellers—tend to regard funny songs and their singers as uncool.

Of the thousands of humorous songs released over the past century, most are rarely heard today, and most of the people who wrote and sang them languish in obscurity. However, there's one amazing exception to that rule. Nearly forty years after his first hit record, "Weird Al" Yankovic continues to sell out concert tours. His songs are in demand on streams, downloads, vinyl, and CDs, and he is frequently seen as a guest star on a variety of TV shows and video platforms.

People who first heard Weird Al as children or teenagers are delighted to see he's still as funny as ever and are happy to introduce their own children—or grandchildren—to his videos and live shows. They know he'll keep the whole family entertained with a wealth of clever, energetic, up-to-date—and kid-friendly—humor, presented with first-class musical skills and production values.

There's nobody else like Weird Al, and there never has been. There've been other brilliant and hilarious comedy musicians, some of whom have managed to sustain careers for a decade or two, but Al is in a class by himself. He became the most requested artist on *The Dr. Demento Show* almost as soon as I began playing his music, and he's remained the most requested artist ever since. Others have had huge hits on the show, but Al has never been seriously challenged as the number one artist of comedy music today (and perhaps of all time).

How does Al do it? Like other successful people, he does it with inspiration and perspiration, in something close to equal proportions. He could probably have been successful in any number of other pursuits. He skipped a grade in elementary school. In high school he was the valedictorian of his class and the star of the debate team. After showing early talent for draftsmanship, he prepared for a career in architecture and got his bachelor's degree in that field at California Polytechnic University (Cal Poly) in San Luis Obispo.

There were no professional musicians or comedians in his family before Al, but his parents were fans of the accordion-playing Polka King Frankie Yankovic (no blood relation). On the day before Al's seventh birthday, they bought him an accordion, along with some lessons, and he quickly learned some of the instrument's standard repertoire. He enjoyed making music, but the popularity of polkas and other accordion music was on the decline in the 1970s, so that repertoire didn't promise a great deal of long-term inspiration.

I'm very, very proud that at that point I provided something that did inspire young Al. Starting in 1970 I'd developed a weekly radio show featuring rock 'n' roll oldies especially geared to a contemporary rock audience. From the start, the show had included some of the novelty songs that were heard every so often on Top 40 stations in the 1950s and '60s—songs like "The Purple People Eater," "Monster Mash," and "Transfusion." Listeners requested more and more of those, and I was happy to oblige them.

In 1972 *The Dr. Demento Show* was picked up by KMET-FM, which was on its way to becoming the most listened-to rock station in Los Angeles. Al began listening to the show around 1973, by which time the show was dominated by funny music, and Al discovered such artists as Spike Jones, Tom Lehrer, Stan Freberg, and Allan Sherman. Meanwhile, he began experimenting with playing contemporary rock music on his accordion and taught himself by ear to play every song on Elton John's double album *Goodbye, Yellow Brick Road.*

To publicize my show, I put on programs at local high schools, and in 1973 I came to Lynwood High, where Al was a sophomore. While he was too shy to introduce himself after my appearance, he was inspired enough to start making up comedy songs to sing and play on his accordion. By 1975 I was occasionally playing new tapes of comedy songs made by listeners, including a few who were around Al's age. "I can do that," he thought, and eventually he came up with a song he thought worthy of being played on the show and sent me a cassette.

"Belvedere Cruisin'," a song about tooling around his hometown in the Yankovic family sedan, wasn't the greatest song he ever wrote, but it had some brash and funny lines, and the accordion definitely caught my ear. The words fit the music and were easy to understand, the performance sounded confident and energetic, and the voice and accordion were balanced just right. Al got the kind of results with an inexpensive mono portable recorder that many others never achieve with far costlier multitrack gear.

Of course, that wasn't his first attempt. He'd perfected his micro-budget recording technique by trial and error. That's the "perspiration" part. After he enrolled at Cal Poly, his woodshedding continued while he studied architecture, spun records on the campus FM station, and performed periodically in the campus coffeehouse. One day he happened to play his accordion in the restroom across the hall from the station and loved the way the sound bounced off the walls. He borrowed a microphone from the station, ran a cable across the hall to the station's tape recorder, and recorded his parody of the Knack's number 1 hit "My Sharona." "My Bologna" became the most-requested song on my show and was released on Capitol Records, bringing Al his first taste of national fame. Another song parody, "Another One Rides the Bus," became even more popular, and yet another, "I Love Rocky Road," led to his first LP. Further triumphs followed in rapid succession.

You can read about his gold and platinum records, his Grammys, his feature film *UHF*, and his many concert tours in chapter 1 of this book, but the main thing Lily Hirsch has accomplished in these pages is to reveal the depth and breadth of the creative talent behind Weird Al's wealth of hits. While it's true that most of Al's best-known songs are parodies built upon the foundations of other people's music, many of his records are arguably superior to the originals—and the same goes for his videos. Moreover, about half the tracks on each album are Yankovic originals, with both lyrics and music by Al.

Lots of people come up with ideas for comedy songs, but only a few actually manage to write great ones. Once again, it's inspiration plus perspiration. While writing "I Want a New Duck" in 1984, for example, he spent hours at the library researching ducks, writing down duck facts in a big blue notebook he carried everywhere he went. Nowadays he uses a laptop, of course, but the exhaustive attention to detail is still there, and it extends to every aspect of his songwriting, arranging, and performing, right down to the costumes and props for his videos and stage shows. Next to Frank Zappa, Al is the greatest workaholic I've ever met. He holds his work to the highest of standards, producing songs and other creations that are fall-on-the-floor funny yet reveal new and fascinating depths with repeated listening.

Every so often, Al discovers something new that he can do. Other people produced his first few albums and directed his first few videos; now Al does that all himself. Lately he's become so much in demand for television guest appearances that he hardly has time to write songs, but his concerts continue to sell out and amaze audiences across the country.

Did I see that all coming when Al sent me that first tape with "Belvedere Cruisin'"? Of course not, but his career and his talent have continued to surprise his coworkers and delight his fans, of which I am definitely one. As a person who once aspired to become a professor and still gets a lot of pleasure from providing factual context to comedic entertainment, I'm honored and pleased to introduce a book whose time has truly come, the first carefully researched and insightful analysis of "Weird Al" Yankovic.

Dr. Demento

ACKNOWLEDGMENTS

Many of my previous project brainstorms have involved Bob Fink. This book was no different. I am grateful to have such sage and trusted counsel at my disposal. There are also many friends who reacted with excitement to the idea of this project, urging me on. Some shared their favorite Weird Al songs or moments; others simply encouraged the sharp left turn my research was taking. On this list, I must include Ryan Mitchell and Cori Hall Shechter. Thank you to Ryan for showing me a video of Weird Al dancing at one of his shows on top of my friend and old roommate Kelly Mitchell. Kelly, you were danced on by greatness! And thank you to Cori, a true individual, for embodying so much of what it means to be a Weird Al fan. Their energy added to the fun of this project. Josh Ottum contributed in this way as well, but he also helped me supplement my musicological education with a crash course on music technology. I am forever appreciative. I would like to acknowledge Alec Grossman, for thoughtfully reading a draft of the manuscript; Joshua Duchan, for sharing his experience interviewing Billy Joel as I prepared for my own celebrity interview; and Chuck Garrett, for discussing with me the challenges of writing about humor and reviewing the book's early chapters. Katie Sticca deserves honorable mention here, for adding a new word to my vocabulary: While once a more traditional academic, I have now become forevermore an "Al-cademic."

I would like to thank Kelly Phillips for contributing her Weird Al artistic experience to this project, and the great Dr. Demento, a true legend, for generously writing the foreword. I also want to acknowledge editor Lynn Weber, who improved my writing more than I'd care to admit, as well as Natalie Mandzuik, my editor at Rowman & Littlefield. A leisurely conversation with Natalie about dream topics inspired me to chase the chance of writing about "Weird Al" Yankovic—with his involvement. And that involvement would not have happened without his longtime manager, Jay Levey. Levey responded to my many messages with consistent kindness. I cannot thank him enough for making this all happen. Yankovic seems to surround himself with the same niceness for which he himself is known. His drummer and archivist, Jon "Bermuda" Schwarz, fits the pattern. He kindly and thoughtfully answered my questions—interviews by e-mail on August 18, 2018, and November 22, 2018—and generously sent me material, granting me permission to reprint some of his collected pictures. I cannot thank him enough.

Then, of course, there's Mr. Yankovic himself. I would not have written this book without his participation. At the same time, I felt at times an overwhelming sense of responsibility once I met him—a need to do justice to his work. He opened his home to me, considering my many questions, big and small. I interviewed him there, in Los Angeles, on July 23, 2018, and by phone on September 26, 2018. There was also an e-mail correspondence on July 2, 2019. Many quotes in the book come from these interactions. In return, he never requested anything of me. In *Weird Al: The Book* (2012), written with fan-author Nathan Rabin, Yankovic stated, "If you're going to hire somebody to write a book about you, it's always a good idea to choose somebody who doesn't think you *suck*." Well, I wasn't hired. Though Yankovic never asked, I don't think he sucks. I owe Yankovic my sincerest thanks for his trust in me—with no strings attached.

I would also like to acknowledge Yankovic for a particular learning moment with my seven-year-old daughter, Elliana. While writing chapter 3, she helped me look for puns in his lyrics. When we came across his play on the word *stripper*, in his parody "Handy," she asked, "What's a stripper?" The awkward answer I gave traumatized us both. So, yes, thank you, Weird Al.

Finally, I have to thank my husband for his unwavering support. Two kids, one dog, and four books in, he remains a true partner. I am especially grateful that he introduced our son, Grant, to the music of Weird Al early. At five years old, Grant could sing the whole of "Amish Paradise" and, remarkably, "Albuquerque." He's the biggest Weird Al fan I know and was often by my side as I took notes watching Weird Al online footage, music videos, and interviews. Because of his excitement, this book was one of my most rewarding writing projects to date. Thank you, Grant, for reminding me to live in each moment, appreciating the joy in each day and, of course, the music of "Weird Al" Yankovic.

INTRODUCTION

Still Weird Al

On May 18, 2018, "Weird Al" Yankovic stopped in Turlock, California, a small town in the Central Valley, as part of his Ridiculously Self-Indulgent, Ill-Advised Vanity Tour. He performed at the Turlock Community Theatre, a local historical landmark that was once a high school auditorium. It was a surprising setting in some ways, hardly the typical pop star destination. But the tour as a whole was meant to be intimate, "like we're just hanging out, playing in your living room," Yankovic explained in a Facebook post. Gone was the over-the-top production that has defined Yankovic's live performance—with choreographed video and elaborate costume changes. Despite the casual approach and low-key venue, the energy outside the auditorium was electric. Waiting in line, I first noticed the colors: A woman wearing a dress with a bright red lobster print; a middle-aged man in a patterned collared shirt, the motif a collection of golden corgis; a teenage girl with paisley leggings and, on her black hat, a standout yellow flower. Though the group was predominantly white, the age range was noteworthy—from the very young to the very old. And many seemed remarkably friendly. As we entered through the heavy doors, the man behind me thanked the volunteer ushers for their help. A young girl in the bathroom stood smiling, wearing brilliant gold shoes. I said to her, "Cute shoes." She could barely contain her excitement as she lifted her foot toward me, showing me a messy signature in black ink. She had been able to get Yankovic's autograph.

When Yankovic appeared on stage with his trademark Hawaiian shirt, the crowd was primed to enjoy the set—a set meant to showcase deep cuts. On the June 24, 2018, episode of the podcast *Comedy Bang! Bang!*, Yankovic described the tour's focus as the "songs that were never hits. The ones you barely remember," like "She Never Told Me She Was a Mime." But of course, the audience remembered. This audience was devoted, grinning throughout the show. And the warmth was contagious. I found myself smiling as well. When someone yelled, "I love you Al!" Yankovic didn't hesitate: "I love you too, my friend." In a 1999 episode of VH1's *Behind the Music* chronicling Yankovic's career, his longtime bassist Steve Jay observed that Yankovic "projects heart." His fans in turn "love him like a friend, not like a celebrity." To the *Hollywood Reporter* in 2014, Jay Levey, Yankovic's steadfast manager, made a similar observation, recounting an early experience dining with Yankovic at a pizzeria: "'Eat It' has just been released and has ignited the airwaves. Suddenly he is recognized everywhere. A small boy, maybe 8 years-old, is walking past our table, notices my pizza partner, and in an easy, friendly voice says 'Hi Al,' and continues on his way. No gushing. No nervousness. No autographs. Just 'Hi Al.' It's always been like that." Based on the Turlock show, not much has changed. The audience was once again singing along with Yankovic, their beloved friend.

To date, Yankovic has produced fourteen studio albums featuring his parody songs, original compositions, and accordion medleys. His most recent, *Mandatory Fun* (2014), was the first comedy album to debut at number 1 on the *Billboard* Top 200 chart and won him a Grammy Award for Best Comedy Album, adding to a Grammy collection that began in 1984 when "Eat It" won for Best Comedy Recording. In total, he has had sixteen Grammy nominations and five wins, including the 2019 Grammy for Best Boxed or Special Limited Edition Package for *Squeeze Box: The Complete Works of "Weird Al" Yankovic*. He has had a song in the Top 40 in each decade since the 1980s—only the fourth artist to do so. He created the 1989 cult-hit film *UHF*, AL-TV on MTV, and *The Weird Al Show* on CBS in the late 1990s. He has also appeared on *The Simpsons*, *30 Rock*, *The Goldbergs*, and, as cohost and bandleader, *Comedy Bang! Bang!* on IFC. He's also done voiceover work for a diverse array of animated entertainment, from *My Little Pony* to

Pig Goat Banana Cricket. And this list is woefully incomplete. Since releasing his song "My Bologna," a parody of the Knack's "My Sharona," in 1979, Yankovic has maintained a fame few have rivaled. On the eve of his sixtieth birthday, he wrapped up his sixteenth tour. His fifteenth, The Ridiculously Self-Indulgent one, was a huge success, despite the title's misleading self-deprecation: Most of the seventy-seven shows were sold out.

Unless you are already a Weird Al fan, this list of achievements may seem startling. Especially based on his press. In 1992, *Los Angeles Times* journalist John D'Agostino declared that Yankovic's "schtick" was "tiresome." Starting that year, headlines made clear a sort of astonishment that Yankovic was "still" in music, "still" going, "still" weird. An *Austin American-Statesman* headline from July 13, 1992, announced, "Weird Al Still King of Parody." A *Chicago Tribune* headline on August 2, 1997, exclaimed, "Yankovic Still Weird, Still a Master of Parody." Fourteen years later, the headlines had hardly changed. On November 7, 2011, the *Modesto Bee* declared, "Performer Weird Al Yankovic Still a Master at Musical Manipulation." Why the consistent emphasis on "still," the adverbial "even now"? The "still" seems to betray a certain insult, as if Yankovic's career was in doubt from the start. Even after several decades of success, the doubt remained. A thriving career seemed to do little to dispel the disbelief about his talent and enduring popularity. Somehow, his success was not enough to prove he was in fact successful.

When I interviewed Yankovic for the first time—in his sleek, modern West Hollywood Hills home in the heat of July—I brought up this consistent "still." Yankovic revealed, "It's kind of a running joke with me and my crew that every single album that I've put out is a comeback album." Laughing, he summed up the sentiment: "Can you believe it? He's back again."

It seems Yankovic's career was never expected to last long, and predictions started early that his popularity would soon wane. Reporters felt compelled to underscore his unlikely longevity. Even Yankovic's bio on his own website begins by highlighting a similar disbelief—a disbelief that he ever made it all: "Few would have guessed that 'Weird Al' Yankovic—who as a shy, accordion-playing teenager got his start sending in homemade tapes to *The Dr. Demento Radio Show*—would go on to become a pop culture icon and the biggest-selling comedy recording artist of all time." In the "Ask Al" forum on his website, Yankovic does little to set the record straight. In 2006 a fan asked, "I thought I had heard a rumor about the upcoming album being your last one. Is there any truth to this?" His answer: "Absolutely not. 'Poodle Hat' was my last album. My upcoming album is my next one. I don't know how these silly rumors get started."

But alongside this astonishment at his success and enduring popularity, other headlines make clear the greater surprise: his ongoing humor and weirdness, the substance of his fame. Not only is Yankovic still going, he's still going in the same vein. On June 6, 2003, in *Desert News*: "Yes, Al Is Still Weird—and Witty"; on July 16, 2010, in the *San Antonio Express-News*: "Yankovic Still Weird, Still Funny"; on June 12, 2015, in the *Baltimore Sun*: "Weird Al Yankovic is Still Laughing." Was Yankovic supposed to do otherwise? Was he supposed to change course, opting for a new sound and style? One headline, in the *Evansville Courier & Press* on May 3, 2000, gets at the issue directly: "Al Still 'Weird,' Despite His Age." Apparently Yankovic was expected to grow up and grow out of comedy, or at the very least opt for more mature jokes about gun violence or war (oh wait, he *did* do that—see "Trigger Happy" and "Christmas at Ground Zero"). He wasn't, for heaven's sake, supposed to make more jokes about food—proof, for Chris Willman, writing in the *Los Angeles Times* on July 27, 1992, of a pre–Peter Pan complex: "Weird Al Yankovic is willfully stuck in a state of arrested development way, way pre-puberty, focusing with the single-minded intensity of an infant on another extremely basic instinct: food."

It's true that Yankovic has repeatedly mined the culture around eating in song. Many of the songs in this category ("I Love Rocky Road," "Lasagna," "Fat," "Addicted to Spuds," "The White Stuff," "Spam," and "My Bologna," among others) were brought together in his 1993 *The Food Album*, despite Yankovic's misgivings—his feeling that the rerelease was just his record label's attempt to make a quick buck. Before becoming a vegetarian (and sometimes vegan) in the early 1990s (inspired by the book *Diet for a New America*), he was also often filmed assembling and downing disparate combinations of processed foods (in *UHF* as well as on AL-TV, including his famous Twinkie Weiner Sandwich, a hot dog in a twinkie covered in spray cheese). And his 1984 breakout hit "Eat It," a parody of Michael Jackson's "Beat It," for many turned him into "The Eat-It Guy," which remained part of his Twitter handle until very recently. I had to ask him if food symbolized something for him—perhaps comfort or commonality. "I don't even know what the real answer is," he admitted. "I've got so many joke answers to that question . . . : I've been a starving artist for so long that I've been obsessed with it." Good one. But, Yankovic continued, food is "universal subject matter." It's a common core of cultural routine, a relatable touchstone for fans of all ages. "It's one of those things that everybody can relate to," he observed. And in that space, there is just a hint of rebellion too, as Yankovic champions fare with few, well, champions: spam and bologna. Food in Yankovic's music isn't, then, just food, a basic instinct—it's a means of communication. As philosopher Roland Barthes observed, "People may very well continue to believe that food is an immediate reality (necessity or pleasure), but this does not prevent it from carrying a system of communication."[1]

To be fair, Yankovic has contributed to the rhetoric around his supposed extended adolescence. In the article "Weird Al Still Waiting to Be Adult" (*Chatham Daily News*, October 6, 1999), Yankovic claimed, "I thought by now I'd be an adult and have a real job." But Yankovic also seems to be working against an expectation of aging, the idea that we become more serious over time. In her 2013 *Atlantic* article "How Happiness Changes with Age," Heidi Grant Halvorson offers some foundation for the assumption. "We all grow up," she writes, "and for many of us, what it means to be 'happy' slowly evolves into something completely different." She continues, "Happiness becomes less the high-energy, *totally-psyched* experience of a teenager partying while his parents are out of town, and more the peaceful, relaxing experience of an overworked mom who's been dreaming of that hot bath all day." Hormones change, as do our dreams, some dashed in pursuit of a livable wage. With a partner and kids, we may become predictable, to some, dull. According to one study, this transformation reaches its apex, or "peak boring," around thirty-nine for men and thirty-five for women.[2] Our silliness is then sedate. Yankovic was supposed to follow the pattern, opting for tea over glee. When I mentioned this supposed natural progression, Yankovic revealed, "I'm still more of a shower person than a bath person," though "I do a bath every now and then." Well, at least there's hope.

Of course, part of the incredulity around Yankovic's longevity has to do with a musical bias: the idea that true art is serious. Humorous music, in contrast, is seen as frivolous and unworthy, subject to flippant dismissal and irrelevance. As Iain Ellis observed in *Rebels Wit Attitude*, it is typically "underappreciated" and "underestimated," unfairly judged light and trivial.[3] Comedic song is further disparaged as novelty music, an "ephemeral art form," as Yankovic says. That specific charge, Yankovic recalls, made it especially difficult to get a record deal at first. Why invest in a musician with little staying power?[4] But humorous music is also seen as somehow less lofty. It's not transcendent art but music with mass appeal, potato chips for potato chip people. As philosopher Theodor Adorno believed, humor "appeals to deformed consciousness and confirms it." Yankovic is well aware of this bias as well as the fall-out for the comedic musician. In 2017, Yankovic told Randy Lewis of the *Los Angeles Times*, "Humor is such an important part of the human experience. I just don't know why showcasing it makes people think, 'You're not a real artist.'"

Music scholar Charles Hiroshi Garrett noticed the hierarchy in his study of humor in jazz, concluding that humor in jazz is almost always seen as contrary to the core values of jazz and its artistic legacy.[5] In an interesting twist, analysis of humor in connection to classical music is less of a problem. Comedy in the classical context is more acceptable since the artistic merits of classical music have seemingly been long cemented. Based in notions of the supposed canon or Romantic transcendence of the masterworks, classical music can withstand the threat of comedy. British singer Anna Russell, who trained as an opera singer before turning to comedy, was thereby able to parody classical music without undue consequence or negative response. Not only that, her association with classical music may have upped her comedy credentials. Regarding Russell, Garrett claims, "Ironically, it appears she was marketed as the best in the world at her craft of musical parody in part because of her engagement with high culture."[6] Victor Borge, the Danish-born pianist, benefited from the same association. He had many gags—famous one-liners ("I don't usually do request numbers—unless, of course, I am asked to do so") and staged falls (the punchline, a seatbelt attached to his piano bench). But he could also execute classical compositions brilliantly, as he did at the Kennedy Center in 1987 during a performance of Leonard Bernstein's *Candide* overture. His stature was enhanced by his abilities in both comedy and "serious" music, though the "serious" music was part of the joke. On the edge of their seats, listeners waited for the music to break, revealing the gag. But he just kept playing. That *was* the gag.

Yankovic's funny songs play on popular culture rather than music deemed high art. Through parody, he has taken on Chamillionaire, Coolio, Eminem, Queen, George Harrison, Green Day, Iggy Azalea, James Brown, Madonna, MC Hammer, Michael Jackson, Lady Gaga, Lorde, Miley Cyrus, Milli Vanilli, Nelly, Nirvana, Puff Daddy, R. Kelly, Robin Thicke, Taylor Swift, and Usher, among others. Popular rather than classical, these diverse performers have done little to improve Yankovic's artistic standing. Nor has his facility on music instruments. In March 2018, Yankovic made his debut on the guitar, playing a cover of Neil Young's "Cinnamon Girl" or, more specifically, Young's one-note solo, at the Apollo Theater in New York. (Yankovic's guitar performances in videos like "Smells Like Nirvana" and "The Saga Begins" were pretend.) But his primary instrument, the one central to his act, is the accordion—an instrument with its own baggage in reception. Yankovic has fun with the issue in "Ask Al": "You can never be too rich, too thin, or have too many accordions!"

His bold and colorful Hawaiian shirt habit doesn't help either. In 2015 Yankovic told Paul Bowers of the *Charleston City Paper*, "I've always had a love for those kind of shirts, and I'm sure they'll always be associated with me in some way." But looks matter in serious art. Customary concert dress is black, sometimes formal tails, the opposite of the casual, patterned display associated with the traditional Hawaiian or Aloha shirt. Yankovic has a home in Hawaii and with it some connection to the shirt's serious side—an artistic, spiritual, and multiethnic history.[7] But the flipside, far more prevalent, is the shirt's standing as a symbol of the tacky tourist. The shirt—let's face it—is leisure wear, the antithesis of high fashion. Every day can be casual Friday when you're Weird Al, and it's hard to take anyone seriously on casual Friday.

In a 2013 interview for the *Omaha World-Herald*, writer Kevin Coffey told Yankovic, "You and your band are tight players." "I really appreciate that," Yankovic responded. "A lot of people, because it's comedy, they think it's maybe not up to par or not as good as 'serious music.'" One side effect of this perception is Yankovic's aversion to karaoke (though he recently made an exception for James Corden's popular segment Carpool Karaoke): "[M]y detractors or some reviewers that have been less than kind in the past have referred to me as a 'glorified karaoke act.' So that sticks in my mind, and if I were to do karaoke, I just wouldn't be able to enjoy it as much as other people."[8] In our first conversation, Yankovic shared a question that has often bothered him, an insult embedded in a compliment: "You're so good at what you do. Have you ever thought about doing real music?" He balances the dismissal with his own commitment to what he does and who he is: "Well, I enjoy doing what I do. I love the genre that I've chosen and the career that I've carved out for myself. So I don't feel like I'm excluded but I definitely feel like doing comedy music puts me into a category where I'm second class."

His recourse to the music of others, part of parody, has done little to dissuade the naysayers. Writing on the topic, John Thomerson defines parody as a new work "created through musical borrowing."[9] Like cover songs, parody songs can be seen as derivative, less creative than original art. In her study of parody, Linda Hutcheon colorfully clarifies the issue. Parody is "the philistine enemy of creative genius and vital originality." It has even been called "parasitic," implying a certain malice; parody supposedly exploits its host. Hutcheon contextualizes the criticism: "What is clear from these sorts of attacks is the continuing strength of a Romantic aesthetic that values genius, originality, and individuality."[10] The real artistic genius is supposed to create from nothing, like a god. Their art has no model, no earthly point of origin. In part, capitalism drives this thinking, then and now: a desire to commodify and possess art. How do you determine the ownership of art reliant on the work of others?

But these notions of humor and parody in music are misleading, and they distract from the serious impact and meaning of Yankovic's music. Humor has purpose, as does parody. As Garrett writes of jazz, humor "assumes a variety of shapes—as a mask for social critique, a display of comic artistry, a mode of communication, a fount of pleasure, and sometimes all of these at once."[11] As a social phenomenon, humor reveals much about the society that in turn laughs and can even influence social values and meaning. Jokes are also everywhere. They are part of our everyday social interaction—breaking the ice in so many different contexts—and a shared sense of humor can create a powerful bond. Cheap and easy, humor itself is a sort of universal healthcare. It provides relief, often an audible release, and that laugh can lower stress, changing the body's chemistry for the better. It can also offer a much-needed psychological lift. Yankovic told Alex Nino Gheciu, writing for *Sharp* magazine: "I've had more than a few people come up to me and say they were in a very bad place in their life—some of them were suicidal, in fact. And listening to my music snapped them out of it; they were able to move on and get through whatever sombre phase they were in. Sometimes, when I think what I do is somewhat pointless, I remember those people and how even my stupid music served a real function for them."

Parody, for its part, plays many roles. It can denigrate, criticize, and mock. It can be funny and playful. It can also offer up tribute or homage. With these various intents, parody has been a major force in art in a variety of historical contexts and genres, from ancient Greece to hip-hop. Today, it too is omnipresent, central to American popular music. As Thomerson maintains, parody is "the compositional technique most familiar in the musical experiences of Americans."[12] On *The Michael Des Barres Program* in 2014, Yankovic himself pointed out just how American parody really is, explaining that the national anthem is itself a parody. Its composer, the lawyer Francis Scott Key, borrowed the tune from an old English drinking song. As a technique, parody is also no less creative and original than so-called original art. To varying degrees, in fact, all art relies on preceding works, existing practice, and cultural customs. We create by responding to our surrounding culture, making certain decisions about the art we already know. Has there ever been a so-called original composer or musical tradition? Does the lone artistic genius even exist? Maybe not.

Philosophers and writers, like artists, build on past work, molding "existing patterns of thought."[13] This book, in some respects, could then be viewed as parody. I am writing an introduction, which you are now reading. It's an established part of a book's formula: table of contents, introduction, and so on. I am obviously aware of preceding norms, but I may be using them in my own way. After the introduction, you might find "Chapter Fun," complete with a nauseating repetition of the professor/author's favorite words—"discourse," "Derrida," and much, much more. Is this work a reliable retread of previous convention? Or is it a flippant subversion of the academic study, an "Al-cademic" book instead?

In 1994, the US Supreme Court in *Campbell v. Acuff-Rose* showed some awareness of parody's value. The case alleged that rap group 2

Live Crew's song "Pretty Woman" violated copyright as a parody of songwriter Roy Orbison's "Oh, Pretty Woman." But the court reasoned that parody "can provide social benefit, by shedding light on an earlier work, and, in the process, creating a new one."[14] Building on the 1976 Copyright Act, the court, in the end, ruled: "Parody, like other comment and criticism, may claim fair use." For this reason, Yankovic is not legally required to seek out permission for his parodies from the original artists—and, by original, I mean "initial" rather than "lone genius." And yet he does, careful to stay in good standing with his fellow artists.

But what about his artistic standing *in relationship* to his fellow artists? That, I have to say, is harder to navigate or explain. In 2003, in response to an "Ask Al" question, Yankovic confessed, "I think my chances of ever making it into the Rock & Roll Hall of Fame are about as good as Milli Vanilli's." There are now multiple online petitions designed to overcome the supposed odds, including an effort titled "Make the Rock Hall 'Weird.'"[15] Referencing his 2003 quip, I asked Yankovic, "Do you still think that's true?" "Well, my stock answer to that is I'm not going to hold my breath about ever getting into the Hall, but if they put another curly-haired accordion-playing parody artist in before me I'll be a little upset," he said, seizing another opportunity to make me laugh. Yankovic was recently honored with a star on the Hollywood Walk of Fame. On August 13, 2018, he announced on Twitter: "The time has finally come . . . On Aug. 27 at 11: 30 AM I'll be getting my very own star on the Hollywood Walk of Fame." His star neighbor, Mark Hamill, tweeted his congratulations the next day, calling the honor well-deserved. And it really was, especially after thirteen years of trying. The star was the result of another fan campaign, which began in 2005. Fans raised the necessary funds and submitted Yankovic's application each year, patiently waiting for the acceptance they felt Yankovic had earned, undeterred by the yearly rejection.

Awards do not determine greatness. Other significant musicians snubbed by the Rock Hall include Tina Turner, Björk, and Devo—the latter the inspiration for Yankovic's anthem "Dare to Be Stupid" (1985). Award or no award, Yankovic has established a unique place in music. For many, he is synonymous with parody itself. As Yankovic himself confirmed, in an interview on December 20, 2018, on *Hot Ones*, "If it's a parody it's Al." A tasteless spoof of Childish Gambino's "This Is America" played on that assumption, implicating Yankovic in a controversial parody, "This Is My Hair I Cut," for which he was not responsible. And the song was certainly not the first offensive parody wrongly credited to Yankovic. For better and for worse, he's the unrivaled prince—even king—of pop parody. DJ and Yankovic mentor Barry Hansen, better known as Dr. Demento, has a matchless grasp on the world of humorous music, with his long-running syndicated radio show spotlighting comedy in music. In 2003 he dubbed Yankovic "the Beatles of my little genre."[16] In 2017 he clarified, "Comedy recording and funny songs go back to the earliest days of the record industry. But Al is unique. There's nothing like him in the history of funny music."[17] Part of that distinction is Yankovic's enduring fame and his long career, which is a credit to his music and Yankovic himself. In 2014, in *The Hollywood Reporter*, manager Jay Levey explained, "The story of Al's longevity as an artist begins and ends with his work. Look—I mean *really* look—at the quality of his wordplay, cleverness, intelligence, innovative rhyming and musicality."

So let's do just that—look, *really* look, at Yankovic's work. Let's listen and talk, *really* talk, about the various aspects of Yankovic's art that merit serious attention. Of course, long-held pseudo wisdom says let's not. As E. B. White famously maintained, "Explaining a joke is like dissecting a frog. You understand it better but the frog dies in the process." One of the few to offer a dissenting opinion is comedian Hari Kondabolu, who finds humor in explaining the joke. But Kondabolu aside, White's sentiment holds sway, as does similar thinking about talk in music. Romantic composer Robert Schumann believed that "[t]he best way to talk about music is to be quiet about it."[18] To me, both oft-quoted lines seem fear based, motivated by a desire to protect a purity in art that does not exist. An unfiltered joke or score is a fallacy; comedy and music depend on performance. And in performance, an entertainer must interpret the joke or music in some way. Not only that, this thinking supports a worn-out cycle worthy of Joseph Heller. We do not take comedic music seriously because we cannot talk about it seriously. And we cannot talk about it seriously because it's comedic music. As Jeremy Dauber wrote in *Jewish Comedy* (*A Serious Study*), "You want a joke book, buy a joke book." I'll take my own cue from the movie *The Princess Bride*. Frog, I say, "You killed my father. Prepare to die." So that you may live.

As we will see in the following chapters, Yankovic's vast output builds on a rich and ongoing American tradition of parody song, with many levels of meaning often at the same time. His songs, including his original compositions, make us laugh but also have a point of view, be it on society, popular culture, politics, race, gender, fame, or words themselves. In his fourteen studio albums, Yankovic is also a master of both musical insult and self-insult, though he maintains a reputation as one of the music industry's good guys. In today's age of incivility (political and otherwise), this "nice guy" persona stands out and has helped win him fiercely loyal fans—fans who have found in his music a certain acceptance and affirmation. This book is for those fans, the young girl with autographed gold shoes. But the book also invites music enthusiasts of all stripes to consider and reconsider Yankovic's music as well as the assorted possibilities of parody and comedy in music: weighty and light, profound and far from it. No laughing, though; this is Weird Al, *seriously*.

I

THIS IS THE LIFE

Alfred Matthew Yankovic was born on October 23, 1959, in Downey, California, of Yugoslavian, Italian, and English descent and with no familial ties to Frankie Yankovic, "America's Polka King," though they met in 1986 setting up the first polka Grammy. His father, Nick Yankovic, served as a medic in World War II, earning a Silver Star and two Purple Hearts. After the war, Nick worked at a steel manufacturing plant. Al's mother, Mary Yankovic, was a professional stenographer.[1] Mary and Nick raised young Al in nearby Lynwood, a multicultural suburb of Los Angeles. Al was an only child and, according to VH1's *Behind the Music,* spent a lot of time in his room. In 1966 Al's parents rented him an accordion from a door-to-door salesman, and he had his first lesson on October 22, 1966—the day before he turned seven—and would continue weekly instruction for three years. Yankovic joked, "My parents chose the accordion because they were convinced it would revolutionize rock."[2] Believe it or not, there were other people who actually shared this opinion. The accordion, which evolved from a free-reed instrument invented in Europe, enjoyed some popularity after World War I, and by 1953 it was a top-selling instrument.[3] With the emergence of rock and roll, there was some hope the accordion would have a prominent place in the new genre. A handsome accordion player named Teddy Randazzo fueled that speculation when he appeared in the 1958 film *The Girl Can't Help It*, playing with the rock band the Three Chuckles.

But the accordion never established a real place in rock—quite the opposite. Writer Marion Jacobson observed, "It was in the early 1960s, with the rise of rock 'n' roll that Western teenagers came to view the squeezebox as the embodiment of everything that was hackneyed, dorky and terminally kitsch about their parents."[4] Its association with the polka led it to be considered (in the United States at least) "unsophisticated," "simple," and "low-class."[5] One accordion player noted that "[t]he accordion had the wrong image. It made you look fat or pregnant. It wasn't much help in getting the girls."[6] So, far from being an expressive addition to the rock supply closet, it became a reliable joke: "What do you call ten accordions at the bottom of the ocean? A good start." "What's the difference between an accordion and a trampoline? You take your shoes off before you jump up and down on a trampoline."

Yankovic riffed on the accordion's image problem when he credited his playing of the accordion to his mother: "My mother decided she wanted me to be a chick magnet in high school."[7] Yankovic would later

Yankovic and Yankovic. *Courtesy of Jon Schwartz*

name as his worst job accordion repo man. When he was a teenager, he gave accordion lessons to children, the accordions on loan. But once a child stopped lessons, Yankovic had to collect the rented instruments. Yankovic joked, "I kept thinking there would be some kind of ugly confrontation, but people were all too happy to give back the accordion."[8]

FROM DEMENTED TO WEIRD

By the age of eight, Yankovic began writing songs for the accordion and changing the words of existing songs for fun: "I think every pre-teen comes up with different words to songs to amuse their friends. . . . I just never grew out of it."[9] To me, he further qualified, "I'd barely call them songs. . . . [T]here was a book of popular song hits from the '60s. And I would go through all the songs. And I would change the words in the book and make them just stupid. . . . [T]hey certainly weren't clever, but . . . they were the seeds."

Yankovic had little exposure to popular music as a kid, but he remembers well his parents' recording of Johnny Cash's "Boa Constrictor," about a man being swallowed by a snake. At the end, the man is gone and the snake burps. "To my 5-year-old brain, this was hilarious. The snake was belching on the record!" Yankovic recalled.[10] Yankovic was also attracted early to the music of Elton John, who helped him imagine the accordion in new ways. In the extensive liner notes accompanying Yankovic's compilation *Permanent Record: Al in the Box*, Yankovic explained, "I was into Elton John a lot during the 70s, and that was partly how I learned to play rock 'n roll on the accordion, by playing the *Goodbye Yellow Brick Road* album over and over and trying to play along with it on the accordion."

His influences were not, however, limited to "respectable" musicians like Elton John, but extended to figures from a brilliant culture of funny music, including entertainers like Spike Jones, Allan Sherman, Stan Freberg, and Tom Lehrer. The 1970s were also the heyday of parody institutions like *Mad* magazine, another big source of inspiration. But most important of all was the cult radio show *The Dr. Demento Show*— "a life-altering discovery," Yankovic told David Segal of the *Washington Post*. As Barry Hanson, Dr. Demento was a student of music with a master's degree from UCLA, his thesis on the evolution of rhythm and blues. His radio program began in 1970. Before the show was syndicated, he sounded locally in Los Angeles on KPPC before his move to rock station KMET. He featured rock 'n' roll and oldies but also rarities, novelty songs, and other comedic gems from the past. It was often these songs—humorous ditties like Sheb Wooley's "The Purple People Eater" or Elmo & Patsy's "Grandma Got Run Over by a Reindeer"—that listeners requested again and again. "Before long," Hansen recounted, "those old funny songs had taken over not only *The Dr. Demento Show* but my whole life as well."[11]

At age twelve or thirteen, Yankovic heard *The Dr. Demento Show* for the first time: "Every Sunday night I'd tune in and I just thought this was my kind of music, this is what I wanted to do."[12] But after his mom reacted to a few off-color choices, like "Dave's Dinghy" and "Bounce Your Boobies," he had to keep the habit a secret: "I immediately loved it and my mom hated it." Yankovic learned to listen in bed Sunday night with a blanket covering him and the clock radio beside him.[13] On *Behind the Music*, Yankovic described the magic of those nights listening to the radio—how it allowed for imagination—a "circus in your head," and his blanket was the big top housing it all. After Dr. Demento spoke at Yankovic's high school, Lynwood High, in 1973, Yankovic approached the ringmaster for an autograph. In the *Permanent Record* liner notes, Dr. Demento remembers Yankovic as one of the few students to do so—though "he was too shy to say much."

Through the show, Yankovic was exposed to Jones, Lehrer, Sherman, and Freberg, among others. He was immediately attracted to their music. "It was the comedy," he told me. "I mean, I wasn't used to hearing that kind of material on the radio. And it just struck a responsive chord with me. I just really appreciated the sensibilities."

Tom Lehrer was a Harvard math student who performed his comical songs at local parties. He was Jewish but, in his own words, "Jewish by ancestry—more to do with the delicatessen than the synagogue."[14] He wrote "Fight Fiercely, Harvard" in 1945, a mock fight song (Yankovic years later would write a similar send-up, his 2014 "Sports Song"). Lehrer's song lampooned the supposedly refined nature of the Harvard athlete—one who might invite the "whole team up for tea." Another favorite was the song "The Elements," written in 1959, which Yankovic later covered. The song, a parody of "I Am the Very Model of a Modern

Major-General," from Gilbert and Sullivan's *The Pirates of Penzance*, rattles off the chemical elements in rapid, rhythmic succession. Despite his unexpected popularity—his first album sold 350,000 copies—Lehrer would opt for university employment over showbiz. As he put it, "What good is it having laurels if you can't sit on them?"[15] He retired from his position as mathematics professor at the University of California, Santa Cruz, in 2001.

Stan Freberg's time in musical comedy was also limited. His decision to leave, however, had more to do with the recording industry in the 1950s, which began demanding full albums rather than the singles Freberg preferred. He explained, "I had to lie down. I mean, the idea of doing twelve single-record cuts in an album!"[16] Before Freberg made his exit plan, he created popular parodies that pushed musical style to the breaking point. Rather than changing the lyrics, in his take on Elvis's "Heartbreak Hotel" (1956), he zoned in on the King's slurring and overuse of echo, bringing out those effects to a level of comedic absurdity. He would go on to a successful second career in advertising. Yankovic wrote a salute to Freberg in *Variety* in 2014, recalling a song made up of only two names—John and Marsha—repeated with varying emphasis: "The first time I was exposed to the work of Stan Freberg was when some prankster in my middle school played his famous soap opera parody 'John and Marsha' over the public address system during class. It was unexpected, inappropriate and just plain weird; it had everyone in hysterics." Soon, with Freberg on Dr. Demento's playlist, Yankovic heard many other Freberg hits and Freberg "became one of my all-time heroes."

Allan Sherman, another idol, would have a musical career cut short, much like Lehrer and Freberg. And yet his departure from parody was by far the most tragic. He was Jewish, influenced early by exposure to Yiddish theater thanks to his grandparents. His 1962 album *My Son, the Folk Singer* put a Jewish twist on folk song. "Frère Jacques" became "Sarah Jackman," with the song's "dormez-vous" transformed into the "Jewish English" "How's by you?"[17] Another popular parody was "Hello Muddah, Hello Fadduh," which turned Amilcare Ponchielli's "Dance of the Hours" into a letter home from summer camp. In 1963 Sherman's album *My Son, the Nut* reached number 1 on the *Billboard* 200—it wasn't until 2014, with Yankovic's *Mandatory Fun*, that another comedy album attained the top spot. But shortly thereafter, Sherman's popularity declined as he battled personal issues made worse by his poor eating habits and alcoholism. He died of emphysema in 1973, at the age of only forty-eight.

Sherman biographer Mark Cohen noted that parody is "almost synonymous with American Jewish humor itself."[18] Although Yankovic is not Jewish, he was no doubt influenced by the massive cultural power of Jewish humor and parody in the United States and elsewhere.[19] In the eighteenth and nineteenth centuries, for example, parody thrived in Germany and became central shtick in German cabaret during the Weimar era and even into the Third Reich—a response for many Jews to their outsider status as well as a cultural interest in language. Yankovic is often mistaken for a Jew: In the writeup "6 Celebrities Everyone Thinks Are Jewish," Yankovic comes in at number 5—"No. Really. Weird Al is not a Jew! Not even with that hair."[20] But the appeal of humor and parody are universal, bolstered by Yankovic's own feelings of being different as well as his love of language. When he heard the music of Lehrer, Freberg, and Sherman, "It just struck me as funny," he explained to me, "And it was at a very impressionable age, so it got me thinking, 'Well, maybe I'll try this.'"

In 1976 Yankovic scored his first minor musical triumph with the song "Belvedere Cruisin'," which he sent into *The Dr. Demento Show*. The song, a comedic original, celebrated his family's big black car, a 1964 Plymouth Belvedere with red upholstery. It was voted into Dr. Demento's Top 10. Dr. Demento remembers thinking, as he listened to the song, "This kid has some talent." In the song, Yankovic compares his ride to all its failing rivals. The accordion was a draw, as Dr. Demento writes in this book's foreword, but he also responded to one line in particular: "There's something about a Comet / That makes me want to vomit."[21] Hearing the song on air took Yankovic by surprise. In a 2011 interview with Nathan Rabin for *AV Music*, Yankovic set the scene:

> I was in my bedroom, living at home with my folks, listening to *The Dr. Demento Show*, as I did every Sunday night, and the song came on. It took me several seconds for my brain to acknowledge it, because I recognized it was my song, but I thought, "How did my tape player get turned on?" and when I put the pieces together and I realized that my song was actually coming out of the speakers and it was on the radio and other people were hearing it too, I think I did

some kind of giddy jig around the house, and started screaming my head off.

"It was all the encouragement I needed," he has said. [22]

Despite this early boost, after high school Yankovic initially pursued another path, one he had settled on when he was just twelve years old. A guidance counselor reasoned that, since he was good at math and had excelled in a junior high drafting class, he should become an architect: "So when I was 12 years old I made the decision to be an architect," he explained, "and I planned to go to Cal Poly which had one of the best architecture schools in the country. At that point I had my whole life figured out." [23] Must have been nice.

At the age of sixteen, Yankovic graduated high school as the valedictorian. He was a straight-A student, earning entry, as planned, into California Polytechnic State University, San Luis Obispo, where he would earn a degree in architecture. Though Yankovic completed his studies at Cal Poly, he quickly realized architecture wasn't his real passion. He has said of his fellow architecture students, "They had a fire in their belly about architecture, and they'd look at a building and say, 'Oh, look at the negative space and the positive space, and the form following function!'" His reaction, in contrast: "Yeah, it's a building. Great." [24] In an interview for *The Dinner Party Download*, Yankovic recalled his thinking then, as he moved away from architecture and toward his real passion: "Well, do I wanna be mediocre doing something that I'm not really that excited about for the rest of my life?"

At Cal Poly, Yankovic nonetheless worked hard to complete his degree. Dr. Demento recalled, "I didn't hear much from him during his first year, as he immersed himself in architecture." But soon Yankovic had another Demento hit as well as a taste of success—meat-flavored, no doubt—beyond the radio show. The building, no matter how great, would have to wait, indefinitely. To quote a song by Art Garfunkel—another architect turned musician—"So Long, Frank Lloyd Wright."

"MY LITTLE HUNGRY ONE"

Yankovic recorded the song "My Bologna" in 1979 in the bathroom across from the university radio station where he worked as a DJ—the campus Dr. Demento, so to speak. The song was a direct parody of the song "My Sharona," by the Knack, a song created as an ode to a girl named Sharona whom lead singer Doug Fieger had decided was his soulmate. Many viewed the band as a novelty act, but in 1979 "My Sharona" reached the top of the charts. Yankovic turned the initial line of the original—"Ooh, my little pretty one, my pretty one"—into "Ooh, my little hungry one, hungry one." As Fieger pursued Sharona, then with someone else—"Never gonna stop, give it up"—Yankovic chased lunch meat—"Never gonna stop, eat it up." The instrumentation was far from faithful, replacing the guitar and percussion of the original with accordion. Yankovic sent his version to Dr. Demento, and on September 27, 1979, Dr. Demento wrote to Yankovic:

> Hi Alfred (would you rather I called you Al on the air?) much belated thanks for your wondrous sausage music. It has made a big hit with my audience, to put it mildly. It's been on my KMET Top Ten twice. Ditto for the Top Ten on my new show on KSAN in San Francisco. On my national show it will be #1 on the show just taped for broadcast two weeks from Sunday. A producer from Capitol Records, Bruce Ravid, called and asked for a copy for The Knack.

After sharing contact information, he signed off with his signature "Stay Demented."[25] In the *Permanent Record* liner notes, Dr. Demento recalled, "The response I got when I played it on the air dwarfed not only that for all his earlier tapes, but practically everything else I played the whole year." Yankovic did get the song to the Knack, and Feiger loved it. The group's record label, Capitol Records, signed Yankovic to a six-month contract, releasing the song as a single just before Christmas that same year.[26] In the announcement Capitol Records declared, "For your holiday distraction, we give you a fine recording that's emerged as a genu-wine killer on Dr. Demento's playlists over the [last] couple of months." Yankovic was thrilled but sure he had somehow peaked. Reflecting on that first brush with fame, Yankovic told Kyle Anderson of *EW*, "I thought, 'Well, it'll never get better than this.'"

Yankovic did not drop everything to take his shot at stardom. He continued his coursework, graduating college in 1980. That same year, he scored again with "Another One Rides the Bus," a direct parody of Queen's "Another One Bites the Dust." Like "My Bologna," the rearrangement features the accordion. Rather than playing a homemade recording, this time Dr. Demento debuted the song with a live Yankovic performance. Jon Schwartz, Yankovic's longtime drummer and unofficial historian, happened to be in the studio that day, scheduled to perform "The Woodsy Owl Song" with some friends—a song promoting Woodsy Owl, known for the message "Give a hoot—don't pollute!" He offered to play percussion for Yankovic, banging in time on Yankovic's accordion case, a do-it-yourself premiere effort. To Anderson, Yankovic said, "That was the only recorded version, the live sound check of that performance on the show. That became the record, and that was an hour after I met my drummer."

"Were you looking for a permanent gig when you met Mr. Yankovic on *The Dr. Demento Show*?" I asked Schwartz. "Not at all," he revealed. "I had a day job and was also in a band and had other musical work. I didn't go to the show with any expectations and didn't know that Al would be there." But Yankovic retained the setup and even gave Schwartz his own nickname. "Weird Al" Yankovic and Jon "Bermuda" Schwartz performed on television for the first time on April 21, 1981, on Tom Snyder's *The Tomorrow Show*. In his introduction, Snyder could not be bothered to note the title of the song Yankovic and Schwartz were about to perform: "I can't find the title," he says in the clip, looking to Yankovic, who helpfully supplies "Another One Rides the Bus." Yankovic, with his then-trademark look of glasses, mustache, and a halo of reddish-brown curls, sings in earnest, with his whole voice, while Schwartz adds slapstick percussion, including clown horn.

Shortly thereafter, Yankovic assembled a permanent band. With the support of a menial day job, he decided to give music a real go. Dr. Demento had invited him to perform along with him at a nightclub in Phoenix. Manager Jay Levey was there that night and witnessed the excitement Yankovic generated from the stage. Levey remembered, "It was amazing. Al was introduced, and he comes out with his accordion and pours all of his energy into a set of parodies and originals. The crowd went wild and rushed the stage. I'm blown away. After his set, he comes off stage and I ask him if he ever thought about putting a band together and having a real career." Yankovic answered simply, according to Levey in the *Permanent Record* liner notes, "Well, sure." Yankovic had already enlisted Schwartz as drummer, but after auditions, he added to the lineup bass player Steve Jay, who had unique experience recording traditional music in Africa, and guitarist Jim West, with whom Jay had already worked.

Addressing those early days, I asked Yankovic, "Did you have a favorite early gig?" "Well," he answered immediately, "most of the early ones weren't very favorite." He laughed, "None of the really early gigs went particularly well." He described a 1982 gig opening for the New Wave group Missing Persons at the Santa Monica Civic Auditorium— the newly formed band's first major debut. Yankovic shared, "It was our first sort of big gig, and we were opening for the group Missing Persons, which at the time was a very popular kind of alternative rock group, getting a lot of airplay on KROQ in LA. And we thought, 'Oh, this is great.' We're getting to open for Missing Persons, and we thought their audience would just love to hear some accordion-based parody music." They "were sadly mistaken," Yankovic admitted. "Literally, from the moment we hit the stage, we were pelted with anything that wasn't nailed down." Yankovic can still remember making his way back to his car after the performance. In the *Permanent Record* liner notes he wrote: "Later that night, after suffering that humiliating defeat, I was walking to my car in the parking lot, and this 12 year old boy comes up to me and says, 'Are you Weird Al?' I said yes, and he said 'YOU SUCK!'" Salt in his wounds.

The audience in Santa Monica might not have been prepared for Yankovic that night, but Weird Al was on the rise. He was starting to make a living doing something he loved. And he had his father's wisdom as fuel: "If you're happy, you're a success."[27] With the popularity of "I Love Rocky Road," a parody of "I Love Rock 'n Roll," popularized by Joan Jett, Yankovic earned himself a contract with the California-based Scotti Brothers label. He also inadvertently found himself a megawatt star producer when, setting out to record professionally, he decided to pursue permission for his ice cream parody. He contacted Jake Hooker, a member of the group the Arrows, which had originally recorded "I Love Rock 'n Roll." Hooker responded, in Yankovic's words, "Well, that sounds like a great idea, and by the way I happen to manage Rick Derringer, and I think Rick would be really interested in being part of this project."[28] Derringer worked as a producer and had been in the band the McCoys, with the 1965 hit "Hang On Sloopy." In 1976 Derringer created his Derringer Band, which would release four albums, but he also worked with a slew of top artists, including Alice Cooper,

Debut Performance. *Courtesy of Jon Schwartz*

Todd Rundgren, Steely Dan, Cyndi Lauber, KISS, and Barbra Streisand, among others. Under the Scotti label, he would produce Yankovic's first album, the self-titled 1983 release *"Weird Al" Yankovic*, as well as his next five. The album also boasted engineer Tony Papa, who would be another longtime Yankovic collaborator. Yankovic toured with the album, his first, aptly named The First Tour.

"Weird Al" Yankovic sold moderately well, eventually certified gold, but it was with the next album, *"Weird Al" Yankovic in 3-D*, released the following year, that Yankovic found real fame, starting a platinum streak. The album included "Eat It," his first Grammy win. In a *Rolling Stone* tribute to Michael Jackson, Yankovic recounted how he reached out to Jackson's camp with his idea for the "Beat It" parody: "The first time I pursued Michael Jackson about a song parody, it was a shot in the dark. We're talking about the most popular and famous person in the known universe, and here I was, this goofy comedy songwriter. He not only returned our phone calls, but he approved it. He thought it was a funny idea." That same year, in 1984, Yankovic had the thrill of a lifetime when Paul McCartney recognized him at a party. "He saw me

and said, 'Oh, Weird Al!'" then turned to his wife and said, "Look honey, it's Weird Al!" "It completely blew my mind that he even knew who I was," Yankovic shared.[29]

His new celebrity status would take some getting used to. In 1984 Yankovic told the *Los Angeles Times*, "I never thought people would be treating me like a star. But with me things happen weirdly, not like they would for the normal star. I'm the kind of guy who gets mobbed at Burger Kings." But who wants to be "normal"? After *"Weird Al" Yankovic in 3-D*, Yankovic would produce twelve more albums—a prolific feat for any star, "normal" or not.

THE SAGA BEGINS AGAIN

In 1985 Yankovic released *Dare to Be Stupid*, the first album of comedic music ever released on compact disc. It included the song "Dare to Be Stupid" (see chapter 4) as well as "This Is the Life," a tongue-in-cheek ode to excess that Yankovic originally wrote for the 1984 film *Johnny Dangerously*. After his The Stupid Tour, he put out the less popular *Polka Party!* in 1986. The album cover features a smiling Al in full traditional polka dress, surrounded by a much more aggressive assembly of hip revelers. The divide, according to Nathan Rabin, was part of the album's popularity problem: "If Al had deliberately set out to sabotage his album's commercial chances, he couldn't have done a better job." The polka look was not a fashionable draw. The album would reach only 177 on the Billboard Top 200; the cover's hipster gap may have played out as fact.

His next album, 1988's *Even Worse*, rebounded with yet another Michael Jackson parody, "Fat." Yankovic poses on the album cover as Jackson, copying the dress, hairstyle, and expression of the Prince of Pop on the cover of his 1987 album *Bad*. Jackson himself approved both the lyrics of "Fat" and the album cover. He also let Yankovic use his own "Bad" video subway set for the "Fat" video, which required a dramatic Yankovic makeover. "It was pretty grueling," Yankovic told the *Los Angeles Times* in 1988, "Every morning, it would take three hours for them to put me in my fat makeup." As an expression of appreciation, Yankovic told me, he approached Jackson when he was playing in Los

Angeles and presented him with an *Even Worse* gold album. "Another record for the pile," Yankovic laughed, "but he was very gracious."

That year, Yankovic also issued a special release of classical music for children, Sergei Prokofiev's *Peter and the Wolf* and Camille Saint-Saëns's *The Carnival of Animals*, the music arranged by the innovative Wendy Carlos. In his Prokoviev version, Yankovic added to the original a new character, Bob the Janitor, represented by the accordion. The narration points out that Peter is "afraid of a lot of things, such as nuclear annihilation and flunking algebra . . . but not wolves." The recording was nominated in 1988 for a Grammy for Best Children's Recording.

In 1989 Yankovic's movie soundtrack, *UHF—Original Motion Picture Soundtrack and Other Stuff*, was released, accompanying the movie *UHF*, which tested well with preview audiences before failing at the box office. The movie's failure was doubly unfortunate because in order to work on the film, Yankovic had turned down an offer to open for Michael Jackson. Often cited is the movie's casting of Michael Richards, pre-*Seinfeld*, in the standout role of Stanley Spadowski. But the star of the show was Weird Al as lovable loser George Newman, who turns his uncle's failing local television station into an unlikely success, inciting the wrath of evil Channel 8. The premise was a setup for Yankovic's parodies, part of the wild programming that ultimately saves the station.

Yankovic wrote the script with Jay Levey, who also directed. In the oral history of *UHF* for *AV Film*, Yankovic recalled, "My manager Jay Levey and I started conceptualizing the movie in '85. You know, at that point I'd had a couple fairly popular albums, and as managers do, he was thinking, 'Well, what's the next big step?' And the consensus was, 'Well, it's time for a Weird Al movie.'" Yankovic figured he could learn as they went, as he often did, and after eight months they had the script's first draft in hand. Producer Gene Kirkwood had recently completed a rather depressing film, *Ironwood*, with Jack Nicholson and Meryl Streep, and was ready for something completely different. Picked up by Orion and with Kirkwood onboard, the movie was filmed in Tulsa, Oklahoma. Along with Richards, Yankovic was happy to work with Victoria Jackson, Fran Drescher, and his friend Emo Philips. The film as whole was never subject to the whims of multiple production parties, rewritten or reconceptualized. Instead, Yankovic and Levey's original vision became *UHF*, the movie. And that vision seemed a clear winner when the movie tested through the roof—"the highest test screening numbers since the original *RoboCop*," Yankovic maintained in the film's oral history. For a brief moment, Yankovic was Hollywood hot. "When a movie tests like that, that's how Hollywood works: They thought we were the next big thing," Levey explained. But in the summer of 1989, the film's release coincided with a number of other huge films, including *Indiana Jones and the Last Crusade*, *Batman*, *Lethal Weapon 2*, and *Do the Right Thing*. The competition proved too much. Yankovic recalled, "We all expected the movie to do well. And then after opening weekend, when it didn't perform up to anybody's expectations, I was basically a ghost." The fall from grace was surprisingly fast. But *UHF* eventually found its audience—one remarkably devoted. When it came out on DVD, *UHF* was a top 10 release. It's now a bona fide classic, a favorite movie reference, with fans committed to their go-to scene picks. "Spatula City," says Ryan Mitchell, a reference to a madcap commercial complete with Yankovic song: "My, where did you get that lovely spatula? / Spatula City, we sell spatulas, and that's all." For others, Emo Philips's buzz saw mishap or "Raul's Wild Kingdom," featuring a failed poodle flight both tremendous and tragic.

After the disappointment of *UHF*, Yankovic found his footing again in 1992 when he took on the cultural craze that was Nirvana. Grunge had taken over American music with the release of Nirvana's 1991 *Nevermind* and the appearance of bands like Pearl Jam and Soundgarden, all radically altering the pop music landscape. Yankovic's response, *Off the Deep End*, was the first Yankovic produced himself, breaking with his previous producer, Derringer. Yankovic had a distinct vision and the discipline to execute it himself. Derringer might have forced the decision, according to engineer Tony Papa. At the time, Papa revealed to Geoff Edgers of the *Washington Post*, Derringer was not in top form: "He would do a line of coke, then mellow it out with a joint and then drink. A lot of times Rick would fall asleep. I think that's when Al realized he didn't really need Rick."

The cover art for *Off the Deep End* was a parody of the iconic album cover of Nirvana's *Nevermind*, which showed a naked baby, underwater, a dollar bill dangling in front of him like a carrot. *Off the Deep End* mimics the image with a submerged Weird Al chasing a doughnut. The album's Nirvana parody song, "Smells Like Nirvana," a takeoff of "Smells Like Teen Spirit," was Yankovic's biggest score since "Eat It."

In Christopher Weingarten's "An Oral History of 'Weird Al' Yankovic's 'Smells Like Nirvana,'" Yankovic recalls meeting Nirvana front man Kurt Cobain in person. Though he had talked with Cobain by phone, securing his permission for the parody, Yankovic met Cobain only once in person, by chance, at a restaurant in Los Angeles: "He just happened to be eating at an adjoining table with his friends. This was after the parody had come out, so I got to go over and thank him in person. I just profusely thanked him and said, 'Anything I can do for you, let me know.' Kurt extended his hand to me and said, 'Polish my nails.'" In his journal, Cobain called Yankovic "America's modern pop-rock genius."

Yankovic followed up in 1993 with *Alapalooza,* aping the name of the quintessential alt-rock music festival Lollapalooza, which had just hit its stride. The album parodied many grunge and alt-rock favorites, as in the Flinstones–Red Hot Chili Peppers mash-up "Bedrock Anthem." The album was a massive hit, certifying gold and winning a Grammy Award for Best Short Form Music Video for the clay animation video of "Jurassic Park." The following year, Yankovic's continued popularity brought him an offer to appear on the celebrity edition of *Wheel of Fortune* along with James Brown and Little Richard. He realized during taping that Brown had no concept of the game. Asked to name a consonant, Brown replied, "Oh . . . uh . . . Europe."

The album *Bad Hair Day*, released in 1996, sold nearly 2 million copies. It reached number 14 on the *Billboard* Top 200 and stayed there for fifty-six weeks. Fifty-six. The platinum-selling album featured the breakout hit "Amish Paradise," a parody of Coolio's "Gangsta's Paradise," and, in the supporting video, some outlandish hairdos with Yankovic playing a hybrid Amish Coolio. In *Weird Al: The Book*, Yankovic wrote, "I've worn these Coolio braids three times in my life: once for the album cover, once for the 'Amish Paradise' video shoot, and once for when I was co-presenting with Coolio at the American Music Awards. I don't recommend them—they're *excruciatingly painful*." "Amish Paradise" would be one of the few to court controversy, with a notorious diss from Coolio himself (see chapter 7).

A year later, Yankovic realized a long-standing vision when he coproduced and hosted a Saturday morning children's show for CBS called *The Weird Al Show*. It featured Harvey the Wonder Hamster: "He doesn't bite and he doesn't squeal / He just runs around on his hamster wheel." Each episode began with a lesson, and Yankovic often had special guests, musical and not. The show ran for one season on CBS. Yankovic recalled, "We first started pitching a 'Weird Al' children's TV show in 1984, around the time of 'Eat It.' My manager and I felt my personality and energy would lend itself well to a kids show, but it wasn't until the mid-Nineties where things seemed to click."[30] The talent involved was remarkable, including voice artist Billy West, writer Ron Weiner, and even Stan Freberg in a guest role, as J. B. Topper-smith—according to Yankovic in *Variety*, "the cantankerous head of the network who would constantly make my life miserable by giving me ridiculous notes and suggestions." The gag wasn't too far from the truth, and the show suffered due to network involvement and FCC regula-tion. It ultimately became, in Yankovic's mind, a "show for nobody."[31] Still, Yankovic never gave up on entertainment for children. In addition to his voiceover work and musical contributions to animated hits like *Captain Underpants: The First Epic Movie*, he has written two books for children: *My New Teacher and Me!* (2013) and *When I Grow Up* (2011).

Yankovic's own experience as a father has no doubt influenced this work. In 2001 Yankovic married Suzanne Krajewski, and the couple had a daughter, Nina, in 2003. He is a devoted father and speaks of Nina—now his "harshest critic"—with great admiration and love. In his 2014 interview with Andy Greene, he described her as "an ideal kid": "She likes playing outside, animals and nature. I was always watching TV at her age. Where did we go right?" In 2011, with Nina about to turn eight, Yankovic told *Live Journal*, "Kids are extremely creative and imaginative by nature, so as long as we don't crush their spirits—as long as we keep reminding them that it's okay to think differently and ex-press themselves in unconventional ways—I think they're going to be fine."

Despite the quick end of *The Weird Al Show*, 1997 was a big year for Yankovic. His label, Scotti Brothers, dissolved in 1997 and Yankovic found himself working with a new label, Sony. He also found himself a new look. For the album cover of the 1999 release *Running with Scis-sors*, Yankovic dropped his signature glasses (he had laser eye surgery) and grew out his hair. He came to be compared to another musician, the sax-wielding Kenny G, who in 2019 tweeted a picture of himself next to Yankovic with the caption: "Winners of best hair by a duo at the Grammys this year." Of his new look on *Running with Scissors*, Yankovic has said, "If Madonna's allowed to reinvent herself every fifteen minutes, I figure I should be good for a change at least once every twenty years."

Yankovic's next album, *Poodle Hat*, won the Grammy for Best Comedy Album in 2003. Explaining the four-year gap between albums, Yankovic cited record contract negotiations and a busy personal life. In an interview at the time with Len Righi of the *Morning Call*, he clarified: "I also fell in love, got married, bought a house and reproduced." On the album cover, Yankovic wears a suit and tie, expression serious, with his own dog, a grey poodle named Bela, on his head. In 2003 Dan Aquilante of the *New York Post* asked, "Where does poodle hat come from?" "Maybe you didn't notice," Yankovic responded, "but on the cover of the album, there's a poodle on my head. . . . She lives with me and works cheap." The surrounding crowd is a cross-section of people from his everyday life. In his "Ask Al" column, he singled out a few: "The guy in the surgical scrubs is my friend Joel Miller. The woman in the foreground with her legs crossed is my first-cousin-once-removed Tammy," summing up: "The overwhelming majority were friends and family members that just wanted to come to the shoot."

Yankovic had his first ever top 10 pop hit with "White & Nerdy" (see chapter 7) on his 2006 album *Straight Outta Lynwood*, which also features a dog on the album cover. The shot by Michael Blackwell, known for photographing hip hop stars, shows Yankovic as a "gangsta," a takeoff on NWA's *Straight Outta Compton*. Before he was called to duty, the dog, a pit bull, was a passerby on a walk with his owners. "White & Nerdy," a parody of Chamillionaire's "Ridin'," was a personal declaration with which many listeners identified. In its first three weeks online, the "White & Nerdy" video had 6 million hits. In the *Washington Post*, Richard Harrington claimed, "It's probably responsible for the accompanying album, Straight Outta Lynwood, debuting at No. 10—Yankovic's highest chart debut ever." Before Yankovic could put out his video, Chamillionaire posted it on his MySpace page. Yankovic told Harrington, "At first I was, 'Hey, I'm gonna world premiere that myself!' Then I thought, how cool is it that Chamillionaire himself wanted to put it on his page."

Yankovic followed *Straight Outta Lynwood* with *Alpocalypse* in 2011. In Rabin's book, Yankovic called the album cover his "might-be" favorite. In the nightmarish photo by Robyn Von Swank, the biblical

horsemen of the apocalypse appear, with one prominent substitution—
a smiling Yankovic waving at the camera. The album's centerpiece was
"Perform this Way," a parody of Lady Gaga's "Born this Way." The
album also featured the Doors-inspired song "Craigslist," with the direct participation of Doors musician Raymond Manzarek. In 2011 Yankovic told the *Pittsburgh Post-Gazette*, "That was a real thrill. I decided
that I wanted to do a song in the style of the Doors but about Craigslist.
I don't know why but the juxtaposition of those two things seemed
funny, seemed wrong on so many levels. The first thing I did was I
called Ray and said, 'Hey, you wanna play on this?' and he was like,
'Yeah! Sure!'" The album would prove his highest charting to date.

Just three years later Yankovic would top himself again, winning the
Grammy for Best Comedy Album for *Mandatory Fun*, which dominated the pop charts in a new way. The album title, Yankovic told NPR in
2014, "was just an oxymoron that I've always been amused by." But it
also signaled the end of his contract obligation. The popularity of You-
Tube, Yankovic revealed in a 2014 interview with the *New York Post*,
uniquely shaped his approach to the album's music: "I don't have the
luxury of going for the most obvious idea. Someone's already thought of
that and it's already up on YouTube. With the new album, there's some
songs that have been parodied to death already. I think I've taken a new
tack with them. That just helps me step up my game." Listeners agreed.
At the time, Dalson Chen, in an interview for the *Windsor Star*, asked
"How did it feel when *Mandatory Fun* hit No. 1 on the Billboard
charts?" "It was surreal!" Yankovic responded. "It was beyond my wild-
est dreams. I never dared to think I'd have a No. 1 album—I thought it
was beyond the realm of possibility. Comedy albums just don't do that.
The last time a comedy album hit No. 1 was 1963!"

Still, Yankovic has called *Mandatory Fun* his last album. Like Freberg, Yankovic finds the album format a burden, favoring single song
release instead. Comedy, after all, is all about timing. Waiting for
enough songs for an album, hoping the songs remain relevant, seems an
unnecessary gamble. In 2015 he said, "I feel like, for the kind of music
that I do, releasing things digitally as soon as I think of them is a bit
more efficient in terms of getting my music out."[32] In 2016 he confirmed, "I think I'm going to be utilizing a singles format or possibly an
EP format moving forward."[33]

In 2014 TruScribe created an homage to Yankovic's remarkable collection of album covers, to some a lost art, with an animated redesign of all fourteen, created on whiteboard right before our very eyes. The animation team had collaborated with Yankovic in the making of the video for his song "Mission Statement," on *Mandatory Fun*. The homage was, in part, thanks. At the end of 2017 Yankovic released his complete albums in the retrospective box set *Squeeze Box: The Complete Works of "Weird Al" Yankovic*, issued in an accordion-shaped box. His 2019 Grammy win for *Squeeze Box* acknowledged the artistic design of the project. In his acceptance speech, Yankovic said, "I've kind of been playing the long game—I never really wanted to be a recording artist. I just did it for forty years so I could win a Grammy as an art director."

But enough about the art. In his music, parody plus accordion has been an unlikely formula for long-term success. For Yankovic, it has been key to a fame far more enduring than that of his predecessors Lehrer, Freberg, and Sherman. He is a lone character—combining music, comedy, Hawaiian shirts, and so much hair. It's been Weird Al, just Weird Al, for forty-some years. Celebrating the release of *Mandatory Fun*, Jaime Weinman announced in the Canadian magazine *Maclean's*: "Song parodist 'Weird Al' Yankovic is back! Again!" The headline on August 14, 2014, in *Rolling Stone* read: "The Triumph of Weird Al: Inside the Parody King's Amazing Comeback." The headlines once again confirmed Yankovic's running joke—that every album he does is a "comeback" album. But here's the thing: Yankovic never really went anywhere. He's been here all along, creating new material, producing fourteen studio albums, making parody his own, his alone. But how? And what does parody actually mean? Like a lot in music, it's easy to use the lingo without really understanding the techniques behind it. In the next chapter, let's dig into the music by discussing parody, Yankovic's approach to parody, and how his approach has changed, making possible a career decades long, the saga ongoing.

2

THE PRINCE OF POP PARODY

Parody is part of growing up. Children, after all, love to mimic. But they like to break with the copy as well, testing out a budding sense of self or just blowing off steam.[1] Parody was part of Yankovic's childhood, as it was part of mine. I especially enjoyed the common, childish refashioning of "Happy Birthday to You," with the alternate ending of "You look like a monkey, and you smell like one too." The unexpected transformation to something inappropriate or taboo made my friends and I roar with laughter, at least a few times. I am not surprised that the prince of pop parody played with the song himself. In his mock autobiography *The Authorized AL*, which was written to accompany *The Compleat Al*, a faux celebrity documentary created in 1985 in collaboration with film producer Robert K. Weiss (of *The Naked Gun* franchise), he turned the traditional version into a money-making scheme:

> Happy birthday to you,
> Happy birthday to you,
> Happy birthday Aunt Elsie,
> Now gimme a dollar.

He opted for a more violent take with his 1983 song "Happy Birthday," from *"Weird Al" Yankovic*, with a new sound and text: "Well, what's the matter little friend? You think this party is the pits / Enjoy it while you can, we'll soon be blown to bits." Against lively instrumental accompaniment, the chorus, "Happy Birthday," fires on repeat, rhythmically reiterating the same note. The verses encourage us to celebrate despite the millions who can't and the chaos and greed that will, in the future, make sure we don't: "I guess you know the Earth is gonna crash into the sun / But that's no reason why we shouldn't have a little fun."

Changing the traditional tune and its lyrics, the song upends the "Happy Birthday" song as well as the very possibility of a happy birthday. Yankovic would later do something similar with his take on Christmas music. Adding to a collection of humorous holiday tunes, including Lehrer's "A Christmas Carol," Sherman's "Twelve Gifts of Christmas," and Freberg's "Green Chritma," Yankovic penned "Christmas at Ground Zero" (1986). Both horrific and horrifically funny, the song is set after an imaginary atomic bomb explosion. Yankovic sings, seemingly happy-go-lucky, with jolly sounds of the season, sleigh bells, and harmonized "ahhs": "We can dodge debris while we trim the tree / Underneath a mushroom cloud."

In a second contribution, "The Night Santa Went Crazy" (1996), Santa himself is the agent of destruction: "And he smiled as he said, with a twinkle in his eye / 'Merry Christmas to all, now you're all gonna die!'" Yankovic serenely sets up the joke describing Santa through a wholly original word combo: with traditional boots and beard, he has a ton of ammo, "a big fat drunk disgruntled Yuletide Rambo."

Yankovic explained to me the inspiration behind his first Christmas song. His record label, Scotti Brothers, was pushing him repeatedly for a Christmas album, what he saw as "the quick cash-in." Yankovic recognized the thought process: "Well, while he's still popular, we've got to get that Christmas album, and get those Christmas bucks." With his gruesome response, he would show them. But to me, Yankovic also credited his predecessors as inspiration: "Dr. Demento would play nothing but funny Christmas songs for two or three weeks before Christmas every year. So I knew that that was a rich mine."

But are all of these songs parodies, the simple text change at the end of "Happy Birthday" as well as the newly composed ode to a deranged Santa? And, if so, what exactly is parody?

PARODY IN ACTION

Parody is far from simple. By definition, parody unites the old with the new: A new work incorporates an older work, repurposing the text, the music, or the general style. But there is an ambiguity in the relationship between the past and the present inherent in the word's root, the Greek noun *parodia*. "Para" has two meanings—"counter" or "against" as well as "beside." In parody, two works may be "counter" (at odds), or simply "beside" (connected or unified). According to English professor Robert Chambers, there is a dualism in parody, "a beside-or-against doubling up of material to create confounding, ambiguous contrasts."[2] Parody, then, can work in two ways, even at the same time. We can identify a work as a parody, but parody is also a verb, an action—we parody another work or its cultural backdrop and norms. The juxtaposition of two works has an aim, perhaps more than one. Yankovic's various versions of the Christmas and "Happy Birthday" songs are all parodies, but these songs are not created equal. They serve different ends, rich with effect.

One function of parody is to offer comment on an initial work, paying tribute to or mocking that foundational work or its related culture and convention. Parody in this way reaches backward, resurrecting a past work or tradition. The initial work becomes relevant again. Yankovic's song "Generic Blues" (1989) is a nice example of this simultaneous movement forward and backward. Rumored to be one of B. B. King's top ten favorite blues songs, "Generic Blues" uses traditional blues phrasing and instrumentation as the lyrics lay out the problematic plight: no money, "I'm just walkin' down the road." Yankovic then shines a new light on the blues tradition, perhaps introducing some listeners to the genre for the first time. As one fan named John put it, "I guess one thing [Yankovic] did of significance is introduce people to songs and genres they may have otherwise never listened to."[3] This was true for Austin Roelofs, who experienced Weird Al as a gateway to Nirvana: "Al took me from the Beatles to Nirvana when I was ready."[4] And on the podcast *Conan O'Brien Needs a Friend, Hamilton* hitmaker Lin-Manuel Miranda explained that, as a Weird Al fan, you "learn to love different kinds of music." Then again, Yankovic creates an unusual treatment of the conventional blues' subject matter, with recourse to the underlying issue:

> I guess I got a pretty low self-image
> Maybe it's a chemical imbalance or something
> I should probably go and see a doctor about it when I've got the time

The blues is arguably cathartic—a means of uplift through confession and communication. But rarely does it address self-help so directly. In the song, Yankovic combines the dark subject matter with a candid consideration of self-care.

The combination of two works in parody is often the source of another effect: parody's humor. There is an incongruity, a particular expectation and its subversion. The surprise reversal can make us laugh. Yankovic maintains, "As has been said many times, a lot of comedy is the element of surprise. It's taking you down a road and then making a sharp left turn."[5] That left turn is at the heart of much of Yankovic's music, including the parody song "Couch Potato" (2003). In it, Yankovic substitutes new lyrics for Eminem's 2002 "Lose Yourself." Eminem's song is full of raw, rhythmic energy. That energy builds from a repeated rhythmic pulse in distorted guitar to a crescendo of synthetic strings and then percussion. It's an anthem of contagious motivation and we are ready to take our "one shot," to go after our dreams. Lost in the music, you can "seize everything you ever wanted." Yankovic's song has the same swelling pulse, a percussion match created by Jon Schwartz. A listener may enjoy recognizing the original, which is a basic element of the fun—*Hey, I know that song!* Some listeners may even like the parody simply because they hear and like "Lose Yourself." In repetition, there is the ready appeal of familiarity, valuable commercially too. But getting the joke, for others, is the real thrill. Against that building vigor, Yankovic promotes another sort of "shot"—taking the opportunity to "sit on your lazy butt, and watch all the TV you ever wanted." The juxtaposition of Eminem's aspirational message and Yankovic's ode to laziness is incongruous and thereby funny, potentially. But even without knowledge of Eminem's original, Yankovic's song can get that laugh. Eminem's vigorous beat clashes in Yankovic's song with his couch potato celebration. And that uncomplicated humor—based on a discrepancy within the song that doesn't require outside comparison—is important to Yankovic: "I like to think that my parodies are funny even if you're not familiar with the original song material."[6] The incongruity exists either way, and so, then, does the humor.

But parody's incongruity can also work as criticism. Through parody, the original song or artist appears in a new light—and that light is not always flattering. Flaws stand out afresh. The societal values that gave rise to the original also emerge from the shadows, offered up for judgment. Yankovic's song "Trapped in the Drive-Thru" is illustrative. From the 2006 album *Straight Outta Lynwood*, the song is a direct parody of "Trapped in the Closet," R. Kelly's 2005 "hip hopera." The R. Kelly song is already humorous, in unintended ways. It's surprisingly long; Kelly repeatedly extended the saga, even as late as 2012. The tale would expand to include over-the-top tales of sex, infidelity, corrupt cops, and even dwarf strippers. And the song's excessive drama is only heightened by R. Kelly's vocal stylings, dramatic embellishment, and modal play. The attention to detail ("Seven o'clock in the morning / And the rays from the sun wakes me / I'm stretchin' and yawnin'") is silly, as is the rapid singsong back-and-forth between characters, all voiced by Kelly. As a 2014 *Rolling Stone* "Readers' Poll of the 10 Best 'Weird Al' Yankovic Videos" put it, "How do you mock something that's already completely ridiculous?"

Yankovic found a way. For one, he stretched some of the existing drama and absurdity, the inadvertent humor. Clocking in at almost eleven minutes, Yankovic's song is long, like Kelly's. He also voices different characters, singing the banter between a man and his wife in excruciating detail. The music is similar, with the same opening keyboard passage, water drop–like sample, sine wave whistle, and synthetic bass boom. Yankovic's singing is backed by a chorus of "oohs," recycling Kelly's lush vocal soundscape. Yankovic's tale too starts at seven o'clock, but this time in the evening. Instead of Kelly's sexual drama, however, Yankovic's story is that of a couple deciding what to eat for dinner. Kelly's expressive vocal slide down highlights hunger in Yankovic's version and a misunderstanding about liver. Like the male character in Kelly's song, Yankovic's male protagonist receives a call, but this time it's from cousin Larry, the name alone far less glamorous or self-important than anything in Kelly's tale. Yankovic's everyday decision making collides with Kelly's theatrics, topped off with a cameo cut from Led Zeppelin's "Black Dog" (1971), which sounds over the car radio when Yankovic's couple finally sets out for food. The legendary Zeppelin song ups the contrast. Like Kelly's, it's a song about sex, but one far shorter, blunter, and more immediately effective. The first line gets right down to business: "Hey, hey, mama, said the way you move / Gonna make you sweat, gonna make you groove." As with "Couch Potato," the humor of Yankovic's parody does not depend on knowledge of the original. Yankovic recycles Kelly's dramatic vocal style, with regular multinote flourishes. In Yankovic's song, the musical setting also creates its own hu-morous clash with the lyrics and the scenario they conjure. We laugh at the theatrical rendering of a basic trip to the fast-food drive-thru: "Here in line at the drive-thru / Did I mention the drive-thru?"

The incongruity between Kelly's drama, heightened by the music itself, and Yankovic's quest for food is certainly funny. (And don't just take my word for it. Listening to these songs while reading is highly encouraged.) But the incongruity also offers criticism, underscoring the excessive length, drama, and detail of Kelly's original. There is an im-plied critique, which might extend to Kelly himself. On the June 24, 2018, episode of the podcast *Comedy Bang! Bang!*, host Scott Auker-man asked Yankovic about Kelly's ongoing sexual scandals, which have included salacious details of Kelly's abuse of underage girls. Yankovic referred to his song "Trapped in the Drive-Thru" in response. Though it was a seeming joke, there's a certain truth in Yankovic's answer. Yankovic's song finds humor in the gap between regular routine, in this case getting dinner, and the sexcapades of Kelly's song. To me, Kelly surfaces tinged as abnormal, even deviant. Before Yankovic's 2005 song, there were reports of Kelly's abusive proclivities, including news of a 1996 suit filed by Tiffany Hawkins alleging "personal injuries and emo-tional distress." Three more cases followed in 2001 and 2002—all with young women alleging sexual abuse: a sex tape, a forced abortion, and a controlling, "indecent sexual relationship." But Yankovic's song argu-ably highlighted Kelly's deviance well ahead of the more recent, high-profile news coverage: the #MeToo movement, R. Kelly's 2019 arrest, and the #MuteRKelly campaign, aimed at excluding Kelly from the entertainment industry.[7] And what better way to mute R. Kelly? Through parody, Yankovic replaces Kelly's voice with his own.

While an original song, style, or artist is often targeted in these ways, Yankovic can also parody events and ideas. On the website College Humor, Yankovic takes on the sinking of the RMS *Titanic* in a hilarious original entitled "Weird Al Yankovic on a Boat (And the Band Played On)," posted on July 15, 2011. Like the iconic musicians who pledged to play music to calm passengers as the ship went down, Yankovic with his band heroically vows to provide "some peace" through music as his own ship sinks. Seemingly serious, they launch into their song, Yankovic singing, "No hope is left of being saved / The icy sea will be our grave." As the desperate passengers panic, Yankovic offers some other inspired songs to drown by, including "Survival Is a Statistical Improbability" and my personal favorite: "Deep Sea Crabs Will Eat Your Face."

PARODY BY TYPE

In Yankovic's songs, these varied targets and effects—tribute, humor, and critique—come in various types. On his fourteen studio albums, Yankovic has released a dozen polka medleys. But most of the songs are either direct parodies or style parodies. Yankovic's writing process is far from random. He methodically matches up the right topic with the right music: "A lot of times, I'll keep a document on my computer of things that will be fun topics to write a song about. Or situations or basically a one-line description of, 'This would be a funny song.' I'll keep another list of genres or artists whose genre or style I might want to appropriate. A lot of times, I'll draw a line from column A to column B and see what makes the most sense."[8] For Yankovic, concentration is crucial. While other artists spin the creative process as a burst of sudden inspiration, Yankovic is honest about the work art requires and his wife's related displeasure. In 2011, he clarified, "I can spend anywhere from a few days to a few weeks writing a song. It doesn't just flow out of me naturally. I wish it did, but it involves a lot of heavy thought. My wife doesn't care for it when I'm in my writing mode, because I'm kind of oblivious to anything else. I'm like a zombie, apparently."[9]

The style parodies are original compositions that make allusion to the musical style of a specific genre or song. Yankovic's Christmas songs are style parodies, for example, as is his "Sports Song" on the 2014 album *Mandatory Fun*. With newly composed music, the song points to the customary fight song, complete with marching band, but plays up the underlying message for laughs. The vocal line ascends and then descends to underscore the sentiment: "We're great and you suck." He thereby stretches convention.

When his style parodies target a specific artist, study of the artist comes first. It's quite a lot of work, really, Yankovic explained on *The Michael Des Barres Show*. And it requires research. In an interview with Dalson Chen of the *Windsor Star*, Yankovic detailed: "I take artists and bands who I admire and I kind of deconstruct them. I listen to their entire bodies of work and I make notes. I try to figure out, 'What exactly

is it that makes their songs recognizable as theirs?'" His song "Bob,"
from the 2003 album *Poodle Hat*, was in this way an unusual case. The
song replicates a musical style associated with Bob Dylan—harmonica,
a pronounced nasal voice, and vocal attacks marked by scooping. At the
same time, Yankovic capitalizes on Dylan's first name as a palindrome:
"Was it a car or a cat I saw?" When I first asked Yankovic about his
approach to composition, he used "Bob" as an example: "I think mostly
I come up with the lyrics first and then figure out what kind of genre to
apply to it. Or sometimes I come up with a concept and I know what
kind of genre I'm writing. But I don't usually write the music first."
"Bob" was in part inspired by the year 2002, itself a palindrome. With
palindromes a topic, Yankovic thought, "Well, I wonder if I could write
a song completely out of palindromes? . . . So I started putting the
rhymes together and putting the verses together and basically making a
poem out of these palindromes." He continued, "And I looked at them
and I thought, 'Well, this . . . this is really just random jumble, but it
looks like it should mean something.'" The pseudo-poetic nonsense
struck him as similar to the lyrical invention of Bob Dylan. With a
booming laugh, he described to me the realization, how he looked at his
palindromes and thought, "I've written a Bob Dylan song."

Once the musical idea and lyrics are in place, it's often the band's
turn. Jon Schwartz filled me in on the group's role in Yankovic's original
composition:

> The first step is a demo that Al records for the band. Sometimes it's
> very specific as to parts, and other times there's a sort of blank space
> where he says, "Do something appropriate here," where the style of
> the song dictates the part. Next, after everyone has lived with his
> demo for a little while, the band rehearses and parts are massaged
> further, and Al is pretty receptive to input from us. The band then
> records a demo with Al, which is usually very close to what the final
> track will sound like. We chew on that a little, and there are a few
> inevitable tweaks, and everyone is basically ready to go into the stu-
> dio at that point.

Yankovic's writing process is different for his polka medleys. In them,
Yankovic rearranges various popular hits for accordion and supporting
ensemble. Yankovic's "Hot Rocks Polka" (1999) reinterprets the music

of a single group, the Rolling Stones. It's a medley of the band's songs and a reference to their compilation album *Hot Rocks* (1964–1971). The humor is in the clash between rock and polka. For Yankovic, however, it was an easy pairing. As he revealed, "Everything I play on the accordion—anything from rock to reggae—winds up sounding sort of like a polka to many people." And thanks to his Elton John remixes, Yankovic "learned early on that there was humor to be gleaned from the juxtaposition of rock and roll and polka music."[10]

Most of the other medleys play for laughs with the music of more than one band. It's a mash-up of multiple songs and often genres. In "Polka Face" (2011), Yankovic moves from an excerpt from "Womanizer" (Britney Spears) to "Right Round" (Flo Rida) and "Day 'n' Nite" (Kid Cudi). In "Polkarama!"(2006) Yankovic begins with "The Chicken Dance" and somehow makes his way, toward the end, to 50 Cent's "Candy Shop." The combination of many often disparate preexisting songs in a single work is not new; it is part of classical collage and general hip-hop practice. Even in the sixteenth century, composers did something similar, arranging several songs in a complicated simultaneous mix (known as quodlibet).[11] But while that construction was vertical, Yankovic's fusion unfolds horizontally, each song segment performed in succession. Brooding alternative rock or hard-edged rap, revamped as polka, only boosts the humor quotient. As Frankie Yankovic used to say, "Polkas are the happiest music this side of heaven."[12] The happy polka norm is a far cry from the more aggressive or moody sound. In joining the two, Yankovic creates a hilarious party mix of loathing and teen angst that feels like a coherent whole despite the various different songs involved. The "art of mash-ups" is this unity in incongruity.[13]

As in parody more generally, the medley's humor can include homage. In his "Polka Power!" (1999), Yankovic quotes Spike Jones's "Der Fuehrer's Face." Jones, a musician and bandleader, was known for humorous music, including musical rearrangements such as his "The Nutcracker Suite: With Apologies to Tchaikovsky." He debuted the song "Der Fuehrer's Face" in 1942 while the Nazis fought to capture Stalingrad. Jones replaced the words of the Nazi anthem "Horst Wessel Lied" with his own text, one that mocked Hitler, accompanied by irreverent sound effects, including a rubber "razzer":

Ven Der Fuehrer says,
"Ve iss der Master Race,"
Ve Heil! *phbbt!*
Heil! *phbbt!*
Right in Der Fuehrer's Face. [14]

Yankovic, in his version of Jones's song, replaces Jones's instrumentation with accordion as well as muted trumpets and tuba. The remix is parody, a juxtaposition of two songs—actually a parody of a parody. It also has purpose, primarily comedic. There is humor in the juxtaposition of the quote and the surrounding tunes, including the song "Ghetto Superstar (That Is What You Are)" (1998), by rapper Ol' Dirty Bastard and singer Mya. A song insulting Hitler fuses with a popular dance hit. [15] But the medley pays tribute to Jones, another early influence, as well. There is reverence in the inclusion of Jones's tune and in the reshuffle more generally. Yankovic has said, "[M]y medleys owe as much to Spike Jones as they do to traditional polka music." [16]

The comedic effect of the polka medley in many ways depends on familiarity with the original song. But the humor in Yankovic's direct parodies does not. These songs retain some version of an initial song's music while their lyrics are replaced with Yankovic's new text. Still, Yankovic's direct parodies target familiar songs, with "a musical or lyrical hook on them," most often those that are high on the charts. That popularity increases the likelihood a listener will recognize the full range of the parody's humor. In fact, most of the songs Yankovic chooses to parody debuted within the two or three years preceding his own version. The most overt exceptions are his direct parodies that deal in myth—superheroes, *Star Wars*, and the return of dinosaurs: "Yoda" (1985), a play on "Lola," by the Kinks (1971); "Jurassic Park" (1993), a parody of "MacArthur Park," by Richard Harris (1968); "The Saga Begins" (1999), a new version of "American Pie," by Don McLean (1971); and "Ode to a Superhero" (in this case, Spider-Man), initially "Piano Man," by Billy Joel (1973). Parody often relies on relevance, but with these latter songs, there is a significant gap between the making of the original and the parody. Instead, the original songs are classics, timeless like myth itself. They arguably help listeners suspend the current moment in favor of a story or legend that never really was. In our conversation, I mentioned the time gap and Yankovic recalled consciously carving out that space for "The Saga Begins," a summary of the film *Star Wars: Episode 1*, which Yankovic famously wrote before he saw the film, based on Internet rumors alone: "I kind of felt like Star Wars was such a ripe, weighty franchise I wanted to pair it with a weighty, classic rock song instead of just whatever happened to be the popular song that month." Of course, the film's contemporary significance could make up for any missing musical currency with its huge prerelease hype—a high destined to dip.

In the making of direct parodies, Yankovic's re-creation of an initial song's music has changed over time. For his first album, Yankovic joked, the guiding mantra was just, "Oh, let's have accordion in everything." The strategy was part of his earliest song successes, on *The Dr. Demento Show* and after. "I mean, there's a certain charm for songs like 'Another One Rides the Bus,'" Yankovic said to me, recalling the early effort. "It's so obviously not anywhere close to the right instrumentation but it's just kind of goofy and fun." But the charm evidently wore off, giving way to a more faithful rendering: "What I like is to trick people into thinking when my song comes on the radio that they're hearing their favorite pop song and then, 'Wait a minute. These aren't the words.'"

"It heightens the comedic effect," I summarized. "Yeah, it's a left turn," confirmed Yankovic.

Yankovic's guitarist Jim West has described the band's role in the process, explaining that each player attempts to make the music of the parodies "as authentic as possible and kind of trick people into thinking it's the real thing."[17] Yankovic made sure I was aware of his team's effort in this regard, calling the re-creation "forensic" group work: "Well, I'm very fortunate enough to work with very talented people. I've had the same band since the early '80s, and I work with talented engineers. I've been doing this myself for a while, so we've got a good team in the studio, and we just dissect it. It's like a forensic kind of thing where we really dig deep and we try to figure out everything that the original musicians did in the studio. And if we're baffled, sometimes we'll approach the original musicians." Of his band, Yankovic told me, "They'll find out what kind of original guitar pickup has been used or . . . where a specific sample came from and we would take great pains to get it as close as possible." That direct approach helped Schwartz get the percussion part just right in the song "Inactive" (2014), a parody of

Imagine Dragons's 2012 song "Radioactive." "I remember my drummer contacted the guy from Imagine Dragons," Yankovic said, "like, 'How'd you get that effect on the snare drum?'"

In our correspondence, Schwartz called the creation of Yankovic's direct parodies "an exercise in backwards-engineering"—one that "becomes more challenging with each project as mainstream music and sounds evolve, and production is cutting-edge." With the evolution of music technology, Schwartz's approach too has changed. It has had to. He shared, "For me, matching acoustic sounds has always been simpler." But he found he could reproduce early technological innovation, at least for a while: "With programmed songs in particular, in the eighties, synth drum sounds were more easily identifiable, and somewhat easy to match or get very close to. Later, as artists and producers began using computers to modify and create sounds from scratch, it was sometimes impossible to determine what sounds were used, and the band's job became more difficult. My approach changed from 'what did they do' to 'how would I make that sound?'"

In final production, the engineer tweaks the group's effort, a last step toward the sound match. Schwartz shared with me: "While I could get the sounds and vibe in the ballpark, our engineers deserve a lot of credit for dialing in the sound with EQ and effects as needed."

Still, a few variances remain, even in the later albums. In an interview with Kevin Coffey, Yankovic explained, "I generally like to make my parodies a couple beats per minute faster than the original song, just for a little energy boost. Also, I find that the comedy usually plays better if the tempo is a little quicker."[18] Parodies of songs sung by female singers are also a particular challenge. Yankovic revealed to me: "The obvious thing is, usually, I can't sing as high as female singers. So we, in many cases, have to change the key of the song, which makes it sound not quite identical to the original." He had to make a similar concession to his voice in his imitation of Michael Jackson. He recalled, "Even when we did 'Eat It,' I think it was maybe a bit higher than my range so we changed that one." The most significant difference, then and now, however, is Yankovic's voice. Like *UHF* co-stars Fran Drescher and Victoria Jackson, Yankovic's voice stands out—an unmistakable sound. Tune in; after all, there's no tuning it out.

A WINNING WHINE

Often described as "a nasal whine," Yankovic's vocal sound is the most distinct element in his parodies.[19] Yankovic has not worked to alter that natural quality, though early on he had misgivings about his voice.[20] He has had a few vocal lessons, from Eric Vetro, "Vocal Coach to the Stars," and friend Lisa Popeil, daughter of the inventor and salesman Sam Popeil, the subject of Yankovic's 1984 song "Mr. Popeil." The goal, he told me, was to avoid losing his voice while on tour rather than changing vocal quality or sound. And why should he? A nasal voice is not uncommon in popular music. In her study of vocal timbre, Kate Heidemann cites Willie Nelson's singing as a classic example of the nasal timbre—with "strong vibrations in the nose." But she admits that production of this timbre as well as perceptions of it are rather complex.[21] While Nelson's long and lauded career might represent a point in favor of a nasal sound, others have viewed the vocal type as a weakness. Outside of music, according to research published in the *Wall Street Journal*, a nasal or raspy tone can even have a negative effect on a person's career.[22] Want a promotion? Try speaking smooth and deep, apparently—more Cronkite than Kermit.

But Yankovic has never publicly doubted the nasal voice and, for purposes of comedy, he has even pushed the effect: "When I started out, I was embracing the whole novelty act thing and being more obnoxious and nasal than I needed to be."[23] Apart from comedy, the distinctive sound provides a fundamental service, signaling to listeners that they are in fact listening to a parody, style or direct. His voice also draws attention to the lyrics as the site of Yankovic's humor, especially in his direct parodies—further supported by the prominence of his sound in the recording, his voice often higher in the mix than the vocal part in the original song. As Schwartz explained to me, "Except for the lyrics, or possible comedic sound effects, you wouldn't know a funny song from a serious one. For us, the music is normal, and we approach that seriously. When Al's vocals come into play, then the song becomes funny." The laugh is in the incongruity between the sound and Yankovic's lyrics or the expected original lyrics and the new ones Yankovic creates. The absurd lyrical scenarios or wordplay only add to the fun.

In popular music, lyrics don't normally mean that much. As music sociologist Simon Frith writes, "In songs, words are the sign of a voice."[24] It's all about the performance rather than the words or their literal definition. "To be blunt," writes music philosopher Theodor Graycyk, "in rock music most lyrics don't matter very much."[25] Sound counts, not the words. But in Yankovic's music, the opposite is often true. Words matter very much. And Yankovic's voice is the sign of those words, urging listeners to pay attention. It's a unique inversion of the popular music norm.

Even with close attention, however, there are many different potential interpretations of a Yankovic parody—be it style parody, direct parody, or medley. Listeners interpret a parody based on their various previous experiences with music as well as their familiarity, or lack thereof, with the parody's targets. While Yankovic most often has humorous intentions, those intentions exist alongside other effects, some intended and others unintended. While I laugh at Yankovic's bleak "Happy Birthday," my daughter is rightfully horrified. While many laughed at "Christmas at Ground Zero" in 1986, the reviews were decidedly mixed after 2001 (as we will discuss in chapter 4). These songs are still parodies, but in different ways for different people—some recognizing his humor, some recognizing his message, some recognizing neither.

That message, in many of Yankovic's songs, revolves around language. Words are central to Yankovic's approach to parody but also a central topic of his parody. As we will see, words form and inform the joke. In so doing, Yankovic at times becomes the English teacher we all wish we had. And, in chapter 3, class is in session—though, with Weird Al in charge, it still feels like recess.

3

POLICING AND PLAYING WITH LANGUAGE

Yankovic cares about words. They have been a means of humor, the focal point in his direct parody songs and his original compositions. But they have also been a puzzle—like his palindrome construction in "Bob." Yankovic never created a building, despite his architecture degree, but he builds in another way. The art of architecture exists in his songs. Fitting words into their proper—and sometimes deliberately improper—place, Yankovic is aware of the power of words in his music's construction. And he respects language in his song's execution. Making clear his words, the site of his musical humor, he is careful to enunciate. But, to further the effect of his parody, he also often adopts the style of other artists or particular genres, with characteristic pronunciation or accent.

With this attention, Yankovic has made language the very basis of his art. The results often seem humorous and light. In the *New Yorker* article "Weirdly Popular," Sasha Frere-Jones discusses Yankovic's song "Word Crimes," insisting, "Every aspect of his art is enthusiastic and cheerful, a throwback to an earlier era of comedy and pop culture, when lightness had validity." In his work, there is "something sweet and unchallenging," Frere-Jones writes. But as philosopher Jürgen Habermas theorized, language is the medium of "the life-world."[1] Language has weighty significance. It is our means of interaction—good and bad—and the way we name societal concerns and values. It in turn affects who we are and how we act. Language is then a serious topic and, in Yankovic's music, seriously funny.

Yankovic's handling of language builds on his early models as well as his experience in high school debate. But perhaps his most significant influence is *Mad* magazine, which exposed him to humor in multiple languages. Prepared in these ways, Yankovic in his music takes on poor diction, grammar violation, and the abuse of words and phrases, while playing with the many possibilities of words themselves.

WORD HEROES, CAPED AND IN ALL CAPS

Yankovic's literary inspirations, the basis of his wordplay, include such diverse actors as Dr. Seuss, Shel Silverstein, and even *The Twilight Zone*'s Rod Serling. Dr. Seuss, as a children's writer, focused on substantial subjects, surprising to some—topics like life's purpose (*Oh, the Places You'll Go!*), environmental abuse (*The Lorax*), and discrimination (*Horton Hears a Who!*).[2] Silverstein too is known for writing for children, especially collections like *Where the Sidewalk Ends* (1974) and *A Light in the Attic* (1981). Silverstein also wrote songs, including Yankovic's early favorite "Boa Constrictor," which appeared on Silverstein's album *Everybody Loves a Nut* (1966), and "A Boy named Sue," which Johnny Cash included on his album *Live at San Quinten* (1969). Silverstein also released "A Boy Named Sue" on his own album, *A Boy Named Sue and Other Country Songs* (1969), his second after the 1962 album *Inside Folk Songs*. On these albums, Silverstein's literary voice stands out, but his vocal sound does as well. Friend William Cole described Silverstein's singing as a "yelp—made by a dog whose tail has been stepped on."[3] Some friend.

Serling's rich, deep voice easily distinguished him from Silverstein. As a child, Yankovic heard Serling on the television series *The Twilight Zone*. "I thought Rod Serling was pretty cool," Yankovic told me. Serling was a screenwriter as well as the narrator for the show, which originally aired from 1959 to 1964. Looking directly into the camera, sometimes with cigarette in hand, Serling eloquently summarized the episode, describing in "He's Alive" "a sparse little man who feeds off his self-delusion," before pausing to deliver the final three words, in "the Twilight Zone." Quotes attributed to Serling are as hip and otherworldly as his on-air persona: "Every writer is a frustrated actor who recites his lines in the hidden auditorium of his skull."

Yankovic worked to perfect his own speech delivery while in high school, where he was active in the National Forensic League, now the National Speech and Debate Association. The association's events involve policy debate, congressional debate, public forum debate, original oratory, and even humorous interpretation, the memorized performance of a comic text written by someone else. Yankovic excelled in his league events, humorous interpretation, and expository speaking. In his high school valedictorian speech (an excerpt is available on YouTube), Yankovic's resulting ease in front of audiences is evident. He clearly announces to the crowd, "If we want a better future, changes are imperative." Yankovic has continued this performance of words in voiceover work, in *Milo Murphy's Law*, *Wallykazam!*, *Teen Titans Go!*, *Gravity Falls*, *Adventure Time*, *Back to the Barnyard*, *The Grim Adventures of Billy & Mandy*, *Lilo & Stitch*, and *The Simpsons*, among others. Through his work, Yankovic has also taken on others who don't give elocution the same attention. On AL-TV, ostensibly a pirate takeover of MTV, Yankovic had "four-hour blocks of programming to basically do anything in the world I wanted to do."[4] With this freedom, he regularly spliced together mock interviews between himself and music celebrities, using existing footage of the stars and new footage of himself to create hilarious conversations that never really happened. In a 1996 clip, Yankovic highlights the British mumblings of rocker Keith Richards. Yankovic looks on incredulously as Richards seems to say, "Here we are, here we go, UFO."

Yankovic takes a similar jab at singer Kurt Cobain in his direct parody song "Smells Like Nirvana," from his album *Off the Deep End*. In the parody, Yankovic targets both Cobain's word delivery in "Smells Like Teen Spirit" as well as the original song's jumbled lyrics. Yankovic claims an affection for the grunge movement that coalesced around Cobain and his band, Nirvana, in the late 1980s and early 1990s. He has said, "It's hard to articulate for me exactly what I loved about Nirvana. It was the energy, the attitude. I liked the sound of real instruments. I like guitars. I like people screaming."[5] In his parody, Yankovic matched that screaming as well as the original song's signature flood of guitar sound, made possible through distinct use of the chorus pedal. Dressed in the video and in performance in a Cobain-esque sloppy striped shirt and floppy blond wig, Yankovic replaces Cobain's first verse—"Load up on guns, bring your friends / It's fun to lose and to pretend"—with what some listeners might have been thinking: "What is this song all about / Can't figure any lyrics out." Guns, loss, a dirty word—Cobain covers a lot in that initial verse, but to what end? And Cobain's lyric diction may have further muddled meaning. Before the final verse, Cobain sings, "Here we are now, entertain us / I feel stupid and contagious." Yankovic, with his retooling, made his point clear: "Here we are now, we're Nirvana / Sing distinctly, we don't wanna." The initial vocal line itself contributes to the confusion, with jagged jumps that give way to a repeated half step. That repetition, in the original, supports: "hello, hello, hello." Who is Nirvana greeting? Yankovic's answer, set to the same half-tone repetition: "don't know, don't know, don't know." And the chorus doesn't help. With an extreme leap in register, Cobain screeches in his highest voice, "With the lights out, it's less dangerous." With his own high-pitched shriek, Yankovic narrates, "Now, I'm mumblin' and I'm screamin'."

When he asked for permission to do the song, catching Cobain when Nirvana was scheduled to perform on *Saturday Night Live*, thanks in part to then-*SNL* player Victoria Jackson, Cobain responded with his own question, "Is it going to be a song about food?" Yankovic said no, "it's going to be a song about how nobody can understand your lyrics." In the *Permanent Record* liner notes, Yankovic recalled Cobain's response: "Oh, that's a funny idea, go ahead!" An early draft of the song, saved by Jon Schwartz, highlights the joke with the title "Sounds Like Teen Gibberish." In the lyrics, Yankovic likens the effect of Cobain's gibberish to "marbles in my mouth," and the accompanying video, which hews closely to the original with the same gymnasium and janitor, gives the claim a visual dimension, with marbles spewing out of Yankovic's mouth as he sings, with added subtitles. Mimicking Cobain's garbled delivery, in the parody's recording Yankovic sang with cookies in his mouth.[6] Yankovic's speech teacher surely wouldn't have approved, but through the word mangling, Yankovic successfully makes his point—a league win.

"Smells Like Nirvana" Live. *Courtesy of Fred Olderr*

MAD FOR FOREIGN LANGUAGES

Yankovic's time in speech helped him hone a useful skill set, backed by the example of Seuss, Silverstein, and Serling. But the writing in *Mad* magazine was in some ways a more obvious muse, the evidence everywhere in Yankovic's approach to language. Yankovic confirmed that, in his youth, "I was absolutely obsessed." In an interview with Michael Cavna for the *Washington Post* in 2015, Yankovic maintained, "Mort

Drucker [who worked for MAD] was one of my all-time favorite artists during my teenage years. And the MAD sensibility bored into my brain at an early age." *Mad* magazine burst onto the scene in 1952 as "Tales Calculated to Drive You MAD—Humor in a Jugular Vein." Harvey Kurtzman, a Russian Jew born in Brooklyn in 1924, was responsible for the idea of *Mad*, a satirical comic book/magazine. And the fourth issue found its intended readership with Kurtzman's parody of Superman, "Superduperman!" Under his initial leadership, the publication would skewer pop culture, including figures like Mickey Mouse, Joe McCarthy, and Norman Rockwell. It would also take on the mundane, much like Yankovic. One *Mad* tale concerned "He-Man Adventures of People Who Don't Get to Do Much More Than Hang Around."[7] For Yankovic, it wasn't just the "smart stupid" comedy that hooked him. *Mad*, for him, was also a way to think about the world. He explained to Cavna, "It's a way of dealing with a distrust for authority figures. It's about always questioning things, and it's about not taking things at face value."

In 1961 *Mad* itself dabbled in parody music, putting out forty-six parodies of popular songs, including "I Swat You Hard on the Skin," a new version of Cole Porter's 1936 song "I've Got You under My Skin." With *Campbell v. Acuff-Rose* well in the future, *Mad* immediately faced a lawsuit, accused of copyright infringement in the interests of the original musicians, including such seminal music figures as Porter, Irving Berlin, and Richard Rodgers. In 1963 the case came before Judge Charles M. Metzner, who ruled that two of the twenty-five songs listed in the case were indeed a violation of copyright. The decision was overturned on appeal in March 1964. Judge Irving R. Kaufman explained: "[W]e believe that parody and satire are deserving of substantial freedom—both as entertainment and as a form of social and literary criticism." But the Supreme Court eventually reinstated the initial ruling. *Mad*'s experiment in parody song was, for a time, over, though music was still fair game.[8] In 1985 the magazine angered the enigmatic singer Prince with "A Fairy Tale We'd Like to See." In it, a princess kisses a frog and subsequently a rather unflattering caricature of the Purple One appears.[9]

Still, the magazine's diverse play with words left a clear (and audible) mark on Yankovic's music. Early on, *Mad* made use of foreign words as well as words newly invented, adding to the expressive language of the magazine as a whole. *Mad*, after all, had deep roots in foreign lands, with some Jewish staff from Nazi Germany, and thus a natural connection to foreign words and phrases. In one letter, reprinted on a "Mad Mumblings" page, a reader demanded, "Please tell me what 'furshlugginer' means."[10] Other puzzling words published in *Mad* included *potrzebie, ganef, veeblefetzer, farshimmelt,* and *halavah*. In his creative wordplay, Kurtzman relied on and repurposed many words from Yiddish, what author Maria Reidelbach calls "an especially expressive language with more than its share of words with humorous possibilities."[11] Indeed, Yiddish boasts many descriptive words that convey character types: from *schlemiels* to *nudnicks*. And many of its words contain meaning, emotion, and humor—simultaneously. "To schlep," for example, means "to carry," but it also conveys the feeling of weight, the effort of carrying, as the speaker forces his or her way through the word's many initial consonants. The effect, to some, is comedic, and the sound is fun to produce with the tongue thrusting forward mid-word.[12]

Yankovic noticed the novel and expressive words. As he told me, "*Mad* magazine was sprinkled with Yiddishisms." The influence of *Mad* on Yankovic is evident in specific phrase constructions as well as his own use of Yiddish, another connection to Jewish parody that supports the mistaken rumor that Yankovic is Jewish. The language appears in Yankovic's 1999 song "Pretty Fly for a Rabbi" (to which we will return in chapter 7), which includes words like *schlep, shmeer, schlemiel, shul,* and *nudnicks*, among many others. In "The Plumbing Song" (1992), a parody of the music of the ill-fated German export Milli Vanilli—specifically their songs "Baby Don't Forget My Number" and "Blame it on the Rain"—Yankovic also sings about a "mensch with a monkey wrench." The Yiddish *mensch*, meaning an honorable person, becomes an unlikely rhyme with "wrench." In "The Night Santa Went Crazy," Yankovic uses the word *gentile*, which is not a Yiddish word but stems from the Hebrew word *goy*, meaning a person who is not Jewish. The song begins, "Down in the workshop all the elves were making toys / For the good Gentile girls and the good Gentile boys." The word connects the Christmas song to Jewish traditions, making the relationship or nonrelationship apparent. It's another example of Yankovic's recourse to Jewish worlds through language, language he encountered early in *Mad*.

Yankovic employs several other foreign languages in his songs, expanding his lyrical possibilities exponentially. He easily exploits his years of high school Spanish—he had three—especially in the parody "Taco Grande" (1992). Like the original song, "Rico Suave," the use of Spanish is quite extensive: "Yo quiero chimichangas y chile Colorado / Yo tengo el dinero para un steak picado." In other songs, Yankovic manages to work in pseudo-languages, business-ese and horoscope-speak, as well as more conventional options like French and Italian. In "Mission Statement," Yankovic sings, "We must all efficiently / Operationalize our strategies." In his 1999 song "Your Horoscope for Today," he tells the Pisces, "You are the true Lord of the Dance / No matter what those idiots at work say." In "Perform this Way," Yankovic announces: "And for no reason, now I'll sing in French / Excusez-moi, qui a pété?" ("Excuse me, who farted?"). In "Genius in France" (2003), it's a similar mix: "They think I'm c'est magnifique"; "Sign my poodle, s'il vous plait." And in "Lasagna" (1988), a direct parody of "La Bamba," he throws in the Italian "Mangia, Mangia!" ("Eat, Eat!"). Yankovic, who is part Italian, had actually wanted to do the whole song in Italian. He makes clear in the *Permanent Record* liner notes, "I was actually going through Italian phrase books and dictionaries until I realized that the humor would be lost on 99% of the audience, so I decided to do the whole thing in English but with kind of a bad Italian accent."

In his 1983 song "Ricky," a play on Toni Basil's 1982 "Mickey," Yankovic relied early on accent, mimicking the speech of Ricky Ricardo in a duet between Lucy and the Spanish-speaking Cuban from the television show *I Love Lucy*. In the accompanying music video, his first, Yankovic has his hair straight and slicked back, imitating the look and dress of Ricardo, played by Desi Arnaz. Yankovic builds on the multilingual humor of the show, itself a unique blend of Spanish and English, especially when it premiered on October 15, 1951. On the show, both Lucy's attempts at Spanish and Ricky's distinct accent were played for laughs. Jess Oppenheimer, producer and writer for the series, recalls of Arnaz, "[S]even or eight times a week he would say something during a rehearsal that came out funny because of his accent, and the people on the set would throw it in."[13] Yankovic played up the gag in his song, with his over-the-top pronunciation: "Hey Lucy, I'm home." One special fan, series star Lucille Ball, sent Yankovic a note of appreciation, saved today in Yankovic's collection of mementos.[14]

High on Yankovic's early list of career aspirations was writer for *Mad*. In "Ask Al," he confirmed, "When I was about four, I used to design miniature golf courses (with a crayon and a big pad of paper). I also thought it would be really cool to be a professional fireworks maker. A few years later I got interested in cartooning, and then I wanted to be a writer for *Mad Magazine*." The message of Yankovic's children's book *When I Grow Up* would have spoken to young Al. The story's eight-year-old protagonist imagines a dizzying array of future careers, but he learns that you don't have to pick just one. And thankfully, Yankovic's parents were always encouraging and never pressured him to discount one dream in favor of another. To Marah Eakin, writing for *AV Music* in 2014, Yankovic recalled, "They just wanted me to be happy, which was the best thing they could have wanted for me." And yet, in some ways, he had chosen his path early, even before his decision at twelve to devote himself to architecture—and it stuck. He would later describe his music to Cavna as a "sort of audio version of *Mad Magazine*." In honor of the influence, *Mad Magazine* appointed Yankovic its first ever guest editor in 2015. *Mad* editor John Ficarra, who became associate editor in 1980, explained to Cavna, "I've always been a big fan of his work. And when the idea of a guest editor came up last year, Al's name rose to the top." Just four years later, *Mad* officially ended; after sixty-seven years, the publication stopped. On July 3, 2019, Yankovic offered his tribute on Twitter: "I can't begin to describe the impact it had on me as a young kid—it's pretty much the reason I turned out weird. Good-bye to one of the all-time greatest American institutions."

This influence helped shape Yankovic's career aspirations and approach to language in parody. But Yankovic has also made his interest in language the subject of many of his songs. On a basic level, Yankovic is concerned with proper use of words. In *Weird Al: The Book*, Yankovic helpfully corrects the grammar of other musicians: Rolling Stones's "(I Can't Get No) Satisfaction" becomes "I Can't Get Any Satisfaction" and *Grease* duet "You're the One That I Want" turns into "You're the One Whom I Want." But in 2014, he turned the issue of grammar, far from the pop fare norm, into a popular triumph with his song "Word Crimes." On his 2014 album *Mandatory Fun*, another clever play on words, the song was the breakout hit, a surprising win for language lovers everywhere.

GETTING SCHOOLED IN SONG

"Word Crimes" is a direct parody of Robin Thicke's "Blurred Lines," a 2013 *Billboard* Song of the Summer. The initial song bemoans the supposed "blurred lines" that keep a good girl from giving in to her supposed animal nature: "But you're an animal, baby it's in your nature / Just let me liberate you." These lines arguably make consent a problem, sanctioning real-life situations that nullify "no": "I hate these blurred lines / I know you want it." Given the endemic of date rape on college campuses, several universities banned the song. One that didn't, the University of Exeter, nonetheless issued a statement from the student guild, printed in 2013 in the *Guardian*: "A song that implies a woman is 'an animal' who 'wants it' because of the way she is dressed is not acceptable." The video, shot against a white backdrop, features several scantily clad women (completely nude in the unrated version) and the fully dressed Thicke. This is a common strategy in music videos—we gaze at the female body while the male body, in clothes, is virtually erased. The contrast is in some ways ridiculous: On what occasion would men and women mingle so differently dressed (or undressed)? But the frequency of the pairing in music videos has helped render the image normal—if not accepted then at least expected.

When the song was released, the sexual implications of the song and video were not the only point of controversy. Songwriters Thicke and Pharrell Williams were accused of copying Marvin Gaye's 1977 song "Got to Give It Up," violating copyright. In testimony, expert musicologists drew attention to similarities between the two songs' lyrical phrases as well as the pairing of bass and keyboard in the style of reggae or ragtime. In March 2018, the Ninth Circuit Court of Appeals confirmed that Gaye's estate was indeed entitled to compensation for the copyright violation, awarding it 50 percent of all "Blurred Lines" royalties.[15]

Yankovic had no delusions about "Blurred Lines," calling it, in a 2017 interview with Jesse David Fox for *Vulture*, "an extremely catchy kind of Marvin Gaye pastiche." And his humor depended on the "sexually charged" subject matter of the original. He played on the "bizarre juxtaposition" of sex and rules of grammar. His music video—one of eight successive videos supporting *Mandatory Fun* released on eight successive days starting on July 14, 2014, and supported by the memorable hashtag, #8videos8days—did so as well. It was a marketing ploy and internet spectacle compared to Beyoncé's surprise online release of her 2013 *The Visual Album*, though Yankovic had actually done a similar release before Beyoncé with his 2011 album *Alpocalypse,* with videos for each of the album's songs. In the "Word Crimes" video, Yankovic replaces Thicke's almost naked women with dancing punctuation marks. In some ways, the joke was kind to the "Blurred Lines" singer, given the original song's more controversial fodder for parody. "I think [Robin Thicke] was glad I went in that direction," Yankovic said in a 2014 interview with Hadley Freeman for the *Guardian*. He could have created a very different parody. And he revealed to Fox that he had other ideas, what he has called "really horrible ideas": "Dessert Line" and "Absurd Mimes," among others. But he never considered playing up the overtones of sexual aggression in the original, the approach many amateurs took on YouTube. Like the original song, these other parodies, were, in Yankovic's on-the-nose wording, "rapey."[16]

The music of "Word Crimes" adheres closely to the original, as is customary for Yankovic in later albums. The parody song relies on the original song's lively percussive drive, defined by a simple dance beat in a two-measure loop, with a prominent bell part. The vocal layers, with punctuating "woos," skew toward the original in lyric as well, despite the change in subject matter. Thicke's line "You're an animal / baby, it's in your nature" becomes "Gonna familiarize you / with the nomenclature." The original line and the parody replacement rhyme: "nature" and "nomenclature." The chorus, too, sounds alike—"I hate these blurred lines" and "I hate these word crimes." Yankovic does not believe a sonic connection between the lyrics is "essential," but, he claimed in the interview with Fox, "the closer you can keep to the original source material while tweaking it to a whole different subject matter, I think that makes the comedy play better." More important than similar-sounding words, to Yankovic, is his lyrics' syllabic correspondence with the original text. He strives to create a new line that fits the original line spatially and rhythmically, with the same syllabic count as well as a similar accent. Again to Fox, he explained, "There's a meter to every line and if you get the accent on the wrong syllable, it doesn't flow that well." Following these parameters, in "Word Crimes" Yankovic presents a string of grammar lessons, drawing attention to the difference between "less" and "fewer," the meaning of "it's," the correct use of "to whom," proper application of quotation marks, the definition of "literal" versus "figurative," and the problematic substitution of numbers for words. The latter is a texting habit, he sings, only allowed for seven-year-olds or Prince, a reference to the singer's adoption of a symbol in place of his name in 1993.

It's a daunting task to match the patterns established in the original, the accent and syllable breakdown, creating compelling content that fits. "I will come up with a dozen variations for every line in the song," Yankovic told Fox. "I'll go back later and figure out which one rolls off the tongue easiest, or which one is the funniest. It is a bit like a puzzle because I try to make every syllable as good as it can be." An early draft of "Smells Like Nirvana" codifies the process. Writing in all caps, Yankovic has two options for the line "How do the words to it go"—one written above the other in a smaller print. On April 3, 2018, crossword columnist Deb Amlen recognized Yankovic's skill in this regard—his ability to twist and bend words to suit a set arrangement—asking, in the *New York Times,* "Why has the man never made a crossword puzzle?" Thankfully, Amlen continued, "Our long national nightmare is over." On that day, Yankovic, aided by puzzle maker Eric Berlin, debuted a *New York Times* crossword puzzle of his own design, dedicated to cheese. The clue for 20A, "Cheese military drama?" gives way to a pun on the film title *A Few Good Men*—"A FEW GOUDA MEN."

The grammar lesson in "Word Crimes" is at times a bit harsh. It begins, "Everybody shut up!" Yankovic's rules include insult: "Don't be a moron / You'd better slow down / And use the right pronoun." Is the delivery an indication of Yankovic's lived experience? When I commented on the ruthless tone, asking about his early English teachers, Yankovic dismissed the link: "I think pretty much every one of them was a very good teacher, and inspirational, and always encouraged me." Yankovic remembered, in particular, Mr. Higgins, a teacher during his high school senior year. No, the inspiration for the song and its severe air, he maintained, was more recent. He cited decades of written releases from his record labels, sent to him for his approval and littered with obvious errors: "Well, spell my name right first," he said to me, laughing. "And this is written by professional people. It's their job to do these releases. And still, they were doing typos, syntax errors. I mean, I would have to go through like I'm an English teacher and, say, red-line it." He acted out the scenario: "Here, try it again." Yankovic also admitted a less obvious secondary point. While he primarily takes to task those ignorant of grammar, at the same time he mocks those overly concerned about grammar's proper use. The tough tone, in this regard, is necessary, a means to underscore the obnoxious air of those policing other people's linguistic choices. He is playing the grammar Nazi, though sympathetically. "A lot of my songs," he told Fox, "are two-edged in that way."

Other songs from *Mandatory Fun* revolve around a different duality—the duality in language itself. "Tacky," a parody of the contagious 2013 Pharrell Williams song "Happy," is a case in point. Yankovic had assumed "Tacky" would be more popular than "Word Crimes." Though it proved false, there was good reason for thinking so, including the hilarious supporting video, the first of the eight video downloads. It was filmed at Palace Theatre in downtown Los Angeles and featured a string of dancing celebrities, including Margaret Cho, Eric Stonestreet, Kristen Schaal, Aisha Tyler, and Jack Black. All are loudly dressed—Cho in yellow lederhosen with bright blue tights. Yankovic's parody has its own language lessons, demonstrating the various meanings and uses of the word "tacky": "It might seem crazy, wearing stripes and plaid / I Instagram every meal I've had." Tacky, in the song, is both appearance and behavior. Your outfit can be a tacky mismatch but your conduct can also be just as tacky. We're back in school, getting schooled on vocabulary and life.

In another song from the same album, "Foil," a parody of Lorde's 2013 "Royals," Yankovic plays the teacher again. In the song, he outlines two very different uses of aluminum foil. Replicating the surprising vocal harmonies that define the original against percussive snaps, Yankovic celebrates the first, rather mundane, foil function: the proper care of leftovers. He sings: "That kind of wrap is just the best / To keep your sandwich nice and fresh." With such a humdrum initial topic, the second application is startling: protection from aliens, mind control, and other extraordinary menaces. Formed into a hat, Yankovic insists, aluminum foil will ward off every sort of sci-fi conspiracy: "Don't mind that, I'm protected cause I made this hat." In the video, a mock cooking show, the lights dim as Yankovic details his tale of government surveillance and thought police. The once jovial Yankovic, as the would-be celebrity chef, glares into the camera. Having lost control of the talent, his poseur producer, played by comedian Patton Oswalt, throws up his hands in exasperation.

PUN FUN

Part of Yankovic's focus on words and their many connotations and consequences gives way in his songs to the prolific use of a much-maligned joke: the pun. A pun relies on similar-sounding words or different definitions of a single word. *Webster's Dictionary* defines it as "the humorous use of a word in such a way as to suggest different meanings or applications or of words having the same or nearly the same sound but different meanings." As pun champion John Pollack puts it, puns are, then, both homophonic, exploiting "words that sound alike," and homographic, "based on etymologically distinct words, spelled the same, that have more than one meaning."[17] Yankovic's accordion medley "Polka Face," which includes an excerpt of Lady Gaga's 2008 song "Poker Face," features a homophonic pun, playing with the sounds of "polka" and "poker." When Yankovic appeared on Craig Ferguson's *The Late Late Show* on February 9, 2012, he created a homographic pun when he responded to Ferguson's demand that he pick one of his organs to "sell off." Rather than the expected anatomical variant of the word, Yankovic threw out the musical version. "Wurlitzer," he said. When Yankovic set out to create another homographic pun, circa 2010, his audience was in on the joke. In the video, available on YouTube, he saunters on stage intending to "shred" before putting several pieces of paper through a shredder. He stands up after the deed is done, face serious as if the task were momentous, hands up in celebration. The packed audience cheers.

Puns are a signal and a product of the ambiguity in language itself. Many words we use have significance beyond our intended meaning. Language can be interpreted in many different ways, based on a word's multiple meanings as well as various associations with a single word. In some ways, punning is inevitable. Purposely playing on that ambiguity can be seen as clever or funny, a surprise or humorous incongruity. But William Shakespeare, a notorious punster, used puns to both entertain and engage an audience. As Pollack writes, puns invite audiences "to pay close attention to the speaker's intent or miss the moment."[18] The pun was strategy, forcing listeners to actively listen or else overlook the full point or argument. Of course, not everyone is prepared to recognize or understand the pun. Puns, after all, demand more of our brain functioning. We naturally select the most likely meaning of a word—that's part of how language processing works. But to understand a pun, we have to maintain in our mind more than one potential meaning simultaneously—a mental juggling act.

Many famous figures in the United States, from Abraham Lincoln to Henry David Thoreau, have responded positively to the pun, making regular use of the device. Puns have also long featured in music, especially on Broadway. And yet puns have accumulated an elephant-sized collection of negative baggage, dismissed as corny or old-fashioned with a groan or eye roll. As a shirt I gave my father-in-law reads, "Bad Puns Are How Eye Roll." As philosophy professor Gordon C. F. Bearn has observed, "The air of crime clings to puns. . . . By groaning, we punish the punster."[19] But the groan—a noise that both sounds and feels funny—can actually disguise motives that have nothing to do with pun punishment. The groan can be acknowledgment of the pun—*Yes, I got the joke*. It can also act as the expression of frustration, making it clear that the pun or punster is an interruption or otherwise unwanted. With the sound, a listener may even attempt to cover up the fact that he or she simply didn't get the pun. I had this complex reaction while reading the original release announcement accompanying Yankovic's "My Bologna," issued by Capitol Records on December 24, 1979: "'My Bologna' features 'Weird Al' delivering some very meaty vocals."[20] My groans grew even louder while reviewing a passage in *The Authorized Al*, a reflection on the making of several of Yankovic's food-based songs:

> It wasn't easy to get these scrumptious songs recorded, however. Al's sweet dream almost turned sour. First of all, Al had to butter up the top bananas at the record company before he could even get a nibble. Then, after all of that work, all Al got was a polite thank you and would he please just let them digest the idea. Frankly, Al felt they didn't care beans about his music. He was steamed.

And that's not even the end of it. Six more sentences follow in that vein—all hard to swallow. My groan was one of amusement but also an audible protest. This was simply too much of a good thing. Make it stop.

And then the sheer number of puns became the joke, and my groan turned into a half smile. I admitted a meat-based defeat.

In his music, a rather gross pun defines Yankovic's 1983 "Gotta Boogie," an up-tempo song with driving percussion, perfect for dancing. In fact, the initial repetition of "Gotta boogie" seems a clear declaration, a need to dance, until Yankovic completes the sentence: "Gotta boogie on my finger and I can't shake it off." In "Handy" (2015), set to Iggy Azalea's 2014 song "Fancy," the pun is a bit more risqué. Yankovic insists, "Let me be your stripper / Taking off lacquer, no one does it quicker." For advanced punsters, in "Christmas at Ground Zero," Yankovic finds a way to pun on mistletoe, with "missile-toe." Other Yankovic puns, like the titular pun "Polka Face," depend on knowledge of the original song, further supported in the corresponding music video.

In "Eat It," a song that cemented Yankovic's fame, Yankovic's pun relies on familiarity with Michael Jackson's original, "Beat It," which had been released in 1983 and was an immediate hit. The original lyrics were well-known; it was a song about aggression and fight, becoming a man. Yankovic's song—with its insistence that you finish your dinner—is an obvious contrast. Jackson's performance and musical style, jagged lines and cool delivery, are also incongruous with the new text: "Have a banana, have a whole bunch It doesn't matter / what you had for lunch." But part of the success of the parody was MTV. The television channel had only existed for three years prior to Yankovic's "Eat It" video. The fledgling network and Yankovic found a way to help each other. In a history of MTV, Yankovic recalled, "As soon as 'Eat It' went into heavy rotation, my life changed. It was overnight fame."[21] Harvey Leeds, one-time director of video promotion at Epic Records, observed, "MTV loved Al. Because every time he parodied a video, it only served to reinforce the power of MTV."[22] Yankovic's "Eat It" video was a shot-for-shot re-creation of Jackson's own video, with a few clear changes. At the video's start, in the same single bed as Jackson, Yankovic sings, but this time with doughnuts beside him. In *MTV Ruled the World*, Yankovic recalled, "We shot for two days on a soundstage. Michael Jackson's original locations didn't exist anymore, so we had to recreate everything from scratch. Michael's choreographer, Vince Patterson, reprised his role as a gang leader for my video." The many connections to Jackson's "Beat It"—through the musical parody as well as the video—helped support Yankovic's pun: "Just eat it! Eat it! / Get yourself an egg and beat it!" The two songs for many were intertwined sonically and visually, the connection cemented by a pun.

Music video more directly supported another Yankovic pun in 2011, in the parody "Perform This Way." After the influence of MTV had waned in the realm of music video, the channel turning more to reality shows than music videos, Yankovic, like many, shifted to digital possibilities. In 2017, media studies expert Mathias Bonde Korsgaard credited the internet with music video's "second golden age," observing a "post-televisual resurrection."[23] Six years before, in 2011, Yankovic was ahead of the curve when he put out a digital video for his song "Perform This Way," a direct parody of Lady Gaga's "Born This Way." In his version, Yankovic sings, "I'll bet you've never seen a skirt steak worn this way!" Referencing an all-meat dress worn by Lady Gaga to the 2010 MTV Video Music Awards, Yankovic riffs on "skirt steak," a cut of beef. The pun is clarified in the video with Yankovic wearing an actual skirt made of meat.

This clarification was part of the video's "added value." Music videos are promotional in nature and thereby easy to dismiss as commercial. But, as Korsgaard explains, video "adds value to the music, guiding us towards certain 'views' on the music, privileging certain musical elements, perhaps making us aware of something we would not otherwise have heard." The dancing punctuation in Yankovic's "Word Crimes" video have similar value. The video enhances the incongruity between Yankovic's song and Thicke's original. It also in some ways calls out the combination of dressed men and undressed women in the "Blurred Lines" video: Both images appear ridiculous.

For Yankovic, pun creation is a major video benefit, depending, of course, on your valuation of the pun—and not only in the "Perform This Way" video. In his "Amish Paradise" video, Yankovic sings the line, "Jebediah feeds the chickens and Jacob plows." The accompanying shot is that of Jebediah feeding the chickens pizza and Jacob plowing the field. But later in the video, Amish boys covertly skim the fictitious magazine *Amish Babes*, emboldened with the text "Plow My Field." It's a sexual pun unique to the video and to Yankovic's typical family-friendly fare. But the use of video to support a pun is all Al—the value of video can be, for him, based in language.

MAKING SENSE OF NONSENSE

In addition to his focus on specific words, Yankovic also reveals in his songs a fascination with certain expressions or aphorisms, their meaning and construction. Phrases include "one of those days," "when I was your age," "good old days," and "only kidding," the latter a phrase with personal relevance. In certain songs, he calls out the misuse of these phrases. But in one song, "Dare to Be Stupid," he adds to the confusion, tweaking phrases to create bizarre pseudo-wisdom that is in fact wise.

In "Genius in France," Yankovic plays with phrases that colorfully insult another person's intelligence: "A few peas short of a casserole / A few buttons missing on my remote control." The phrases fit the musical line and colorfully illustrate meaning both sonically and visually. The combination of such phrases brings to mind the song "My Favorite Things," by Richard Rodgers and Oscar Hammerstein II, from the 1965 musical *The Sound of Music*: "Raindrops on roses and whiskers on kittens / Bright copper kettles and warm woolen mittens." Each phrase creates its own picture. I wasn't surprised to learn Yankovic had taken note of the Rodgers and Hammerstein original, creating his own never-released parody of the classic in 1979. By phone, I asked him, "Do you remember what you did with that song?" I couldn't find a copy of the song, I told him. Yankovic was relieved: "Good. It was probably pretty bad." In his version, he nonetheless shared, the "favorite things" were far less inviting, no cozy mittens or kittens: "It was basically from the standpoint of some degenerate and everything that he mentioned was just disgusting."

In his 1985 classic "Dare to Be Stupid," a celebration of the individual, Yankovic spotlights similarly descriptive aphorisms, like "Don't look a gift horse in the mouth" or "Don't put your eggs all in one basket." The aphorisms, in effect, have the air of eternal truth. As Ben Grant writes more generally in his study of short phrase constructions, aphorisms communicate a sense that the speaker "articulates a truth that comes from elsewhere."[24] Masked by a facade of authority, an opinion appears as wisdom. But in "Dare to Be Stupid," Yankovic flips the conventional formulation, authority gone: "It's time to let the bedbugs bite / You better put all your eggs in one basket."

When Yankovic upends perceived truth ("Look a gift horse in the mouth"), the effect is strangely freeing but also disorienting. Reality slides into a game or dream world. Grant observes this impish potential, calling aphorisms "small things" that together make "a field of play." He singles out Lewis Carroll's *Alice's Adventures in Wonderland* (1865) as a case in point. "Grinning like a Cheshire cat," a preexisting phrase, becomes in Carroll's work a character, an idea turned tangible. Yankovic creates a comparable "universe of nonsense." But that nonsense makes some sense. Do it your own way, Yankovic's song says. Don't follow the existing script. His 1999 album *Running with Scissors* makes the same inversion a point of pride. The cover art features Yankovic in fitness attire, sprinting with hands raised in victory, holding scissors aloft. A parent's admonishment becomes a winning, yet still dangerous, lifestyle choice.

In his music, Yankovic subverts other phrases through exaggeration. His 1992 song "When I Was Your Age" is a style parody of the music of Don Henley, solo artist and founding member of the Eagles. In the parody, Yankovic riffs on the existing hyperbole and overuse of the titular phrase by stretching its reach even further: "Well, nobody ever drove me to school when it was ninety degrees below / We had to walk buck naked through forty miles of snow." As is typical of many of Yankovic's songs, the scenario quickly escalates: "Dad would whoop us every night till a quarter after twelve," then they'd have to whoop themselves. The chorus: "When I was your age."

The intensification of the scenario is similar in his song "One of These Days," an original composition from his 1986 album *Polka Party!* The song starts reasonably: "Got to work late 'cause my alarm was busted / The boss chewed me out and everybody's disgusted." Tardy to work, Yankovic dismisses the bad day as "just one of those days." The phrase, "one of those days," is often used in this way to write off a wholly ordinary, though less than perfect, showing at work or school. But Yankovic extends the norms of the line's conventional use, with the phrase describing subsequent scenarios both frightening and ridiculous: "The Nazis tied me up and covered me with ants / And I spilled toxic waste on my brand new pants." The humor lies in the easy dismissal of the truly dire. But there is also a comedic contrast between the serious and unserious: toxic waste versus brand new pants, burning crosses versus no more Cheetos.

On the 1988 album *Even Worse*, Yankovic highlights a related phrase, "good old days." In some ways, the phrase is such a cliché that it has lost any real meaning. But it is also a rosy expression that masks the worst of the past—every past. As Petula Dvorak writes in a rebuke of the phrase, "No, those weren't the good old days." She points to the nostalgia conjured by an old hardware store in Purcellville, Virginia, open since 1914. But, she insists, don't be fooled. When that store opened, lynchings still occurred in the Virginia Piedmont region, women couldn't vote, and town leaders punished those even suspected of being gay. "Still feeling nostalgic?" she asks.[25]

Yankovic clearly wasn't. In the song "Good Old Days," a style parody of the music of folk artist James Taylor, Yankovic imitates the quaint comfort associated with Taylor, known for songs like "You've Got a Friend," as he describes a simpler time: "Dad would be up at dawn / He'd be watering the lawn." The accompaniment is light, featuring the acoustic guitar, and the music has an easygoing, wholesome lilt. But, while mom was baking biscuits and pie, Yankovic sings, he'd spend his day in the basement, "Torturing rats with a hacksaw / And pulling the wings off of flies." The music, in a major key, does not alter or modulate to illustrate these darker activities, uniting baking and torture as if there is some equivalence. At the same time, the consistent sound does make clear the chronology: Both the good and the bad happened in this past. The jarring contrast quickly gives way to the refrain, after a silent downbeat, a moment of pause: "Those were the good old days," harmonized in happy block progression. This time, Yankovic undermines the line not through exaggeration but through realism, pitting our glowing picture of the past against the dark deeds that surely occurred then too. It's a humorous clash with a pointed message. Yankovic took that startling mash-up to another level on November 30, 2018, when he sang the song in bed, in solidarity with children who have to spend the holidays in a hospital bed—part of Bedstock, an initiative to support the Children's Cancer Association. With his band in blankets, Yankovic sang for a worthy cause about animal mutilation in front of a huge pink and white stuffed pony.

A final phrase that can cover up all sorts of ills is "only kidding." Yankovic makes the phrase and its abuse the subject of his 1992 song "I Was Only Kidding." The song relies on the punk/New Wave music of Tonio K, whose songs often walk a line between humor and anger, a funny nihilism that earned him radio play on Dr. Demento's show. The singer does not have the same level of mainstream recognition as the musicians Yankovic typically chooses to parody. But Yankovic evidently had a soft spot for Tonio K, who also inspired his 1983 song "Happy Birthday"; "I Was Only Kidding" is, then, a rare stylistic repeat. To Kyle Anderson, in *Entertainment Weekly* (2014), Yankovic explained, "[Tonio K] is not obscure but he's not an artist that a lot of people would immediately recognize. But I'm a huge fan of his."

Yankovic's "I Was Only Kidding" begins like a ballad, backed by a full choir with big vibrato. The choir sings a harmonized "ooo," as Yankovic sweetly croons the first verse:

> When I told you that I loved you
> With those tender words I spoke
> I was only kidding
> Now, can't you take a joke

The choir joins Yankovic, singing "I was only kidding," but the "ooo"s return, supporting the next line, "Now, can't you take a joke," which ascends in a harmonized slide to close the verse. Everything then changes, with a blistering guitar passage that signals the start of the song's punk portion. Yankovic's sweet side disappears to reveal something raw and angry. Not even his explanation, "I was only kidding," can hide the truth of who he is. And for his wronged former lover, with gun in hand, it's clear the phrase does not ease the pain. And still this cruel lothario seems unconcerned, confident in his defense, ending the song with a lively "Hey!"

The phrase is passive-aggressive in Yankovic's song, a way for the offender to confuse the victim by assuming victim status himself. Yankovic's musical setting plays up that subterfuge, with a drastic change in tone that reveals the speaker's darker intentions. But there's something else in the phrase, a complicated connection to comedy that makes it particularly fitting for a Yankovic song. While humor is freeing and subversive, it can also be a means to cover up all manner of transgression—a "homophobic punchline or an act of sexual harassment." It was just a joke. I was only kidding. As musicologist William Cheng observes, it's a "get-out-of-jail-free" card.[26] At the same time, the phrase can work in the reverse. Nothing counts in comedy. The expression says: it's just a joke; he's just a joke. And the connection to children, in *kid*ding, doesn't help. The phrase is a specific threat to humor and the comedian, a dismissal of comedy's serious subject matter. Yankovic himself has been dismissed in the same way, a dismissal that ignores the weight and significance of his comedy. "I Was Only Kidding" therefore feels particularly personal. It features a musical style Yankovic held in especially high esteem and a phrase that undercuts comedic art. Words are part of Yankovic's music and approach to music. But this takedown hints at something more than Yankovic's concern about language. Could the song be one man's attempt to vindicate comedy?

When we met, I tried to better understand Yankovic's focus on the abuse of words: "Are these things that have just annoyed you in your life?" "Yeah, partly that," he acknowledged, "and partly because I saw the comedic potential in it. That's where a lot of comedy comes from. It comes from just airing grievances, airing pet peeves; 'What's your beef?' as Jay Leno would say." In his autobiography *Leading with My Chin*, Leno described the gimmick, a staple of his visits to *Late Night with David Letterman*: "[T]o launch me into some fit of bombast, [Letterman would] usually ask: 'So—do you have any beefs this time out? Anything that's stuck in your craw? Gnawing at you? Eating at you?'" Yankovic's annoyances often just happen to be word-based, the misuse of language—even the inference of words where there are none. In his song "Jackson Park Express" (2014), for example, Yankovic reads increasingly detailed messages into the subtle looks passed between passengers on the bus, a send-up in part of clichéd movie meet-cutes but also exploration of another language abuse: "She looked at me in a way that asked / 'Did you have a nose job or something?'" In Yankovic's music, these aggravations, these beefs, overlap with the comedic potential of wordplay in general. He concentrates on the abuse of words to get a laugh through his own creative attention to language. In so doing, his comedy has consequence—a substance not everyone recognizes.

Perhaps in comparison to Thicke's suggestion of rape, Yankovic's focus on words seems sweet and light, as Frere-Jones maintains. But there is still a challenge in Yankovic's music and in his wordplay. This consideration of language can be weighty. Language is central to the workings of society, a means of interaction and negotiation, influencing how we think about the world and those around us. Language can entertain and create connection, but it can also function as a tool of abuse and manipulation. Through his focus on language, Yankovic creates humor but also makes pointed arguments—arguments concerning the past, attitudes toward humor, and general behavior. Writers like Frere-Jones may miss the point because they have trouble looking past the joke. Yankovic's reputation as a nice guy may also play a role. Yankovic himself has been viewed as "sweet and unchallenging," his persona potentially coloring his music's reception. That image, as we will see, gives cover to more than just Yankovic's significant attention to language.

4

SUGAR AND SPICE AND EVERYTHING ALMOST NICE

In this book's foreword, Dr. Demento compares Yankovic to Frank Zappa in terms of the two musicians' admirable work ethic. But, in terms of nice, Zappa was nothing like Yankovic. With a vicious sense of humor that often came out in his music ("Jesus Thinks You're a Jerk," "Crew Slut," and "Jumbo, Go Away," among others), Zappa was notoriously hard on other musicians (as he himself would admit) and even his audiences, at one concert calling them "pigs." Yankovic, in contrast, is routinely recognized as "nice": nice to work with and an all-around swell guy. In 2015 journalist Michael Hogan writing in the *Telegraph* confirmed that "[h]eld in high esteem by his peers and music fans alike, Yankovic has a reputation as one of the industry's good guys."[1] Singer Bill Mumy (Art Barnes of the duo Barnes & Barnes) views the label as well deserved: "Al's been a pal since before MTV. His videos are always brilliant. He's a really hard worker and a very nice guy. One of the good guys."[2] Andy Samberg and Seth Meyers agreed on *Late Night with Seth Meyers*, discussing Yankovic as the "nicest man on earth." This reputation is part of Yankovic's brand—a rather unusual one, at least in Hollywood.

In his songs, Yankovic has challenged others who are not quite so nice (though never Zappa, whom he actually admired, even creating the Zappa style parody "Genius in France"). His style parody "Why Does This Always Happen to Me?" (2003) is based on the music of Ben Folds, who penned the song "The Luckiest," a love song that Yankovic, in an interview with David Segal of the *Washington Post*, admitted gets him "all weepy." (Me too, sir. Me too.) In it, Yankovic targets people who selfishly view the tragedy of others as their own inconvenience, a tendency he guards against himself: A terrible car accident, "everybody dead," and now "it looks like I'm gonna be late to work. . . . Why does this always happen to me?" In a 2011 interview he told Rabin, "These are real moments where I find myself being horrified by my own brain, having so little empathy for other people."

I had to ask him, "Do you see yourself as nice?" I already suspected that Yankovic's nice-guy reputation was based in fact. When I asked to interview him, through his longtime manager, Jay Levey, Yankovic invited me, a stranger, into his home in the hills of West Hollywood; introduced me to his lovely wife, Suzanne; and offered me something to drink—coffee, juice, whatever I wanted. I set up for the interview in his living room, with a view through the floor-to-ceiling windows of Los Angeles below. Yankovic sat on the couch beside me, with no modern instrument of distraction, a cell phone or other electronic device. He was completely engaged, and as I asked questions, he at times leaned a bit closer to make sure he had heard the question in full. In response to each of my queries, he was both entertaining and thoughtful. He apologized for one short answer: "I'm not thinking of anything . . . sorry." I had to laugh; the apology was so unwarranted. An interview is a forced interaction with the potential to go spectacularly awry (as is evident in online compilations of star-studded face-to-face disasters). But through his generosity, Yankovic made our first interview productive and rewarding. And the cherry on top: he autographed a CD for a five-year-old fan—my son.

Still I continued to pry, hoping to make Yankovic's drummer, Jon Schwartz, my informant: "In work together, is Mr. Yankovic really as nice as they say?" "Absolutely," he maintained. "He's genuinely considerate and kind. I've never heard a mean or dirty word from Al. In fact, I've only seen him get angry once or twice in all these years, and it takes a lot to get him to that point." Schwartz has worked with Yankovic since their first meeting in 1980—so long, in fact, that he has a joke: "that I would be his drummer until he's 'Old Al' Yankovic. . . . That prophecy," he realizes, "is likely to come true." Two other members of the band, guitarist Jim West and bassist Steve Jay, have been with Yankovic since 1982—almost four decades. In 1991 Yankovic added Rubén Valtierra on keyboards to the group. Though he's approaching thirty years with Yankovic, Valtierra will always be the new guy. The band members' choice to maintain their working relationships with Yankovic for all these years appears to confirm Yankovic's niceness—a point I made to the man himself. After all, I commented, "Spinal Tap had thirty-seven members." "Well, they keep dying is the problem," Yankovic humbly responded.

I was more direct when I interviewed Schwartz: "How unusual is it for a band to maintain the same membership for so long, in your opinion?" Schwartz revealed, "It's extremely rare in a business not known for long-term popularity or creativity. Only a few bands have had continual careers longer than Al's, with their original personnel—U2, ZZ Top, and, until very recently, Rush. That's pretty good company!" In the estimation of Reed Fischer, writing for *Rolling Stone*, U2 is indeed one of the longest-running bands, "no breaks, no lineup changes, no hiatuses." Bono, the Edge, Adam Clayton, and Larry Mullen Jr. have been together since 1978. But ZZ Top and Rush actually had early changes in the position of drummer. Aerosmith almost made the list, but the group, too, has had lineup changes: guitarist Joe Perry left the band due to drug issues in 1979 and Brad Whitford, with his own issues, took a break in 1981—though they both returned in 1984. Not only that, Aerosmith has had internal feuds wholly foreign to Yankovic's band. Just in 2009, Daniel Kreps reported in *Rolling Stone*, Perry purportedly wasn't speaking to lead singer Steven Tyler after the group's canceled tour. Though Tyler insisted "Shit's cool," Perry publicly commented, according to Kreps, "All I know is [Tyler's] got to get his act together."

In earnest, Yankovic revealed to me: "Well, I think I'm a nice guy. I'm always a little baffled when people single me out for my niceness because most of my friends are nice. I don't think I'm any nicer than my friends. Most of the people that I meet even in the music business are generally fairly nice people, so I don't know how I got this reputation. I'm glad for it. I'm happy to be known as a nice guy." With a smile, he added, "But I mean, mostly, I just don't treat people like garbage. I try not to be a jerk, and apparently in this town that's good enough."

Yankovic's reputation is especially meaningful today, in our current age of incivility. But he does have several songs that include biting insults. "One More Minute," from his 1985 album *Dare to Be Stupid*, is

The Band in "Amish Paradise." *Courtesy of Jon Schwartz*

a sort of doo-wop throwback with supporting male vocals. In it, Yankovic croons, in a rounder voice reminiscent of Elvis Presley, "Well, I heard that you're leavin'." But no hard feelings; he is supposedly over it, no tears here. In the video, the three backup singers sway behind Yankovic as he sings in the spotlight, head often tilting down and moving slowly around, eyes closed in sentimental excess. But his attempts to cope with an evident breakup move from the ordinary to the extreme rather quickly: from tearing up old pictures to burning down a malt shop. The breakdown is supported by the vocal part, which slowly ascends, peaking an octave above its initial note, in an emotional climax of admitted arson. The malt shop indexes the innocence of shared drinks in a nostalgic past. Still, the heartbroken protagonist is obviously far from fine. Yankovic makes that clear by cramming into the last verse an overload of illustrative imagery:

> I'd rather rip my heart out of my ribcage with my bare hands
> And then throw it on the floor and stomp on it 'till I die
> Than spend one more minute . . .
> With you.

Inspired by an unpleasant breakup, the song fits into a history of insulting breakup songs. Some are rather poetic in their bite, like Carly Simon's 1972 song "You're So Vain," which Simon later revealed was aimed at least in part at actor Warren Beatty. Others less so, like Cee-Lo Green's 2010 kiss-off to his gold-digging ex, "F*** You." Yankovic's song stands out within this subgenre. It's insulting but also remarkably violent, with one of his few sexual innuendos: "'Cause I'm stranded all alone, in the gas station of love / And I have to use the self-service pumps."

Yankovic also composed "I'm So Sick of You," from the 1996 album *Bad Hair Day*, with its impressive list of jabs: "your teeth are all yellow, your butt's made of Jell-O. . . . Hey baby, trust me, you just disgust me." Most of the insults are superficial, having to do with appearance or the body more generally. But they also take on habits—asking "stupid" questions, biting toenails, and drooling. And this song too has violent tendencies: "And when you ask me what I'm thinkin', honey, usually I'm thinkin' / How I'd really like to tie your head completely up in duct tape."

When I attempted to find potential inspiration behind some of these songs and their dark dealings with women, Yankovic explained to me that he didn't get married until 2001: "I was single for a big chunk of my adult life." He continued, "And I had my fair share of dysfunctional relationships." He wouldn't call his songs autobiographical, but he admitted, "I have to say that there are some feelings that I probably picked from my deep subconscious that I covered in comedy and dredged [up] for music purposes."

But men too are subject to insult in Yankovic's songs. In "That Boy Could Dance," from his 1984 album *"Weird Al" Yankovic in 3-D*, Yankovic describes a boy saved only by his ability to dance: "We all used to call him, Jimmy the Geek / He was a dumb lookin', scrawny, little four-eyed freak." And on the same album Yankovic mocks the fictional boxing hero Rocky, who, in the song "Theme from Rocky XIII," is imagined to be well past his prime. In the song, Yankovic parodies Survivor's "Eye of the Tiger," an anthem of inspiration in the *Rocky* film franchise, to portray Rocky, now "fat and weak," as he sells deli meat: "Try the rye or the Kaiser."

How does Yankovic maintain his nice reputation while putting out a whole song insulting an ex or taking down popular culture's most beloved boxer? Insult in parody is especially complex. And Yankovic cannot be held responsible for all of the insult in his songs—some are subject to interpretation and change in meaning over time. But Yankovic's popular standing as a nice guy may also come into play. Does being nice offset any potential blowback? *But it's Al. Nice Al.*

INSULTING AL

In Yankovic's songs, there is name-calling, a rather traditional means of insult. In "Another One Rides the Bus," Yankovic refers to "perverts," "freaks," and "a smelly old bum." In the 1986 song "Toothless People," Yankovic's parody of Mick Jagger's "Ruthless People," Yankovic sings, "Toothless people / Old and feeble." In his 2006 "Canadian Idiot," a take on Green Day's "American Idiot," Yankovic announces the intention to insult Canadians up front: "And do I look like some frostbitten hosehead?" In "You're Pitiful" (2006), a direct parody of James Blunt's "You're Beautiful," Yankovic finds a way to match Blunt's otherworldly high register, replacing the original song's titular compliment with a direct dig: "My life is brilliant / Your life's a joke / You're just pathetic / You're always broke." Yankovic had hoped to include the song on his 2006 album *Straight Outta Lynwood*, but Atlantic Records denied permission, overruling Blunt's initial endorsement. Yankovic instead released the song on his website, explaining to Stephen Thompson of NPR, "If James Blunt himself were objecting, I wouldn't even offer my parody for free on my website. But since it's a bunch of suits—who are actually going against their own artist's wishes—I have absolutely no problem with it." Evidently, he thought the executives at Atlantic Records were, well, pitiful.

But Yankovic's most insulting songs employ more than simple name-calling. I asked Yankovic, "What do you think is your most insulting song?" He thought for a moment, "Maybe 'Achy Breaky Song.'" "Achy Breaky Song" (1993) lists all the terrible music Yankovic would prefer over Billy Ray Cyrus's "Achy Breaky Heart." In so doing, Yankovic created a diss track, musician-on-musician abuse not unlike the famous examples "Hit 'Em Up," Tupac Shakur's 1996 attack on Biggie Smalls and Junior M.A.F.I.A., or Nicki Minaj's more recent "Stupid Hoe," directed at Lil' Kim. Cyrus's song was released on March 23, 1992, and became a number one hit just two months later. The pushback was just as quick. Indeed, Yankovic was not alone in his negative reaction to the invented phrase "achy breaky," despite the fun wordplay. The accompanying video, with Cyrus sporting a pronounced mullet, was fuel to the fire. Writing for *Wide Open Country*, Jeremy Burchard added, "And don't forget that super dramatic moment where he rips off his shirt." To insult Cyrus, Yankovic maligns other perennial punching bags, musicians who are bad but still supposedly better than Cyrus: "You can torture me with Donny and Marie / You can play some Barry Manilow / Or you can play some schlock like New Kids on the Block / Or any Village People song you know."

Barry Manilow is a regular target elsewhere, including within crime prevention—a favorite artist in playlists designed to deter teen loitering. I had to follow up: "Is Barry Manilow really a least favorite?" "No," Yankovic said. "I like Barry Manilow. I mean I've got nothing against Barry Manilow. He plays the accordion, for crying out loud." Like Yankovic's early study, Manilow's musical training was accordion based. Manilow recalled, "My parents somehow rented an accordion. Every Jewish and Italian kid had to play an accordion."[3] In our first interview, Yankovic clarified, outlining the writing strategy informing "Achy Breaky Song": "I kind of went through songs where I'd imagine that a lot of people might be irritated by the artist. In fact, I could have put myself on that list easily. And I actually like a lot of the songs—a lot of the artists that I name-check in the song. It's just that for the sake of comedy, they're sort of the punchlines, punchline names."

Calling "Achy Breaky" the "most annoying song I know," Yankovic in his song professes to prefer violence—being tied to a chair and kicked down the stairs or "a pitchfork in my brain"—over "that stupid song." And yet the whole takedown is a direct parody—and thus imitation—of Cyrus's song. The music is the same, with repetitive percussion and guitar accompaniment. Yankovic even sings with a light country twang. Aside from the addition of a sound akin to pitched duck calls after the chorus, only the text is truly distinct. He is insulting a song that he in turn reproduces. His insult of Cyrus is, then, also a self-insult: "[T]hat nauseating song" is also his own. Still, Yankovic didn't feel great about the song. It's "sort of mean-spirited," he acknowledged. He had crossed a line he had established for himself, so he donated proceeds from the sale of the song to the United Cerebral Palsy Association. In "Ask Al," he revealed, "Both the writer of 'Achy Breaky Heart' and I were a little uncomfortable over the fact that the parody was a little bit, well, mean-spirited. So we thought it would kind of take the edge off of it if we donated all of the songwriting proceeds to a worthy charity."

Yankovic made a similar concession with his song "Perform This Way," which lampoons Lady Gaga's over-the-top dress. Though Gaga (eventually) called the parody "empowering," Yankovic had some trouble getting her permission initially, which he detailed at the time on his personal blog. He also felt somewhat conflicted about taking on Lady Gaga's song "Born This Way," a powerful anthem of self-love despite difference: "I try not to do parodies that are in bad taste, and the fact that 'Born This Way' was a gay rights anthem, I just felt a little strange poking fun at it." He decided to donate the song's profits to the Human Rights Campaign, a national organization devoted to lesbian, gay, bisexual, transgender, and queer civil rights—a way to justify the song "personally."[4] In his blog entry "The Gaga Saga," he clarified: "Based on my concept, I was reasonably sure that my parody wasn't really going to offend anybody . . . but I still decided, as an act of good karma, that I would donate all the money from sales of the song and music video to the Human Rights Campaign."

In 1980 Yankovic went after Billy Joel with the song "It's Still Billy Joel to Me," a direct parody of Joel's "It's Still Rock and Roll to Me," also released in 1980. As with the Cyrus parody, the song is direct in its insult: "What's the matter with the songs he's singin'? / Can't you tell that they're pretty lame? / After listenin' to a couple albums / Well, they all start to sound the same." But Yankovic never released the song; the lyrics are available thanks to Jeff Morris and Annie Satler on the Demented Music Database at http://dmdb.org. In "Ask Al," Homely Bubert asked about the omission: "Never got the rights? Decided it was a bit harsh?" Yankovic answered, "I wrote that in 1980, but even by 1983 (when my first album came out) it felt a bit dated. Also, we figured that Billy wasn't very likely to give us his blessing on that one anyway, so we never even bothered asking."

Some have taken notice of Yankovic's songs in this vein. One writer, Brian Boone, in the article "Weird Al's Mean Streak," notes Yankovic's nice-guy rep but observes, "Yankovic is human, and as such, he's got a mean streak that occasionally, and fascinatingly, rears its curly head." Boone singles out as proof another song, Yankovic's "(This Song's Just)

Six Words Long" (1988). Like "Achy Breaky Song," the insult is also self-insult. The original, George Harrison's 1987 song "Got My Mind Set on You," begins with seven words, repeated four times: "I got my mind set on you." Yankovic spoofs this repetition, highlighting other repeated lines in the original: "it's gonna take money," "it's gonna take time," "to do it (right)." Of course, to insult Harrison's song in this way, Yankovic again replicates some of the techniques he criticizes. The song begins: "This song's just six words long." That's all—six words, repeated four times, like the original.

But it could be worse. In *Weird Al: The Book,* Rabin qualifies, "Weird Al's songs don't set out to skewer anyone: they're more about exuberant silliness rather than any cruel purpose." Yankovic himself emphasizes the role of homage in his parody—as well as the humor, of course. He insists, "The spirit in which a music parody should be created is a personal choice—many parodists and satirists go for the jugular, but I've always gone for humor that was a little less biting and derogatory."[5] To Dan Rather, in his 2015 *Big Interview,* Yankovic summarized, "I'd rather poke them in the ribs than kick them in the butt."

Parody itself can soften the burn, buried as it is in more than one purpose. The insult in parody isn't always central, obvious, or intentional. As Linda Hutcheon maintains, parody's "range of intent is from respectful admiration to biting ridicule."[6] This range is a defining difference between parody and satire. While both rely on a certain distance and implied judgment, satire "generally uses that distance to make a negative statement about that which is satirized."[7] For that reason, parody is a more flexible device. While some of Yankovic's songs can be defined as satire, he favors parody and, with it, the versatility and confusion of multiple effects.

Even without parody, insult can be unclear. Nothing is intrinsically insulting. Scenario determines meaning—who is involved and where. In interpretation, the effect of an insult can be funny, inspiring, or upsetting—at times simultaneously. And a listener might ascribe to a song an insult where none was intended. Yankovic most often intends a tribute or just plain fun, but on more than one occasion, he has had to deal with unforeseen fallout from inadvertent and ambiguous insult.

"HE'S A MIDGET BUT HE MAKES A LOT OF TROUBLE"

Yankovic is careful to ask for permission from the artists he parodies, though legally he is not required to do so—part of his positive reputation, no doubt. Interscope Records gave him permission to parody rapper Coolio's "Gangsta's Paradise," but the result—"Amish Paradise," released in 1996—offended Coolio. Backstage at the Grammys in 1996, Coolio told a reporter, according to Conor McKeon in *Vulture*, "[I] ain't with that . . . I think that my song was too serious . . . I really . . . don't appreciate him desecrating the song like that." Ten years later, Coolio had apparently gotten over it. In "Ask Al," Yankovic recalled, "I was at the Consumer Electronics Show earlier this year signing autographs at the XM Radio booth, when somebody told me, 'Hey, did you know Coolio is in the building?' A few minutes later it was 'Hey, Coolio is in the area' and then 'Hey, Coolio is coming over here to see you!' I admit I was a little nervous at the time, since I don't know if I should be expecting a handshake or a punch in the eye." Coolio's negative reaction was well publicized, in part because it was unusual. Most artists react positively to Yankovic's parody proposals. Often the biggest challenge for Yankovic is simply making contact with the original artist in order to request permission. When Australian rapper Iggy Azalea's management didn't return his calls in 2014, Yankovic checked Azalea's tour schedule. He told Australia's *Herald Sun* newspaper, "I decided to fly down to Denver to see if I could 'bump' into her, talk to her and get her permission on the spot. As soon as she got offstage, I introduced myself, told her what I wanted to do and she said it all sounded fine." With his perseverance, his song "Handy," a parody of Azalea's "Fancy," was a go. But Yankovic didn't have to worry about Coolio at the electronics show: "As it turned out, Coolio couldn't have been nicer—he just walked up to the table and started signing one of my pictures with his own name." A picture in Schwartz's private collection captures the moment. In the photo, Coolio, in a green jersey, holds out his hand to shake Yankovic's, and Yankovic, in a gray Hawaiian shirt with blue flowers, reaches back, smiling. Both men seem to be looking at their outstretched hands rather than each other. Still, bygones were bygones. As reported by Michael Hogan in the *Telegraph*, Coolio later admitted, "I was being cocky and stupid. I was wrong and should've embraced it. The song's actually funny as s___."

Yankovic has also unwittingly offended listeners. In his song "The Saga Begins," the line "Did you see him hitting on the queen?" somehow crossed the line. Radio Disney censored it, changing "hitting on the queen" to "talking to the queen." But language and thus meaning transform over time. More often than not, this evolution has been the real problem for Yankovic. His parodies, after all, rely heavily on language as well as timing, a response to a particular cultural moment. As time passes, his songs can mean something else, informed by new events. The songs may become insulting independent of their original intent. For this reason, Yankovic has called out the use of words like "midget" in some of his earlier songs. Describing Barney Rubble in the "Bedrock Anthem" on the 1993 album *Alapalooza*, Yankovic sings, "He's a midget but he makes a lot of trouble." Yankovic knows now that the real trouble was the word "midget." When he originally used the word, Yankovic told me, it "was just sort of a jokey word and certainly not the slur that it's become. . . . So I certainly wouldn't write a song like that now. Even when I perform songs that have that word in them, I wince a bit. And in fact, one time, I forget which city it was, but I stopped the song in the middle. I was like, 'Look, when I wrote this song, it wasn't that kind of word.'" If Yankovic had been a novelty act, here then gone, he wouldn't have this issue. He wouldn't have to deal with the way parody changes in meaning over time. His longevity has forced him to consider how the significance of his songs changes. It's a unique downside of enduring fame.

He has been particularly sensitive in this regard to the song "Christmas at Ground Zero," written during the Cold War. In late 1979, Soviet forces invaded Afghanistan, and in 1980 President Jimmy Carter boycotted the Olympics in Moscow. With Ronald Reagan's election later that year, his "Evil Empire" speech in 1983, and an increase in military spending, by 1986 the Cold War was in blizzard conditions. When Yankovic's song came out, though a de-escalation of tensions was under way, "Christmas at Ground Zero" was not without controversy. Some radio stations banned it. In a 2013 interview with Jeremy Martin for the *San Antonio Current*, Yankovic joked, "for some reason, they didn't think it was appropriate to have a song about nuclear destruction during the holidays." For Yankovic, that incongruity was the source of the song's humor—the juxtaposition of the grim lyrics and Christmas cheer, signaled by the song's traditional sounds of the season, ringing bells and woodblock percussion evoking sleigh bells and horse hooves.

Decades later, the same incongruous humor remained, but the specifics of the Cold War context were less clear. The new global crisis of terror, following the terrorist attacks of September 11, 2001, for many had become the predominant threat. And the term "ground zero" had transformed in meaning, too, from the site of an imagined nuclear blast to the all-too-real site of the 2001 World Trade Center attack. In a 2014 interview with Mick Stingley of *Esquire*, Yankovic felt compelled to make clear the distinction: "I'd like to stress here for the record, in case it confuses anybody: 'Christmas at Ground Zero' is not in any way, shape, or form about 9/11. I wrote the song in 1986, so ground zero is referring to the center of a nuclear blast." Still, he found it difficult to perform the song after 2001. In a 2011 interview with Nathan Rabin for *AV Music*, he said, "I can't really play the song live anymore because too many people misunderstand the connotations of Ground Zero. It's not a reference to 9/11, obviously. It was written in 1987 [*sic*] when 'ground zero' just meant the epicenter of a nuclear attack."

Yankovic has also had to reconsider the significance of his 1992 song "Smells Like Nirvana." After Kurt Cobain's suicide on April 5, 1994, the twenty-seven-year-old singer's tragic death was mourned globally. And Cobain's death had a major effect on fans as well as the music world in general; one fan, Daniel Kaspar, after attending a vigil by Seattle's Space Needle, returned home and shot himself.[8] When I asked Yankovic about "Smells Like Nirvana" and how Cobain's death changed the song, he responded, "Certainly that song was very difficult to play in the month following Kurt Cobain's death because we were just about to go on tour or to continue a tour. I forget. But I was playing that song in the live show very soon after Kurt died. And in fact, we played it in Seattle a month after he killed himself." Before the Seattle performance, Yankovic was unsure whether he should perform the song or remove it from the set list out of respect. He sought advice from friends and journalists in Seattle. He recalled their verdict: "Kurt loved the song and it's a celebration of his music, and we think you should do it." Yankovic decided to include the song, but with proper preparation: "So what I did, actually, for a month or two following Kurt's passing, I would play the song but it started with a solemn dedication. And I kind

SUGAR AND SPICE AND EVERYTHING ALMOST NICE

of felt like I paid my respects, but at the same time I gave people the song they wanted to hear."

One other moment of unintended insult "really horrified" Yankovic, and this time a change in geography rather than chronology was the culprit. "In 'Word Crimes,' I used the word spastic," he said to me. "Now, in North America, that just means basically a goofy idiot. Outside of North America, particularly Australia and the UK, it's specifically referring to somebody with cerebral palsy. And it's considered a horrible slur. It's like the R-word. And when people in the UK heard that song, they were very offended, and I was horrified." "Spaz" and "spastic" were both playground taunts with little resonance in 2014 in the United States, but, as Ben Zimmer explained in the "Language Log," in the UK both "remain in active usage as derogatory terms for people with cerebral palsy or other disabilities affecting motor coordination." In fact, spastic ranked as the "second-most offensive term for disabled people," right below "retard," in a BBC survey. At the time, Yankovic wrote on Twitter, "If you thought I didn't know that 'spastic' is considered a highly offensive slur by some people . . . you're right, I didn't. Deeply sorry." Indeed, many people did reason Yankovic couldn't have known. To me, Yankovic recalled, "I apologized profusely, and I think I'm largely forgiven because people realize that there's a language difference." One writer, however, excused Yankovic whether or not he knew the word's meaning: "Even if he did know that, we doubt that 'Weird Al' would use offensive terms to bring in listeners; he's classier than that. All the man really wants to do is make parodies, play polka and make people 'LMFAO!'"[9]

Fans did not assume the worst. The default rationale was based in positive perceptions of Yankovic as a person. His standing as a nice guy allows people to give him the benefit of the doubt—sometimes even with insults he actually does intend. Niceness, according to author Carrie Tirado Bramen, has worked in this way for Americans more generally. The idea that Americans are for the most part nice, she explains in *American Niceness*, has masked bad behavior abroad: "Even if they do serious damage in the world, American niceness means that the damage will more than likely be seen as a mistake." Yankovic may be similarly let off the hook, allowed to play with insult because he is seen as nice. Surely, he doesn't mean it. Surely, he insults with good humor. Nice trumps all. Of course, nice has its own potential downsides. Not everyone wants to be seen as nice. But Yankovic highlights the benefits of niceness—a refreshing model at a time when bad behavior by and large dominates the headlines and public politics.

NICE AL

The term "nice" is far from clear-cut. Ruben Aharonian, the first violinist of the Borodin Quartet, said in an interview, "We are not here to perform nice music." Aharonian clarified, explaining that the group's goals are greater than "beautiful music in beautiful surroundings." In performance, the four string players aim instead to represent the composer's intentions as well as the original context of the music's playing. They seek a just rendering of the music.[10] Nice music, they implied, is somehow ineffectual, lacking the weight of history. Nice is surface without substance.

Such negative connotations have tainted the term "nice" from the beginning, including in its Latin derivation, *nescius*. Meaning "foolish" and "silly," nice was initially a diss in definition. During the sixteenth and seventeenth centuries, the meaning of nice split: It could be both complement and counterpunch. While still negative in dictionary definition, in nineteenth-century slang, nice meant "pleasing." Eventually, the slang application became dominant. But nice or pleasing generated its own ambiguity, as in Aharonian's interview. Something pleasing could be something weak. Something pleasing could be something insignificant. In common usage, nice could also be a means of dismissal. "That's nice, dear," a parent says, without looking up. Even worse, "Nice going," you say to yourself after spilling wine on your shirt. And there's nothing nice about sarcastic self-congratulation.[11]

For women, in particular, nice has been a trap. As Joan Duncan Oliver writes in *The Meaning of Nice*, "For women especially, the landscape of nice is littered with outmoded expectations." Little girls are supposedly made of "sugar and spice and everything nice." When women break out of that mode, speaking up or out, they can be punished, labeled a "bitch"—or worse. "If you don't have anything nice to say," we are told, "don't say anything at all." But nice guys have their own problems. The aphorism "Nice guys finish last" comes to mind. The statement is based in fact. If a person is too nice, he or she may shy away from needed conflict, thereby accepting unfair treatment.

Still, niceness doesn't have to be a liability. Through his own success, Yankovic appears to contradict the idea that nice guys finish last. In the last few years, we have been bombarded by high-profile wrongdoing outed by the #MeToo movement as well as incivility, including Twitter insult, in the political realm. Donald Trump offers up inescapable abuse, widely reported, calling Mexicans "rapists," women "fat pigs," and immigrants "animals," in addition to his many insults for individuals ("nasty" and "crooked" Hillary Clinton, "no talent" Samantha Bee, "Crazy Joe" Biden, and so on). Miss Manners, writing for the *Atlantic* in 2017, observed a surprising acceptance of such rudeness today—a change she credits to disillusionment, bad behavior as entertainment, and a new spin on vulgarity as a form of authenticity or sincerity.

Against this backdrop, I suggested to Yankovic that being nice "is almost a political act these days." In 2017 Yankovic made a lighthearted effort to distance himself from other men abusing power in Hollywood and elsewhere. After a Fox News story used the phrase "Weird Al" to insult comedian and politician Al Franken, who had been accused of sexual assault, Yankovic pointed out on Twitter that his name was trademarked. He tweeted, on November 20, 2017, "If you really feel compelled to insult Franken, Sharpton, Gore, Roker, or Pacino . . . PLEASE CHOOSE A DIFFERENT NICKNAME." But Yankovic responded to my political inference with a laugh: "It's just the way I was raised. I mean, I don't think I'm being a political activist by being a nice person." I asked Schwartz, "Do you think being nice means something more today—with the #MeToo movement and high-profile Twitter insults in the political realm?" "Social media has become the tell-all of who's nice, and who's a jerk," he answered. "Unfortunately, the nice people seem to be in the minority, so they do tend to stand out, and it's refreshing."

I myself wanted to write about Yankovic in part because he is nice. Write-ups about kind men have been in short supply as of late. Yankovic, to me, is a prominent reminder to remain optimistic. There's hope for men—and therefore, us all. Others find in Yankovic the same relief. In 2014 journalist Meghan Daum observed in the *Los Angeles Times*, "With bombs, bloodshed and border chaos crowding the headlines, maybe Yankovic is just the cease-fire we need right now." When Yankovic received his star on the Hollywood Walk of Fame, Dr. Demento declared during the ceremony:, "If more people were weird like him, wouldn't we have a much better world?" The crowd cheered.

Yankovic's nice-guy reputation is complex, a balance between his insults in song and the competing connotations of the term "nice." As an artist, he thoughtfully considers the meaning of his songs, careful not to cross a self-determined line while addressing the evolution of his parody's meaning in time and place. As a person, he acts ethically and decently toward others. The proof, in part, is the stability that surrounds him—the band members who have chosen to work with him for all of these years. Together, they have created an enduring base of fans. Yankovic provides for them a safe space and big laughs.

That sense of safety and even refuge is in part a response to Yankovic's insult reversal. When he flips the insult toward himself, he allows his fans to embrace him while they embrace their own flaws. These self-insults (and there are many, as the next chapter shows) help cement the good and goodwill in his music and performance. It's a hallmark of his image, his art, and his humor's serious psychological payoff.

5

THE ART OF SELF-DEPRECATION

While Yankovic is known for his pokes at celebrities, like Donny and Marie and "Achy Breaky"–era Billy Ray Cyrus, self-insult or self-directed abuse easily outnumbers insults of others in Yankovic's songs. It's such a constant that we have to wonder what role self-deprecation plays in the music and performance of Weird Al.

IT PAYS TO SUCK

The comedic potential of self-deprecation is no secret among comedians, many of whom Yankovic admires. *Mad* magazine often relied on self-denigration. It was, according to Maria Reidelbach, "central to the spirit of *Mad*." And the staff embraced it. In its masthead, the magazine's writers and artists are called "the usual gang of idiots."[1] Other early influences also modeled self-insult. In the liner notes of his 1953 album *The Songs of Tom Lehrer*, Tom Lehrer announced, "This recording of the inimitable songs of Tom Lehrer has been issued in spite of widespread popular demand for its suppression." In a performance in Santa Monica, Allan Sherman explained why he looked "short and fat," no longer "exactly like Cary Grant." Tongue in cheek, he blamed publicity consultants, who urged him to adopt the new look, including glasses, in order to sell his songs: "If it works, we'll keep it."[2] Likewise, Yankovic's mentor, Barry Hansen adopted his handle Dr. Demento

Good and Cheap Al. *Courtesy of Jon Schwartz*

after someone commented on his radio show's playlist: "You'd have to be demented to play that."

Comedians have used self-insult as a preemptive defense, a strategy associated in particular with Jewish comedians. It's a means of survival for outsiders. If we laugh first, according to this logic, we'll beat others to the punch.[3] Comedian Jim Gaffigan, however, explains his own reliance on self-deprecation as self-awareness. In "The Psychology of Why We Laugh at Self-Deprecating Humor" (2016), he observes: "Self-awareness is a compelling attribute among other human beings. . . . I think that self-awareness is something that is very similar to observational humor."

Similarly in music, self-insult is everywhere—in music terms, song lyrics, and band names. The duo behind electronic music's Daft Punk found their name thanks to comment comparable to the demented charge—a reviewer criticized their music as "Daft Punk." The song "Creep" (1993) by the band Radiohead is one long ode to the singer-narrator's self-loathing: "But I'm a creep, I'm a weirdo / What the hell am I doing here? / I don't belong here." The musician Beck wrote "Loser" (1994) when he was frustrated with his own musical chops: "I thought, 'Man, I'm the worst rapper in the world—I'm just a loser.'"[4] Much earlier, in the song "Misery Blues," singer Ma Rainey blamed herself for her man's despicable ways: "I'm such a fool, down in my shoes / I've got those misery blues." Self-insulting band names include Garbage, Austin punk group the Dicks, Al Jourgenson's Revolting Cocks, hardcore punk Circle Jerks, and the rap group NWA, which, Ice Cube and Jimmy Fallon made clear, does not stand for Nine White Accountants. For a one-time collaboration, Talking Heads lead David Byrne and folk singer Will Oldham called themselves the Pieces of Shit.

The appeal of self-insult is clear: For comedians and musicians, self-insult takes away the sting of what anyone else can say. Putting themselves on stage, to be judged and potentially mocked in a public way, makes them feel understandably vulnerable. Self-deprecation is a way to overcome nerves, a means of self-protection. Self-insulting names can also be a smart way to be noticed. Musicians fight for attention, and an insulting or offensive name can be one way to get some. As Adam Boult noted in the *Guardian*, in a 2014 listing of the "Top 10 Sweariest Band Names," "it's hard to think of anything as forthright and attention-grabbing, not to mention big and clever, as putting rude words in a band name." And insulting terms can eventually take on positive connotations. The term "Baroque," attached to Western art music composed between about 1600 and 1750, is derived from insult—the Portuguese word *barroco*, which means "oddly shaped pearl." It was a negative descriptor of the ornate music of the period. The term "geek" originally referred to a circus performer who bit the heads off chickens and was for a long time a childhood taunt; now people brag "I'm such a geek" to explain their intense knowledge of pop culture and other passions. There's even a related rock subgenre called geek rock.

More significant for our purposes, in self-insult there is release and relief. Conceding human frailty invites others to do the same. In allowing for that imperfection, there is kinship, relatability, and empathy. And if the self-deprecation is funny, there is an additional sense of camaraderie—everyone is in on the joke. If it's a star or celebrity revealing him- or herself, he or she can seem more accessible. Think Barack Obama, singled out by Adam Howard on NBC News in 2016 as "Comedian-in-Chief," with the many jokes about his rapidly greying hair. Self-insult also levels the playing field for those at the bottom. If it's some-one seen as an outsider, self-insult can counter stereotyping: *He's just like us*. On top of that, self-insult can transform into a point of pride. Self-insult only works in this way, though, if it seems genuine and does not go too far. While we read real disclosure as a sign of honesty, we can spot an attempt at manipulation, mock humility, a mile away.[5] It's a fine line, but one worth walking for comedians and musicians.

WHITE, NERDY, TACKY, AND FAT: WEIRD AL'S SELF-INSULT

The first time I interviewed Yankovic, I brought up the abundance of insult at his own expense. He reasoned, "It's a basic component to comedy. And certainly, for what I do, that helps when I'm tearing somebody else down. . . . I'm not such a bully if I'm pointing the finger back at myself and saying, 'Hey, look, I'm an idiot too.'" For Yankovic, then, self-deprecation helps maintain that nice-guy standing, lessening the bite of some of his parodies. And self-insult can also be, simply put, funny.

But self-insult has a surprisingly shifty character. It can be just what it seems to be—or something more. It can be sincere or misdirected. And it can be read by many different listeners in many different ways. The variety of songs in which Yankovic uses self-deprecation demon-strates all of these possibilities.

The song "I Lost on Jeopardy" (1984) is one of the more straightfor-ward examples of self-deprecation in Yankovic's work. A parody of "Jeopardy," by the Greg Kihn Band, the song substitutes for the original heartfelt chorus—"Our love's in jeopardy, baby"—a confession of an embarrassing failure: "I lost on Jeopardy, baby." The parody, which renewed interest in the game show, featured the voice of the show's actual announcer, Don Pardo, who insults Yankovic at length: "That's right Al—you lost . . . You don't get to come back tomorrow! . . . You're a complete loser!!" In the song's video, Yankovic plays a contestant, staring ahead, bewildered and afraid. A deer caught in the headlights, he somehow stumbles into his seat, pitted against a plumber and an architect, both with PhDs. It's a hilarious send-up of the way all of us have felt at one point or another: hopelessly out of our depth, with all of our limitations on full display. But if you know enough about Yankovic, there's a sly message under the surface: The architect, confident and smooth, is in some ways Yankovic's doppelgänger—the person he could have been if he had continued in architecture rather than veering off course into musical comedy.

Self-deprecation works in a slightly different way in his 2003 song "Genius in France." The song is admission of Yankovic's supposed stupidity. (Whatever, valedictorian.) But he notes sardonically that he has managed to pull the wool over the eyes of the allegedly discerning French:

> (Well,) I'm not the brightest crayon in the box
> Everyone says I'm dumber than a bag of rocks
> I barely even know . . . how to put on my own pants
> But I'm a genius in France (yeah), genius in France

Using colorful expressions, as he often does, he illustrates the problem: his own unintelligence. At the same time, the self-insult is a jab at the French. The French famously considered Jerry Lewis, with his bumbling and stumbling movie characters, to be a comic genius. That they would elevate someone like him, "a few peas short of a casserole," is not a testament to his own secret worth but rather a sign of the French people's gullibility and snobbishness. He's the emperor with no clothes, and the French are his dimwitted courtiers. Hmm, Yankovic thinks, this might be the country for me. Not so stupid after all.

A related type of song is one in which insult is disguised as self-insult. A song like "White & Nerdy" seems like sincere self-deprecation (as we will discuss further), but in other songs he uses self-insult that we suspect has more to do with other people than Yankovic. It's a diplomatic way to criticize, apparently directing the insult at himself while offering a critique of a certain type of person or behavior. For example, in "Tacky" he sings about his own poor sense of fashion, an observation that could be true of the real Al Yankovic: "Wear my belt with suspenders and sandals with my socks." But most of the song is taken up with rude habits that seem, at heart, other-directed, despite the first-person voice. I ask girls if they're pregnant or fat; I threaten waiters with bad reviews: "If you're okay with that, then, you might just be tacky, too." These habits aren't simply misguided style choices—they're evidence of bad character. And since Yankovic isn't known for rude manners (quite the opposite), the listener gets the impression that the song isn't about

Yankovic; it's a critique of others or society in general, masked as self-insult.

More complicated are the self-deprecating songs that focus on nerdiness. For instance, in his song, "White & Nerdy," a parody of "Ridin'" by Chamillionaire and Krayzie Bone, Yankovic plays on the uncoolness of the white nerd stereotype. The sentiment was remarkably appealing—the song was the biggest hit from his 2006 album *Straight Outta Lynwood*, his first single to make *Billboard*'s Top 10. In 2016 William Hughes, writing for the *AV Club*, credited the song with planting "the seeds" for what he dubbed a "'Weird Al' Renaissance," a revival of interest in Yankovic that coalesced eight years later around the release of his 2014 album *Mandatory Fun*.

The popularity of the song stems from how ideas of "nerd" and "geek" have changed in our culture. These transformations have lent layers of meaning to Yankovic's songs about nerds, a particular musical type in Yankovic's vast output of self-deprecating song.

HIP TO BE SQUARE

In the "White & Nerdy" video, Yankovic's nerd receives a wedgie and we see "Alfred"—the name Yankovic went by as a child—written on his underwear. In life, Yankovic embraces his white and nerdy persona. In the 2006 *Billboard* article "'Weird Al' Won't Back Down on Twelfth Album," Yankovic declared of "White & Nerdy": "This is a song I was born to write. I've been doing research my entire life." Indeed, he gathered material from his early years. To Geoff Edgers of the *Washington Post* he noted, "I was two years younger than everybody in school. I didn't go through puberty at the same time. I didn't learn to drive at the same time. I was a straight-A student, a high school valedictorian. I was always the nerdy kid." When Dan Rather asked him to pick from his own output his favorite song, he eventually named "White & Nerdy," explaining it as the "most autobiographical."

In the song, Yankovic sings, "I'm nerdy in the extreme / Whiter than sour cream." And he depicts the hassles he has to deal with because of it—others laughing and rolling their eyes. How did this become one of Yankovic's most popular songs, one with which countless fans happily identify?

In the 1950 children's book *If I Ran a Zoo*, Dr. Seuss uses the term "nerd" to refer to one of several unique characters that the child narrator would bring into the zoo if he had his way: "a preep, a proo, a nerkle, a nerd, and a seersucker too." Seuss's nerd was a comically grumpy and ill-kempt little creature, and while the derivation of the term "nerd" in pop culture is still debated, many find Seuss's character to be the most plausible source. Throughout the 1950s and into the 1980s, "nerd" meant someone fatally uncool, with unfashionable clothes and interests.[6]

But as time went on, the meaning of "nerd" began to shift. The 2004 film *Napoleon Dynamite* celebrated the nerd as someone who is incapable of conforming. In the nerd, there is rebellion and authenticity. That rebellion aligns with a cool detachment, a countercultural ideal central to hipness.[7] In 2007 the television show *Big Bang Theory* debuted on CBS, with a story centered on a group of so-called nerds. No longer peripheral characters, nerds were popular, at least on the small screen—so much so that in 2007 the president of the network CW said, explaining his station's own focus on nerds in programing: "Nerds are really in right now."[8]

The evolution is similar to that of the related term "geek." In a 2017 study of geek masculinity, Anastasia Salter and Bridget Blodgett maintained,

> Geek is a contested term: it is a label that gets applied to others and historically is associated with mockery and outsider status. The term is particularly US centric, and might be understood in other contexts as nerd, fanboy or fangirl, otaku, etc. But over the last two decades it has shifted significantly to become an insider label: a self-identified term that brings with it a connection to an apparent subculture that is increasingly dominant both in popular media and in US economic and cultural structures.[9]

Yankovic's music and persona fit perfectly within the new Nerd Pride. He owns his unique fashion choices and general look. He's enthusiastic about things that have at times been rejected by the mainstream, from puns and silly word play to *Mad* magazine and Dr. Demento. In 2011 linguist Mary Bucholtz studied nerdiness in high school students, many of whom self-identified as nerds. She noticed, among them, "an extraordinarily playful attitude toward language." They were both aware of language and enjoyed playing with it to comedic effect. Their play with language included puns and even newly coined words, in one case a term closely related to Yiddish.[10] With wordplay central to his music, Yankovic fits many of these descriptors, practical markers of nerd identity from the general to Bucholtz's more specific traits. He has authentic credibility as a nerd—and well past high school, where designations like nerd are more significant.

It's important to realize, however, that Yankovic's nerd persona preceded this shift into respectability. I asked his bandmate Jon Schwarz, "Do you think the connotations of nerd have changed during your time working with Mr. Yankovic?" He responded, "With the rise of personal computers and video games over the last thirty years, I'd say the stereotypical image of a nerd has gone from a well-dressed kid with pocket protector and a slide rule to an everyday-looking kid with a tablet. I guess that could be almost anybody. Perhaps with everyone having a smartphone and being more technologically savvy, the nerdist population and the normals have merged somewhat."

In 2006, when Yankovic's song "White & Nerdy" was released, that metamorphosis was not complete. And it certainly wasn't in 1979, when he wrote "Born to Be Mild" (a parody of Steppenwolf's 1969 song "Born to Be Wild"). In the song, Yankovic sings, "Everybody says that you're a nerd, but / They should know that you just don't care." In the never-released song, Yankovic did not assume the nerd character himself—he spoke to a *you*: "You're a nerd." But in 1996, in another "White & Nerdy" precursor, he did assume the character. "Gee, I'm a Nerd," a parody of the Beatles' "Free as a Bird," both defines a nerd and lays out his plight. He's hooked on *Star Trek* and the internet, but "All the jocks and muscle heads / Flip me the bird / Cause I'm a nerd." Yankovic has called Paul McCartney "a good sport," even after he rejected Yankovic's proposed song "Chicken Pot Pie," a parody of the 1990 song "Live and Let Die" (the reasoning: McCartney is a vegetarian). In the case of "Gee, I'm a Nerd," according to "Ask Al," McCartney left the decision to Yoko Ono, who ultimately refused Yankovic's request for permission. Like "Born to Be Mild," the song was never officially released. These songs, as well as his 1999 song "It's All about the Pentiums," a play on Sean "Puff Daddy" Combs's "It's All about the Benjamins" (1997), set up "White & Nerdy" and the nerd as Yankovic's self-professed identity.

Yankovic's proud nerdiness works in two directions: He is both a celebrity and an outsider. His ownership of his nerd status creates an accessibility as well as a sense of communion for other outsiders. It's a point of pride—for himself and others—that allows him to unite with his fans in a constructive common identity. In his music, Yankovic claims the nerd stereotype rather than resigning himself to the attached shame, and in so doing he transforms it. He invites his audiences to do the same—an attractive spin on the label for fans otherwise discouraged by it. They in turn feel a part of a safe space, a like-minded community. For listeners, he models a reckoning with the label "nerd," and there is freedom in that embrace—"free as a bird"—but also connection and self-empowerment. In our culture of bullying, Yankovic's fan empowerment has been especially significant.

FLIPPING THE BULLY TALE

Wielding insult—even self-insult—can be a tricky endeavor, and in some of Yankovic's songs there is a gray area around consideration of weight. In his parody of Michael Jackson's "Bad," his second homage to the Prince of Pop, Yankovic went from being the "Eat It" guy to the "Fat" guy (thanks to a fat suit). In the song "Fat," he sings, "Because I'm fat, I'm fat, come on." The song, however, begins with accusation, though Yankovic quickly removes the sting with personal disclosure: "Your butt is wide . . . well, mine is, too." Eleven years later, Yankovic considered food intake again in the song "Grapefruit Diet" (1999), a fun interpretation of the upbeat 1997 song "Zoot Suit Riot" by the ska group Cherry Poppin' Daddies: "Fudge and Twinkies and deviled ham / Who's real flabby? Yes, I am!" And in "Inactive," a parody of Imagine Dragon's "Radioactive," Yankovic is—yes—"inactive": "I'm waking up, in Cheeto dust / My belly's covered with pizza crust."

There is some potential for offense here, played up in a recent satirical news story on the website 2G1 Reviews. The article, supposedly by Pamela Finkelstein (a shout-out to *UHF* and the character played by Fran Drescher), claims Weight Watchers officially removed a statue of Yankovic from its corporate headquarters due to "an allegation of sizeism against the singer." In the real world, Yankovic's songs about weight poke at America's obsession with a certain standard of beauty. By making himself the one who's fat or flabby, he offers the same kind of affirmation of supposed physical imperfection that he does of nerdiness. In the video for "Tacky," he arguably does the same, in a revelry of tacky costumes and crazy dancing. It's a subtle reaction to our bully culture. But Yankovic isn't always so restrained in response. While songs like "White & Nerdy" lightly touch on bullying (those laughing and rolling their eyes), others unequivocally hone in on the ever-present scourge of such abuse.

Bullying today is a national problem. The problem has been a particular concern for those deemed nerds. A 1996 study concluded that "nerd classification and academic success were often justification for peer to peer teasing."[11] Bullying is also apparently a greater issue for those in the arts. According to a national arts education study, American music and theater students in middle and high school are more likely than their nonartistic peers to be the targets of harassment.[12] The television show *Glee* (2009–2015) dramatized that imbalance, depicting the bullying of various members of its high school glee club, membership a particular point of nerd identification in Yankovic's "White & Nerdy." For the popular character Finn, mere participation in the club was enough to make him a new target; the result, a slushy in the face. It is fitting, then, that musicians have used their music to fight back. In "Brain Damage" (1999), Eminem calls his bully fat: "I was harassed daily by this fat kid named DeAngelo Bailey / He banged my head against the urinal till he broke my nose, soaked my clothes in blood, grabbed me and choked my throat." In the song "Mean" (2010), singer Taylor Swift takes her own stand: "Someday I'll be living in a big old city / And all you're ever gonna be is mean / Someday I'll be big enough so you can't hit me / And all you're ever gonna be is mean."

Yankovic has indeed made allusions to bullying in his own music. In the video for "White & Nerdy," he implicitly references a 2003 case of cyberbullying when he imitates moves made infamous in the "Star Wars Kid" video. The video of fourteen-year-old Ghyslain Raza, practicing choreographed lightsaber play for a *Star Wars* parody, was uploaded in 2003 without Raza's knowledge. Comments attached to the video were vicious, attacking him as overweight and "dweeby." At school, he recalled, the bullying was intolerable, with classmates encouraging him to kill himself: "It soon became impossible for me to attend classes."[13]

But Yankovic addresses bullying most directly in his song "I Remember Larry." The song, from his 1996 album *Bad Hair Day*, is a style parody of the music of Hilly Michaels, a drummer who released two solo albums in the early 1980s. While obscure, Michaels's music stands out, full of energy and fun—"The Cars on speed," according to one writer. After a guitar windup, Yankovic's homage begins, recalling that guy next door, Larry. The verse continues, Yankovic calling Larry "the neighborhood clown," though he was far worse—de-pantsing Yankovic's character and posting pictures all over town as well as dumping toxic waste on his lawn. The song is lively, backed by robust guitar, keyboard, and percussion. Lush, repeated power chords in the guitar punctuate the end of the second line, a segue to the next lyric. To support the last line of the verse, Yankovic includes full, major vocal harmonies. The chorus is likewise harmonized:

> Boy, what a joker
> What a funny, funny guy
> I'll never forget about Larry
> No matter how I try

Yankovic seems to dismiss Larry's actions: He was "always foolin' around." But the chorus hints at the lasting impact of Larry's bullying: "I'll never forget about Larry / No matter how I try." Still, the upbeat harmonization never wavers in the chorus, obscuring that would-be revelation.

In the song, attempts to normalize Larry's actions ("what a joker") give cover to truly criminal behavior. The strategy indexes the old adage "Boys will be boys," a phrase that has consistently been used to dismiss bullying. In the 2014 article "Stop Saying 'Boys Will Be Boys,'" in the *Huffington Post*, Jennifer Hicks counters the thinking: "Let's be clear here. Boys are not a**holes by nature. It's not in their genetic makeup to automatically be mean-spirited or cruel." Eventually Yankovic can no longer ignore Larry's behavior. He snaps, pulling off his own "gag": an apparent kidnapping of Larry as an act of revenge. Though Larry is now stuffed in a plastic bag and left in the forest, the music and energy remain the same. Yankovic's vengeance, the music suggests, is no different than Larry's antics.

In the second repetition of the chorus, following Yankovic's crime, the music stalls as Yankovic holds the final note on the word "guy," in the line "What a funny, funny guy." The following lyric, "No matter how

I try," this time descends in pitch on the closing syllable and the tempo slows. To close, the music offers a chance for introspection. In a psychedelic finale, complete with extra reverb, Yankovic wistfully sings, "Oh, I remember Larry," and the declaration repeats, varied in a counterpoint of layered melodic fragment. It's a meditative section, distinct from the energy of the whole. And, in the song, there is no real closure, as the section fades to nothing.

Yankovic knew bullying firsthand. In a 1995 interview with Joel Rubinoff for *The Record*, he said, "I was one of those kids people liked to throw rocks at at recess." He added, "You can imagine how much fun they had with 'Yankovic' in gym class." In another interview, with John Lekich for the *Globe and Mail*, he joked, "I pretty much kept to myself. I guess I could have just as easily turned into a serial killer." With hesitation, I pressed him for specifics. He expanded, "I definitely got bullied a few times, and I was the prototypical nerd and that made things a bit worse for me." He offered a few examples of the abuse, including tacks on his chair, before politely changing the subject. To Dan Rather, he outlined similar moments of harassment, during middle school PE in particular. It was "not a fun time," he admitted.

The name "Weird Al" grew out of that experience. In a 2012 interview with Dan Schawbel for *Forbes*, Yankovic explained of the name, "I'm pretty sure that nickname was given to me by someone in the dorms during my freshman year in college." A year later, Yankovic took on the name professionally when he worked at the campus radio station. Yankovic was a bit more blunt with Kathy McCabe of News Corp Australia: "People were calling me Weird Al as an insult." At the campus radio station, he needed an on-air name. He wasn't initially playing obscure or "weird" music, but, as he put it in the *Permanent Record* liner notes, "in my heart I wanted to be the surrogate Dr. Demento for San Luis Obispo, so 'Weird Al' seemed appropriate."

The name became more than mere homage to his mentor: "I know when I first took on the name Weird Al in my teen years, it was empowering." He maintained, "I took it on as a badge of honour, a license to fly my freak flag high."[14] As he would later in his music, Yankovic flipped the insult as self-insult. The word itself offers foundation for the reversal. According to Merriam-Webster online, "weird" can be defined as strange or odd, but also extraordinary and fantastic. Yankovic made weird fantastic. With that act of empowerment, in addition to his embrace of nerd culture, Yankovic has become a role model and hero for other outsiders, nerds and otherwise. For many of them, their anthem is another rousing reclamation of insult: Dare to be stupid!

"DARE TO BE STUPID"

On the World of Weird Al Yankovic, a huge online forum for fans, "Dare to Be Stupid" was voted the best song on the album *Dare to Be Stupid* three times over. In Doug Gross's 2010 list of "the top 10 geek anthems," "Dare to Be Stupid" comes in at number ten. Gross admits, "'White and Nerdy' or 'All About the Pentiums' would also have been obvious choices here from an artist with probably as loyal a geek following as anyone. But 'Dare to be Stupid' was a mission statement at a time when Al was still ascending to supernerd status." On February 26, 2013, Yankovic himself joked on Twitter that it might make a good national anthem, after then–secretary of state John Kerry explained to German students: "In American you have a right to be stupid—if you want to be."

One writer, Marc Silverberg, claimed the song was Yankovic's own guiding mantra, a song that "brilliantly sums up his philosophy on life and music."[15] But Yankovic himself seems reluctant to assign the song deeper personal meaning. By phone, he told me that the phrase was "one of those odd things that popped in my head." He had written "Dare to be stupid" in a notebook, and one day he came back to the line and thought, "That's a song." When I pushed for meaning, he added, "I guess, if anybody is taking it seriously, it's saying that it's okay to be different, dare to think outside the box, to do things that other people may not agree with or accept. You've got to follow your own drummer."

The song is a style parody of the music of the band Devo, whose name is an abbreviation of the word "devolution"—the idea that American civilization was regressing, in part a response to the Kent State University shootings in the band's home state of Ohio. With challenging and original music videos, the band was known for a surreal humor. Like their songs "Satisfaction" (1978) and "Whip It" (1980), Yankovic's "Dare to Be Stupid" has a rather sparse, synthetic sound evocative of the era. Schwartz told me that Yankovic wrote the song on his Roland Jupiter-8, a synthesizer made available in early 1981. In final production, the synth accompaniment, produced mainly on the same type of innovative keyboard, combines with a punchy snare drum sound, an effect that recalls the gated reverb credited to musician Phil Collins. In an attempt to re-create Devo's sound, Schwartz had purchased his first drum machine, creating most of the percussion parts on his new Yamaha RX11, the then latest "box of groove." Schwartz told me, "It provided most of the LinnDrum-type sounds associated with Devo, and I played the fills live on my newly acquired Simmons SDS-8 drums."

Yankovic's vocal performance in "Dare to Be Stupid" at times mimics the vocal style of Devo's Mark Mothersbaugh, alternating between a deeper, more resonant voice and his own signature sound. The vocal delivery is at times robotic, with breaks between words. That effect matches Devo's performance in video as well. The performers in "Whip It" and "Satisfaction" are stiff, with quick, sudden movements. In Yankovic's video for "Dare to Be Stupid," he and his band mimic the body contortion, wearing the same yellow jumpsuits donned by Devo in "Satisfaction." Both "Whip It" and "Dare to Be Stupid" are also organized around alternation between solo and group singing, a call and response, an octave below, supporting the main message: "Dare to Be Stupid." Of "Dare to Be Stupid," Mothersbaugh said: "It was the most beautiful thing I had ever heard. . . . I hate him for it, basically."

"Dare to Be Stupid" starts with a driving, rhythmic lead-in on the keyboard. Yankovic then introduces his rallying cry in the vocal style of Devo, a round, almost hollow tone: "Put down your chain saw and listen to me." Like the music of Devo, there's a simplicity to the music. The vocal lines rarely move, repeating the same note as Yankovic begins his aphorism flips: "It's time to let your babies grow up to be cowboys." He in this way questions perceived wisdom, making it clear that you can live your life on your own terms. This particular lyric at the same time references the cowboy characters in "Whip It." He sings, "It's so easy to do / Dare to be stupid." The music supports that ease, with a narrow vocal range and mostly stepwise motion.

Yankovic uses his natural voice when he sings, "You better squeeze all the Charmin you can / When Mr. Whipple's not around"—a reference to a TV ad that ran for two decades (1965–1985), in which a grocer named Mr. Whipple repeatedly scolds costumers for squeezing the Charmin toilet paper. Yankovic uses the ubiquity of the Charmin ad to preach independence and daring. Maintaining his own voice in the next line as well, Yankovic offers advice that counters logic—in this case, getting a tan from the microwave. But when Yankovic returns to popular aphorisms, his Devo-inspired voice, the voice of authority, returns. When he gets to the main message, "Dare to be stupid," the group joins him to emphasize the point.

The video amplifies the lyrics and adds to them its own visual rendering, images of other "stupid" activities. Yankovic and his band members put ice cream cones on their heads, a synchronized stupidity, and feet convert into percussion. There's a communal invitation in the song—We can be stupid together: "Let's go!" That directive results in an instrumental break, movement that might inspire a wider movement. And the possibilities are endless.

Generally, "stupid" is an insult. But in Yankovic's song, "stupid" is a signal of difference—a marker reserved for outcasts, like "weird" or "nerd." Yankovic once again flips the pejorative, and the word becomes a sign of individuality. A stupid person breaks with common wisdom, refusing to conform. To promote the *Dare to Be Stupid* album, in the summer of 1985 Yankovic drove in his Stupid Bus on his Stupid Tour. Individuality was live, coast to coast. In his tour rider, Yankovic decided to include "one unreasonable demand," he explained as he took CBS News on a tour of his closet: one "garish Hawaiian shirt" for every show. Another refusal to conform turned a much-derided shirt into his signature look.

Yankovic redeploys common insults directed at those declared different—weird, nerd, and stupid—identifying himself as such in a positive way. That self-insult is primarily a means of communal uplift and empowerment. We can be weird, stupid individuals together. The message creates a powerful and positive link—a potent reason, among many, to connect with Weird Al and his music.

DARE TO BE AN AL-OHOLIC

Ben Quinn, in "Nerd of Honour" (2017), calls Yankovic "nerd royalty." And Tim Donnelly, in the *New York Post*, calls him a "hero" for "nerdy America."[16] McCabe offers explanation: "For a lot of kids who think they are weird and don't fit in, well, here's the guy who is weird and

YANKOVIC
BEACON THEATRE—OCT. 5

**"DARE TO BE STUPID" THE NEW ALBUM FROM "WEIRD AL" YANKOVIC
ON SCOTTI BROS/CBS RECORDS & TAPES**

Beacon Theatre Ticket info: $16.50 & $14.50 on sale now at the
Beacon Box Office (787-1477) and all Ticketron outlets (977-9020).
To Charge Tickets—call Chargit (944-9300) or Teletron (947-5850)

COME MEET WEIRD AL · SAT OCTOBER 5TH AT **VIDEO SHACK** (Broadway and 49th Street) 1-3PM

"Dare to Be Stupid" Poster. *Courtesy of Jon Schwartz*

different." Yankovic has been sensitive to his responsibility as a hero and role model. A popular quote credited to Yankovic on the website A–Z Quotes: "People that were a little nerdy in high school would look up to me and know it gets better." In his interview with Dan Rather, he explained that embracing his weirdness could send a powerful message to children: It's okay to be weird; it's okay to be you.

Yankovic's dedication to that message plays out in real life as well as his music. Yankovic's powerful self-deprecation marks his public appearances. Self-insult is part of his complete personal presentation to the outside world. At his concert stop in Turlock, California, on May 18, 2018, Yankovic introduced songs with personal disclosure. Before playing his 2003 song "Party at the Leper Colony," he said, "This next song I'm really not proud of." At the end of the night he looked genuinely surprised by the standing ovation. When he received his star on the Hollywood Walk of Fame, he spoke to those in attendance: "My name is gonna be walked on, spit on, and let's face it . . . urinated on for generations to come. That's a legacy, my friends."

More importantly, in 2015 Yankovic came to the rescue of eight-year-old Layla Murphy, who was being bullied at her school in Virginia. A group of girls teased her for liking the *Star Wars* franchise—sci-fi films supposedly meant for boys. The 501st Legion, a group dedicated to wearing *Star Wars* costume replicas, tweeted about the effect: "Layla began to lose herself." With help from the legion, Layla met Yankovic at a concert and received a full storm trooper costume. In a picture, Yankovic smiles next to the girl, who has thick black, bangs. With a shy smile, she is dressed in her new storm trooper outfit.[17]

For all these reasons, Yankovic's fans are especially steadfast. As Yankovic's wife, Suzanne, told the *Orange County Register* in 2002, "He's got the best fans in the world. They are so loyal." On *The Michael Des Barres Program*, Yankovic credited his fans with having his back—eager to defend him in the midst of any controversy. Observing Yankovic's fans in Houston in 2016, Cory Garcia characterized them in the *Houston Press* as "people who love a certain type of comedy who are genuinely excited to experience it with a group of strangers. . . . They're the type who'll start making references to song lyrics hoping that you'll smile the same way that they're smiling. It's awesome." Responding to Yankovic's Twitter posts, his fans—or Al-oholics—are also often quite funny themselves. When Jamie Lee Curtis wished Yankovic a happy birthday on October 23, 2018, posting a picture of her supposed gift, a cruise ship, Yankovic fan Kevin Denelsbeck responded to the subsequent thread, "Would these tweets count as liner notes?" On April 3, 2019, when Yankovic posted a picture while traveling of an ice cream cone covered in gold, part of his new "very restrictive diet," quite a few fans joined the fun. KevinPerryRules posted, "What an Au-inspiring diet." Another posted, "Is that a Goldstone Creamery?" Fans also have inside jokes. One of them is the number 27, which pops up in Yankovic's work, including his jersey on the album cover of *Running with Scissors*. In "Ask Al," Yankovic explained, "'27' is obviously my favorite number and an in-joke with my fans." This topic, among many others, can be discussed at the fan site World of Weird Al Yankovic on www.weirdalforum.com or in the Facebook group "Close Personal Friends of Weird Al."

But these fans have offered more than their adoration and wit. They have also been behind numerous campaigns on behalf of Yankovic. In 2014, sixty thousand fans signed a Change.org petition to nominate Yankovic to perform at the Super Bowl halftime show.[18] While his inclusion in the Rock & Roll Hall of Fame is still an unrealized crusade, fans were successful in their bid to lock up for Yankovic a star on the Hollywood Walk of Fame—a mission one fan, Dave Rossi, began in 2003. The headline to an article by Brittany Martin in *Los Angeles Magazine* says it all: "Weird Al Is Getting a Walk of Fame Star Because Weird Al Fans Really, Really Love Weird Al." Fans have also organized a convention dedicated to Yankovic, called Alcon. In 1998, as described at the website allthingsyank.com, Yankovic apologized for not being there in a video before making a surprise appearance: "From around the video screen came none other than Al himself!" The last gathering took place in April 2002. But a related Fest of Al convened in Denver in 2018. Nathan Rabin, author of *Weird Al: The Book*, was a fan first, and his devotion continues with his blog chronicling Yankovic's songs, *The Weird Accordion to Al*.

A crew of female fans created a fanzine called the *Midnight Star*, which stopped publication in 1998 (it was named after Yankovic's original composition of the same name, a 1984 song about tabloid journalism). This short-lived publication fits within a wider genre of fan fiction, which is often the product of women.[19] One of the magazine's authors, Carlotta Barnes, has followed Yankovic across the country on tour. She has said, according to Heather McCabe in the *Houston Chronicle* (1996), "A lot of women don't understand that Al is good-looking. And those of us who do are not eager to spread the word around." She is not alone in showing up to back-to-back Yankovic concert dates. In 2000 Yankovic observed, "Sometimes I'll look out into the audience and see a lot of the same faces I've seen the last 10 nights."[20] There are many devotional remakes of Yankovic's songs as well. Some of these fan-made videos are listed and linked on his website at http://weirdal.com. There are three versions therein of "Yoda," which is Yankovic's own offering to the *Star Wars* franchise—filking at its finest.

It is hard to pigeonhole Yankovic fans, who represent a wide age range. In the liner notes to *The Essential "Weird Al" Yankovic*, a compilation album put out in 2009, Stephen Thompson, editor of NPR Music, wrote, "Today, my 66-year-old mother, countless teenagers, and I all love 'Weird Al' Yankovic more or less equally, and on more or less the exact same level." In witty online posts, these fans, young and old, seem remarkably intelligent. There are campaigns and videos, "Weird Al" Halloween costumes, imaginative Yankovic tattoos, and Yankovic comics, like Kelly Phillips's "Weird Me." The fans don't just listen to his music passively. They actively participate in Yankovic's career and output in a variety of ways, riffing on his music, organizing meetups, and producing their own related art. Fandom has sometimes been characterized as pathological hysteria: Fans are supposedly pathetic, looking to give their empty lives meaning. But with the advent of the internet, the full creative (and joyous) aspects of fandom have become visible— and nowhere more than with Yankovic's fans.

Phillips remembers the first time she heard a Yankovic song, "The Saga Begins." She told me, by e-mail: "I think the moment the song started, something sparked inside me. It was like finding a kindred spirit. And the deeper I dug into his music, the more I found that I related to or admired about it. He was nerdy, he was smart, he was kind, he was accessible, he was beloved—I felt like I had discovered this huge, delightful secret in the world that had no end, and I wanted more than anything to be a part of it." Though "The Saga Begins" will always hold a special place in her heart, Phillips notes that for many other fans that special song is "Dare to Be Stupid," both a self-insult— perhaps *the* Yankovic self-insult—and an anthem, a call to arms:

It's a song from pretty early in his career, and I think on top of it being pretty emblematic of his style and humor, it's a solid call to action. It's a sentiment that encourages you to be silly, to not take life too seriously, to be bold and unpredictable, to go against the norm. As in all things, his song takes that idea to the nth degree, but the older I get, the more it resonates with me as a reminder to maintain perspective and to stay in touch with that bit of musical magic I felt when I was younger. Plus, it's fun to shout!

Phillips recognizes that fans often discover Yankovic's work at a young age, around thirteen, she estimates. In his book, Rabin confirms: "Buying a Weird Al album has been a rite of passage for young people since the '80s." However, that initial discovery, Phillips told me, does not dictate or freeze a fan's response for life: "On one level, his music very much appeals to a sense of humor that we all share when we're at that age, but I think what sets the lifetime fans apart is that we discover so many deeper levels in his work that we continue to connect with over and over again. It makes for some pretty passionate, die-hard fans." For those fans, the 2002 Orange County Fair included an exhibit devoted to Yankovic's career entitled "The Weird Al Experience." Steven Beazley, deputy general manager for the fair, explained to the *Orange County Register*, "In 2000, [Yankovic] came here on tour. I've never seen a clamor like that before or since. I thought, 'What can we do for people who have this fervor?'" Touring the display, which included his Kurt Cobain wig and his Grammy for "Eat It," Yankovic said with character-istic self-deprecation, "I honestly didn't know I had this much of a career." At his 2018 performance in Turlock, such self-effacement was a revelation. There was acceptance of difference, further celebrated in commerce, with a superhero nerd doll for sale at the merch table.

The cult fandom—the loyalty and enthusiasm of fans over such a long career—has threatened to do what years of school bullying never could: make Yankovic cool. The hipster-nerd now populates the high end of the cool spectrum, even in fashion—as Natalie L. Lapacek-Trout points out in her study of the television nerd and trendy "nerd style glasses,"[21] not to mention the famed popularity of Sheldon Cooper's long-sleeve-short-sleeve message tees. Yankovic, the ultimate nerd, has become cool too. No decided effort could have turned the tide. Cool, like hip, just is. With the popularity of *Mandatory Fun* in 2014, Christ Ford asked in *Diffuser*, "Is it finally cool to like 'Weird Al'?" That same year, Mike Ryan answered in the affirmative, "Somewhere along the line, it became cool to like 'Weird Al' Yankovic." Yankovic himself noticed the change, connecting it to 2006's "White & Nerdy." In an interview with Ryan for *Screen Crush,* he explained, "At that point, people realized, well, hey, nerds are cool and nerds rule the world. And, all of a sudden, people were like trying to establish their nerd credentials."[22] As Rabin wrote in his book, Weird Al "was uncool before being uncool became cool."

Yankovic's position as the ultimate nerd, or, in Tim Donnelly's formulation, "President Al of Nerd America," is a positive symbol for many: the outsiders and the bullied. And his music appeals to fans, an especially creative and active group. And yet, as we will learn in the following chapter, Yankovic has no desire to take this platform beyond Nerd America. In fact, he is hesitant to address politics explicitly in any form. A Hawaiian shirt in the Oval Office? It seems unlikely. But we, as stupid individuals, can certainly upend logic; we can dare to dream. Yankovic 2020!

6

PRESIDENT AL

"Please, please don't pickaxe my star," Yankovic said when he publicly received his Walk of Fame star. A month before, in July 2018, a man had taken a pickaxe to the nearby star of Donald Trump. The culprit, who carried his pickaxe in a guitar case, notified the police of his vandalism—one in a string of attempts to protest Trump by defacing his square on the Walk of Fame.[1] A few weeks later, the West Hollywood City Council voted to remove Trump's star entirely, cited as a reason Trump's "disturbing treatment of women and other actions that do not meet the shared values of the City of West Hollywood, the region, state, and country."[2] Some assumed Yankovic's star would replace Trump's. On August 14, 2018, Rob'em wrote on Twitter, "Happy to hear Weird Al will be replacing Trump's star on the Walk of Fame. Somehow that feels like the most right thing in the universe." But Wyatt Duncan didn't think a star switch-up went far enough. Replace Trump's star with Yankovic's? No, he wrote, "Replace Donald Trump with Weird Al." During his star acceptance speech, Yankovic couldn't ignore the controversy, explaining his initial pickaxe admonishment: "I know it's all the rage these days, but that's not cool. That's rude. . . . Unless," he added, "at some point in the future I do something unfathomably monstrous and evil, in which case, go ahead . . . it makes sense." The statement was funny, but at the same time, it hinted at serious concerns within the political realm. Was Yankovic subtly saying Trump deserved the destruction of his star? Had Trump, in Yankovic's mind, committed a "monstrous and evil" act?

Yankovic rarely makes known his explicit political views. His music is not that of newer parodist Randy Rainbow, whose musical spin-offs are entirely political—Camelot to Kavanaugh. In a 2017 interview with Katy W for *Timeout Los Angeles*, Yankovic explained his take on political humor: "I've always tried to avoid doing that kind of humor. It's divisive. No matter how mild or innocuous your humor is, in this day and age, people will get upset—really upset. I'm very reluctant to make a joke if I think it will infuriate millions of people, and I wouldn't be too keen on losing half of my fan base." In an interview on December 20, 2018, for *Hot Ones*, Yankovic compared politics to performing at the Super Bowl: No matter what you do, some people will hate you. And Yankovic is reluctant to invite into his life that level of ill will. Technology has ramped up the concern, making it even easier to offend. In "Weird Al Takes on Political Correctness," on the website antiMusic, Yankovic noted, "Especially in our online culture, people get addicted to being offended. They look for things to be offended by. And some things probably are very offensive, and some things would probably be better left unsaid. . . . [T]here's maybe a little bit more of that currently in our culture than I personally like." The anonymity of online worlds allows people to say their worst. Internet trolls take shelter in their hidden identities, unleashing their attacks without direct confrontation or the threat of repercussion. Some attacks go viral, compounding their hostile effect.

Other comedians sidestep politics, similarly wary of losing audiences. But even if audience members are sympathetic to the comic's position, some recognize that political jokes in and of themselves can be a turn-off. According to Brian Logan in "Should Comedians Stand Up for a Political Party?" audiences may resent being told "what to think." In a 2011 interview with Michael Kaminer of *Vegetarian Times*, Yankovic described such talk as pedantic: "I don't really look at my music as a way to preach to people, more to entertain them." In parody, political themes have another downside: They tend to date the song. A political song can quickly lose its meaning and resonance over time. Yankovic told David Segal of the *Washington Post*, "Things that are topical in the political arena this week would be old news a month from now, so that's probably not the kind of thing I want to have as part of my catalog."

And yet, in his speech at the Walk of Fame ceremony, Yankovic referenced politics, despite the many reasons not to. He also flirted with politics on Twitter on May 18, 2016, jesting that his name was meant to help Trump. Trump had been tagging his adversaries with one-word descriptors—Crooked Hillary, Lyin' Ted, Little Marco, and so on. Weird Al fit the formula. Yankovic wrote: "The truth is, I only named myself Weird Al because I wanted to save @realdonaldtrump the trouble of coming up with a stupid nickname for me." The playful proposal that "Dare to Be Stupid" become the national anthem is a related tease. These statements were jokes, but to some the jokes are serious. "Dare to Be Stupid" is an anthem—a celebration of individuality. And Yankovic, through the self-empowerment of self-insult, has become a role model: a nice guy at a time when insults and #MeToo revelations dominate the news cycle.

One fan made the logical leap with a Facebook page entitled "Weird Al for President in 2020," and the hashtag #MakeAmericaWeirdTogether. "If 'Weird Al' can dare," read the August 3, 2016, post, "so can you!" In support, the video of "Dare to Be Stupid" was attached. Wyatt Duncan, hoping to replace Trump with Yankovic, was hardly the first to hail Yankovic as presidential material. As Katie Rife observed in *AV News* in 2016, "'Weird Al' Yankovic is, in many ways, the opposite of Donald Trump: He's a humble, self-made success who seems quite secure with the size of his hands, not to mention that he's *trying* to make us laugh when he acts like a fool on TV." When Trump was elected on November 9, 2016, the "Weird Al for President" Facebook page announced: "Looks like we failed again America. At least we finally got an entertainer with no political experience in the White House, just not the right one."

The truth is, Yankovic does reference politics, despite purporting to avoid the topic entirely. And his fans make the connection, pushing for more political investment—including a Weird Al political run. Yankovic's support of specific political issues is not overt, but it is there. He made clear his support of civil rights and equality for all with his donation to the Human Rights Campaign, part of his Lady Gaga parody, as well as promotion of the NOH8 Campaign, which began in opposition to California's Proposition 8, banning same-sex marriage in 2008. On August 11, 2010, on the World of Weird Al Yankovic website, minnick27 commented on Yankovic's NOH8 support: "We know Al follows Obama on Twitter, but this seems to be the first overt political statement he's made. Bravo to him for not hiding his views."

When he was asked about his political views in the interview on the website antiMusic, Yankovic voiced support for free speech: "I'm a big believer in free speech; I think you should be allowed to say anything you want." The issue is no doubt close to his heart, given past litigation around parody as well as ongoing attempts to crack down on music deemed offensive. One fan in "Ask Al," however, noted the contradiction, asking, "Hey Al, I was wondering why you say you don't like to talk about political issues but in some interviews you talk about them anyway." Yankovic responded, "Well, it's true—I really don't like talking about political issues in interviews. But when an interviewer asks me a direct question, I feel somewhat obligated to either give them a direct answer, or make a joke, or perhaps a little combination of both. Unfortunately, it's normally considered pretty rude just to jump out of my chair and run screaming out of the room with my hands over my ears."

Still, that sense of obligation doesn't account for certain political moments in his music—songs like "The North Korea Polka" (2017), "Party in the CIA" (2011), and "Trigger Happy" (1992). The political surely doesn't seep uncontrolled into his work, and Yankovic could easily have run screaming from his own musical-political setups. The fact that he didn't is noteworthy. The fact that he seems like he would is too. How does Yankovic venture into musical politics without seeming like he does? And how political is his music, anyway?

"PLEASE DON'T NUKE US NORTH KOREA"

On August 13, 2017, I settled in to watch the show *Last Week Tonight with John Oliver*. I occasionally clear a space for the show, a satirical news program that the *AV Club* has called a "shining beacon in the eternal shriek that was our daily life." On that night, my effort was rewarded with a musical message from Yankovic to North Korea. Oliver set up the song by addressing the recent escalation of words between Trump and North Korea's leader Kim Jong Un, who had recently tested a missile with the purported ability to reach the United States mainland. After one successful missile test, Kim declared that his country has "the sure capability to attack in an overall and practical way the Americans in the Pacific operation theatre."[3] On August 8, 2017, Trump matched the fiery rhetoric, threatening North Korea from his golf resort in Bedminster, New Jersey: "North Korea best not make any more threats to the United States." As reported by Saba Hamedy on CNN, he vowed, "They will be met with fire and fury like the world has never seen."

North Korea had become known for its threats, but the United States had traditionally opted for "strategic patience."[4] With Trump, the American approach drastically changed. Trump had poked the bear—a bear no one wanted poked. As Oliver acknowledged, many in the United States were scared, imagining a future cut short by nuclear war. The situation, Oliver declared, was serious, "requiring a deft hand." Unfortunately, the president, he implied, was not capable of an appropriate response, with the "temperament of a wet cat." But Oliver himself offered his own remedy, after explaining a bit about North Korea's reclusive leader.

Kim Jong Un, he maintained, operated from a place of "rational self-preservation." In his book *The Real North Korea,* Andrei Lankov characterized the North Korean elite in a similar way, crediting their extreme policies to self-protection: "[T]hey simply do not see how else they can stay in control and protect not only their property (quite meager by current international standards) but, more importantly, their freedom to act and their lives (as well as the freedom and lives of their loved ones)."[5] The strategy necessitated in part the portrayal of the United States as the enemy in propaganda and early education. The two countries were seemingly separate and fundamentally at odds. But some North Koreans found a way to maintain contact, viewing smuggled television shows from the United States, including the crime drama *NCIS.* Hoping his show might also find its way into North Korea, Oliver addressed the dark nation, where the accordion is remarkably popular as the "people's instrument."[6] He spoke directly: "Hi North Korea." A simple opening. He then announced, "I would like to give you, the North Korean people, a sense of how we are feeling right now in a way you might understand and enjoy, and that is through the international language of the accordion." He then introduced Yankovic, who appeared on stage in a collared shirt, trademark Hawaiian motif replaced by stars and stripes. He was backed by a ten-piece band, including a brass section, all dressed in proper polka attire—high socks, shorts, and suspenders.

Yankovic had some earlier experience with dictators like Kim Jong Un, having appeared on the cover of his album *Mandatory Fun* feigning his own version of a supreme leader: With an intense stare, he stands in military dress, hands on hips. Writer Matt Melis summed up the message in *Consequence of Sound*: "Join the party, or else." But his song on *Last Week Tonight*, "The North Korea Polka (Please Don't Nuke Us)," did not replicate his fascist turn. He was congenial and upbeat, a diplomat. With a jaunty melody and matching accompaniment, Yankovic summed up the current mood: "You've got us crapping our collective pants." Countering depictions of Americans as evil in North Korea propaganda, Yankovic offered, "You might call us blood-thirsty dogs / But the metaphor is not very apt." Instead, he made clear, we're nothing to fear, just "goofy dorks," who "probably couldn't find your country on a map." The chorus of the song was a frank entreaty: "Please don't nuke us North Korea."

The concept of the song was funny, especially given the reception of the accordion in the United States—far less positive than in North Korea. But there was a sobering side to the song that matched the gravity of politics in North Korea. Yankovic's music that night was reassuring, a sane voice in a time of high anxiety. The song was also a striking moment of lighthearted political diplomacy, with the accordion functioning as a bridge and common ground. The strategy is notable, and novel in a context of comedy. But the song nonetheless called to my mind a substantial tradition of similar musical effort in the United States.

In 1954, the President's Emergency Fund for International Affairs established the Cultural Presentations Program. Until the early 1970s this program supported American musicians and their concerts abroad—performances devised to better the American image. In the program, there was a tension between propaganda and a noble ideal of cultural exchange. A comparable tension exists in the very notion of diplomacy—both a means of union and intervention.[7] Playing both sides, classical music had a disproportionate role in the program, exported to frame the United States as a particularly cultured nation. But jazz too had a role, often used to downplay notions of American racism. The program supported music from the host nation as well—a true bridge—much like Yankovic and Oliver's collaboration. In March 1958 conductor William Strickland directed the Seoul Philharmonic, performing a composition by Korean composer Sungtae Kim. In 1969 the Duquesne University Tamburitzans toured the Soviet Union supported by the program. They found special unity and recognition with their performance of music familiar to their audiences. In her study of cultural diplomacy, musicologist Danielle Fosler-Lussier writes, "The demonstration of a shared musical repertoire allowed the Tamburitzans to connect with fellow musicians and audiences."[8] But musicians didn't always have to travel to function effectively in the program. Like Yankovic's performance, there were broadcast concerts. Though these concerts lacked direct interaction with the target audiences, they could nonetheless serve transnational ends, changing attitudes at home and abroad. Viewers at home in the United States could imagine connection with another nation, creating a shared world in music.

In the guise of a gag, Yankovic's performance was directed at North Korea in a language intended to create communion. American audiences, too, could feel that closeness with North Korea. Yankovic's performance was reassuring in this way. North Korea could emerge, in the American mind, as a nation of accordion players rather than death, as could the United States for North Koreans. In Yankovic's performance, we could peacefully coexist, if only for a moment.

Yankovic doesn't take complete ownership of this musical-political dialogue. When I clamored for details about the song and its origins, Yankovic explained: "Well, I just got a call from John Oliver's people." In his wording, they explained, "We want to do a bit where you basically come on and play a song on your accordion and convince the North Koreans not to bomb us." Yankovic had to cut a family vacation short and write the song in a day or two, which is not his usual compositional process: "I generally tend not to rush things that quickly. Usually, I like to ruminate on things." But he was able to write the song in a hurry and get to New York, where the band was in costume and waiting: "And it was just an amazing experience, but it all just came together in a couple of days."

The song, with its political message, was a collaboration with John Oliver and his team. Yankovic could put the political onus on Oliver, if he so chose, though he ultimately wrote and performed the song. Not only that: in the song Yankovic does not betray his explicit political views. Oliver's show is associated with a leftist political bent, but the song itself is rather safe, a plea for peace. As Yankovic commented to me, "I don't know how political it is just to ask somebody not to nuke us. I think that's probably pretty nonpartisan." And Yankovic has a point. How political is the song? Collaboration, diplomacy, and humor confuse the message as well as Yankovic's responsibility for that message. Yankovic could make a political plea in music while easily explaining away the effort. Despite the political material, his apolitical reputation was still intact. He was political but didn't *seem* that political.

The same can be said of another Yankovic political venture: his remastering of the third and final presidential debate between Hillary Clinton and Donald Trump in October 2016. The resulting video was again a collaboration—this time with the Gregory Brothers, a music video production team responsible for the Songify the News web series and the earworm-y theme song for *Unbreakable Kimmy Schmidt*. But in the video, Yankovic takes central stage as an arbiter of peace for a second time.

"BAD HOMBRES, NASTY WOMEN"

In the video "Bad Hombres, Nasty Women," Yankovic reaches back to his speech experience in high school, but his role has changed. This time he sits at the desk as moderator. "Good evening," he says in a black suit with black tie; the screen affiliation appears as "UHF Evening News Anchor." To the candidates, he explains that this evening's debate is the "last chance to make an impression." Still speaking, he sets the rules: "Let's do this in B-flat minor." He then opens his mouth wide and the singing begins, one note that accompanies the initial words of the candidates, now digitally manipulated as song. "Such a nasty woman," Trump in this way intones.

Yankovic dramatically sings in a full voice his first question: "We have so many adversaries overseas," the melodic line ascends; "can we all agree to be frenemies?" the pitch descends. Yankovic nods his head as Clinton speaks of cooperation, songified. Trump's response is a repetition of Mosul, a city in Iran that was later the site of a fierce nine-month battle. Trump's words are cut to repeat "So sad" and "So bad"—a rhyme that gives a jumbled answer some artificial coherence. The showdown escalates as the wind, from nowhere, picks up, affecting Yankovic alone. "Why should you run the show?" Yankovic asks against the storm. With the election in two weeks, the stakes are high, and Yankovic, to this end, intends to cover some of the major issues, asking the candidates first to publicize their Supreme Court picks. He adds a caveat, "Please don't say me, I'm a busy dude." He then references gun ownership and the possibility of a new Cold War—both topics present in his earlier parody songs (a subject to which we will return). When Trump offers his infamous insult—"Bad hombres," which sums up his negative view of immigrants—a fiery vortex opens up behind Yankovic.

Was the apocalyptic vision inspired by Trump's insult or his stance on immigration? Does this moment in the video reveal the Gregory Brothers's or Yankovic's views on issues of immigration? Earlier, the topic was a part of Yankovic's song "Buy Me a Condo" (1984), a parody of the music of Bob Marley. In the earlier tune, the immigrant is not from Mexico, which is Trump's focus, but instead Jamaica, and Yankovic displays a sensitivity to the plight of foreigners. He assumes the perspective of this "lonely Rastaman" as well as his accent, singing of all that has changed and will change: "Gonna cut off me dreadlocks / T'row away all me ganja / I'll have a Tupperware party / Maybe join me a health spa." In "Bad Hombres, Nasty Women," it is not clear if the vortex is commentary on Trump's policy or behavior, despite Yankovic's potential opposition to both. In an op-ed, Yankovic and the Gregory Brothers commented, "[W]e can't say we were shocked that songifying the final debate between Hillary Clinton and Donald Trump revealed a terrifying space opera about bad hombres and nasty women. So terrifying, in fact, that it ripped open a wormhole to another dimension, and pulled an unsuspecting Weird Al Yankovic in from his home in a parallel universe to moderate the whole thing. Sorry about that, Weird Al. You deserve better than this. Don't we all?"[9] The address to Yankovic suggests that the Gregory Brothers, if anyone, were responsible for the vortex. The debate itself ends on a lighter note, with Yankovic remarking, "Is it windy here or is it just me?"

Once more, Yankovic does not betray his political views. He appears to be an advocate for peace—supporting a coming together of both sides as "frenemies." But he does promote the proper functioning of the democratic system, urging the candidates to make clear their beliefs in order to help inform voters. And the video as a whole is educational—presenting aspects of the candidates' policies while promoting engagement. In the lead-up to the election, the video advocated for awareness and was a gentle reminder to vote. He would offer another reminder two years later, on October 21, 2018, in a Twitter post. Alongside an "I Voted" sticker, Yankovic wrote, "Some of you might not be aware of this, but when you vote, they give you a FREE STICKER. Not even kidding, they JUST GIVE IT TO YOU. You'd have to be a real IDIOT not to take advantage of this. Just sayin'." That's about as easygoing as political activism gets.

By phone, I brought up Yankovic's collaborative process with the Gregory Brothers: "Did you write the questions you asked in the mock debate?" "No," Yankovic said, "I creatively was responsible for basically nothing." Pointing out that his performance was recorded before the actual debate, he clarified: "So basically [the Gregory Brothers] came up with several generic questions which they were pretty sure were going to be included in the debate. . . . They got everything else in the can and they watched the debate and then they spent literally all night long working on it and making it happen. It was like ten hours later and they had a complete video. They're pretty amazing that way." I was almost skeptical when Yankovic added, "I wish I could claim more, creatively." He once again had a collaborator to muddy the waters of authorship and responsibility. He was political and not, controversial and not. If his politics were coffee, they'd be decaf.

FUN WITH GUNS

Occasionally Yankovic offers a political perspective without the veil of collaboration. Some fans heard in Yankovic's song "Genius in France" a commentary on the war in Iraq. When the song appeared in 2003, cafeteria menus in the Capitol complex in Washington, DC, had renamed French fries "freedom fries" as a rebuke to the French, who would not support the United States's decision to prepare for war against Iraq. Joan Z. Shore, writing for *Huffington Post*, also surmised that Americans were simply jealous of France, with their couture clothing and high-end cheese. But in "Ask Al," Yankovic set the record straight: "I did not write 'Genius in France' as any sort of political statement. I wrote the song long before the war in Iraq started, and it was never my intention to jump on any kind of 'bashing the French' bandwagon. I was bashing the French before it was trendy."

But there are a few undeniably political songs in Yankovic's vaults, most of which focus on violence and the abuse of power.

"TRIGGER HAPPY"

Yankovic's 1992 song "Trigger Happy" tackles gun violence, a theme that appears more than once in Yankovic's work. In his 1989 movie *UHF*, there is an interview with a gun nut, Earl Ramsey, who says, "Gun control is for wimps and commies." Wearing a red hat and camo shirt with a tan vest, he continues, in a heavy southern accent, "Let's get one thing straight: guns don't kill people, I do"—a variation on a common defense of gun ownership: "Guns don't kill, people do." Ramsey creepily looks directly at the camera, pointing a gun at the viewer to make his final argument, the defense slyly morphing into a threat.

In "Trigger Happy," Yankovic makes gun control the central topic. The song title references a person who is primed to shoot, with or without reason. The song, a joyful style parody, emphasizes the feeling behind the phrase, the giddy glee that wielding that kind of power must produce. It mimes the vocal stylings of rock duo Jan and Dean (known for songs like 1963's "Surf City") and the surf sound of the Beach Boys. The Beach Boys's Brian Wilson was obsessed with vocal harmonies, as in the 1963 song "Surfer Girl," and viewed his music as spiritual. [10] Carl Wilson, his brother, observed of "Surfer Girl" and others like it: "We didn't just duplicate parts; we used a lot of counterpoint, a lot of layered sound. We're big ooohers; we love to oooh. It's a big full sound, that's very pleasing to us. It opens up the heart." [11]

"Trigger Happy" has the same rich, sonorous sound, but it's jarring when joined with the lyrical content. In the *Permanent Record* liner notes, Yankovic explained, "I thought it would be fun to juxtapose a Beach Boys/Jan & Dean type surf riff with a song about a gun nut." The frightening topic may nullify, for some, the humor. For others, the song plays both sides—funny and disturbing. The song begins with a full harmonization of "trigger happy," before Yankovic sings the first verse alone, describing a purported comfort in gun ownership: "Got an AK-47, well you know it makes me feel all right." Of course, there is a joke already in the selection of an AK-47 and, in the next line an Uzi, for comfort, the latter a submachine gun and the former an assault rifle.

Both weapons are large, rather excessive choices for a simple feeling of safety. And that goal of comfort, a defense against the world's dangers, is undermined again by the next line: "There's no feeling any greater / Than to shoot first and ask questions later." It's a preemptive and thoughtless strike. This supposed defense is something more sinister, a risky power move with lethal repercussions.

The chorus follows, with complete chordal coordination and background "ooohs." In the next verse, Yankovic references the common refrain supporting gun ownership—it's a "constitutional right." He also stokes fear by citing the communist threat—one on the wane in 1993— and the fear of crime. Later he asks, "Do you feel lucky, punk?" The phrase and song's repeated use of "punk" references the catchphrase of Harry Callahan, played by Clint Eastwood in the 1971 movie *Dirty Harry* and its later variations. The Callahan character is rarely on the defense. He is reactive, a vigilante who uses violence to get what he wants. Assuming the role of Callahan, Yankovic in "Trigger Happy" makes it clear that his gun owner is playing out an aggressive fantasy as a self-styled Dirty Harry.

The consequences of this weaponized power play include accidentally shooting dad—"a lousy flesh wound"—and injuring "little fluffy," a cat filled with lead—"We'll have to use him for a pencil instead." The musical style is upbeat, with easy dismissal of the violence. But the tragic accidents are not far from the reality of gun ownership. In 2012, for example, Jeffrey Giuliano in New Fairfield, Connecticut, shot and killed his son, a fifteen-year-old whom he mistook for an intruder.[12] In an instant, the laugh in "Trigger Happy" collides with reality—the joke shatters in a moment of reflection.

"CANADIAN IDIOT"

Almost two decades later, in 2006, Yankovic addressed guns again in "Canadian Idiot," his parody of Green Day's punk-rock "American Idiot." The Green Day song, which was an immediate hit when it was released on the album of the same name in 2004, called out the dysfunction of the American media and the prevalence of prejudice—what the band tagged the "redneck agenda." Backed by heavy percussion, Green Day vented their discontent in a rageful explosion of guitar. As the group's bassist Mike Dirnt said at the time, "I'm pissed off, and I'm angry, and I feel like I'm not fully represented." The song has most recently received attention thanks to a 2018 British effort to make the song a number one hit ahead of a visit from Donald Trump—the song accompaniment to the UK's "Trump Baby" balloon.

Yankovic's ironic version takes Canadians to task for not being like Americans. "Don't want to be an American idiot" becomes "Don't want to be a Canadian idiot"—each line punctuated by a flood of guitar. While Green Day criticizes American media—"Don't want a nation under the new media"—Yankovic plays for laughs with a number of American prejudices about Canadians—"Don't want to be some beer swillin' hockey nut." The list goes on: Canadians export only maple syrup and snow and "live on donuts and moose meat." Yankovic also brings up Canada's relationship to guns: "And they leave the house without packin' heat / Never even bring their guns to the mall." Without guns, the song says, Yankovic supposedly "[c]an't take 'em seriously at all." But Yankovic's insult song is actually a send-up of the rude American more than the Canadian. Not everyone got that point, with angry comments taking to task a spate of 2006 homemade videos set to "Canadian Idiot." But one young fan, thirteen-year-old Phil McCracken from Columbus, Ohio, heard the song clearly, telling the *Globe and Mail*: "It's really making fun of the Americans and their views on the Canadians." On his blog, Rabin connected the song to a more general wrong: "'Canadian Idiot' is fundamentally about the way we demonize people who are not like us, even when those differences actually make them better than us, not worse." To John Williams of the *Toronto Sun*, Yankovic said of the song, laughing, "It's actually a love letter to Canada." Later in the song, Yankovic begrudgingly shows some of that love, admitting Canadian positives: clean air, national health care, and low crime rates—the latter implying a relationship between gun ownership and crime rather than explicitly railing against gun rights. Yankovic's song has the same shout and hammering pulse as the original, but the message is less overt. Playing with stereotypes, Yankovic suggests the real problem is our fear of someone different, someone who does things their own way. A line admitting that "nervous" fear juts out of the song's setting, as if it were a radioed request for help.

"PARTY IN THE CIA"

"Party in the CIA" is set squarely back in the United States. From the 2011 album *Alpocalypse*, the song is a direct parody of Miley Cyrus's popular 2009 hit "Party in the USA." (First Billy Ray and then his daughter, Miley—Yankovic's parodies are a Cyrus family tradition.) The theme of the song is adjustment—the anxiety that comes with change, ostensibly her move from Nashville to Los Angeles—and it suggests music can beat back the unease: "They're playin' my song / You know I'm gonna be okay / Yeah, it's a party in the USA." Fans have viewed Cyrus's song in patriotic terms, some even hoping it might become the next national anthem (over "Dare to Be Stupid"—try again). In 2011, when President Barack Obama declared Osama Bin Laden dead, You-Tubers celebrated with "Party in the USA," clicking on the song's video hundreds of thousands of times. But in 2017 Cyrus used a performance of the song to take her own political stand. At the iHeartRadio Festival in Las Vegas, Cyrus performed the song as words appeared on a screen behind her: "Dreamers," "Justice," "Hope." Around the same time Cyrus tweeted a message promoting equality: "I won't stop until it's a party in the usa for everyone."

The same guitar riff opens the parody "Party in the CIA," but while Cyrus arrives at LAX, Yankovic makes his move to Langley, Virginia, home of CIA headquarters. Yankovic may be "feelin' nervous," but he has high hopes: "Wanna infiltrate some Third-World place," toppling its leader. But he evidently has the skills for any mission: "a quickie confession" or "waterboardin' session." He lists other questionable activities—tapping phones, shredding files, paying bribes, assassinating targets—but returns to the issue of torture to close the song: "We only torture the folks we don't like / You're probably gonna be OK!" Yankovic portrays these shady endeavors as light and fun for those perpetrating them: "It's a party in the CIA." But the upbeat music clashes with the gravity of the work, an incongruity extended by the clash between Cyrus's topic and Yankovic's. That collision is part of Yankovic's humor. In our first interview, he explained, "I try to have the music kind of play against the lyrics. So if it's a really dark, sick, twisted set of lyrics, I try to match it with something very happy and upbeat which is like 'Party in the CIA,' that kind of thing." Still, there's a message. The potential to party anywhere in the USA doesn't quite square with the violence of its government operatives.

When Yankovic wrote his parody, the issue of torture was especially prominent. Two years before the release of "Party in the CIA," the Obama administration released shocking pictures of prisoner abuse in US detention camps in Iraq and Afghanistan. This discharge followed the 2004 appearance of the infamous pictures of depravity at Abu Ghraib prison. Just before the Obama administration released the new images in 2009, it had made available memos from the Bush administration outlining torture techniques approved by the CIA. As late as 2008, George W. Bush had vetoed a bill banning some of those strategies, including waterboarding or simulated drowning. Democratic senator Dianne Feinstein spoke out against the decision: "Torture is a black mark against the United States."[13] As Stephen Grey put it in his 2006 study of the CIA torture program, torture "is wrong because it degrades our own societies," undermining "the rule of law and our own morality."[14]

Regime change, for some, has been seen as an analogous abuse of power and may have been another Yankovic target. Bernie Sanders, as a presidential candidate in 2016, categorized the war in Iraq as an effort by the United States to effect such change, grouping it with the infamous 1954 toppling of the democratically elected Arbenz government in Guatemala as well as the 1973 overthrow of Salvador Allende in Chile. In a 1970 memo, the CIA deputy director wrote, "It is firm and continuing policy that Allende be overthrown by a coup. . . . It is imperative that these actions be implemented clandestinely and securely so that the USG [United States government] and American hand be well hidden."[15] In 2003 the image of the literal toppling of a statue of Saddam Hussein in Baghdad provided a concrete picture of the American government's involvement or intrusion along these lines. And in 2009 the target was the democratically elected government in Honduras. Yankovic had done his homework when he sang, "No hurry on this South American dictator / I'll assassinate him later." (Yankovic is famous for his careful research. He said in the *Permanent Record* liner notes that for his 1985 song "I Want a New Duck," he "went to the library and read up on ducks for a week.") This investigative habit gives "Party in the CIA" a certain gravitas, an informed foundation. On a Reddit thread called "'Weird Al' Yankovic—Party in the CIA," one poster wrote on May 31, 2016, "Who would have thought that the most poignant critique of government surveillance and regime-toppling would come from Weird Al Yankovic."

And yet the humor of "Party in the CIA" can obscure that weightiness, just as that weightiness can obscure the joke. When his song came out, Yankovic was concerned about the new connection between Cyrus's song and bin Laden's assassination. "It's a little eerie," he said to Dave Itzkoff of the *New York Times*: "I hope people won't consider the song in bad taste." Humor, as always, was the primary inspiration. Yankovic told Rabin in his 2011 interview, "I decided if I was going to do a parody of a Miley Cyrus song, I had to make it very dark. That had to be part of the joke: I'm taking this kind of pop, bubblegum-y fluff of a song, and making it very dark and twisted." That joke can potentially distract from any message. Lost in the interpretive complexities of parody, listeners could also easily miss the point, especially one meant to be sly. I asked Yankovic, was "Party in the CIA" a "commentary on waterboarding or torture"? He admitted, "Well, yeah, I mean, it's so tongue-in-cheek though. It doesn't come off very heavy-handed. In fact, I've met several people actually in the CIA that say, 'Oh, we love the song. We play it in the offices all the time.'" Yankovic's parodies with a political point are, then, safe in a way—they are subtle, subject to interpretation, and thus have built-in refutation; they have "plausible deniability," to use CIA director Allen Dulles's term. Yankovic can be political, in parody song, on his own terms, without risk to his career. At his party, he can have his cake and torture it too.

CLIPS DON'T LIE

Guns have almost mythical status in the United States, connected to notions of frontier life, real and imagined. But the supposed constitutional right to own guns, part of the Second Amendment, is subject to debate. Some insist the Second Amendment grants the individual the right to bear arms for personal use, while others maintain that gun ownership was intended instead for the restricted use of an organized militia. In the latter camp, Patrick J. Charles, author of *Armed in America*, argues, "The fact of the matter is that the Founding Fathers' conception of the Second Amendment had little to do with a right to own, maintain, and use firearms for hunting, shooting, and self-defense."[16] In 1989, three years before the release of "Trigger Happy," there was a debate about the ownership of assault weapons. Bill Clinton helped pass the Brady Act, signed in 1993, to restrict these guns; this was part of his 1992 campaign platform: "We support a reasonable waiting period to permit background checks for purchases of handguns, as well as assault weapons controls to ban the possession, sale, importation and manufacture of the most deadly assault weapons."[17]

This attention to gun control in the 1990s and the ensuing decades provides a contextual foundation for Yankovic's political parodies. His childhood in Cold War America does so as well, revealed by reference to communists in "Trigger Happy" (as well as in *UHF* and even "Christmas at Ground Zero"): "Yeah, I gotta be ready if the commies attack us tonight." In *The Politics of Childhood in Cold War America*, Ann Marie Kordas chronicles the different ways the perceived threat of communism defined growing up in the aftermath of World War II. Throughout the 1960s, parents, teachers, and society at large worked to prepare children to respond to a communist threat. Yankovic would have experienced efforts toward the latter end of this period—the prominent sale of toy guns and a new valuation of guns more generally. Kordas writes, "Toys for male children encouraged them to envision themselves engaging in a variety of 'manly' jobs as adults. The most important of these was the role of a soldier, and toys of the Cold War period designed for boys have a distinctly military theme to them."[18] Children were also encouraged to be "normal" and "other-directed" and thus able to take direction in case of armed conflict. At the time, with this promotion of conformity, there was a pronounced aversion to exceptional achievement, even in school. Cold War America was particularly cold to the nerd, someone who stood out in a crowd.

When I brought up "Trigger Happy," Yankovic didn't connect the song to any specific political debate or the politics of his childhood, instead explaining, "I've just never been a big gun fan." But he did mention his vegetarianism, which he adopted in 1992 after reading John Robbins's *Diet for a New America* (1987). He had mocked vegetarianism and its stereotypical lifestyle a decade before, in his 1983 song "I'll Be Mellow When I'm Dead": "I don't want no part of that vegetarian scene . . . I'd rather have a Big Mac or a Jumbo Jack / Then all the bean sprouts in Japan." Yankovic told *Vegetarian Times* that the song is

now used against him: "This is nearly a decade before I became vegetarian myself. I was poking fun at the whole laid-back Southern California lifestyle, and I guess vegetarianism was part of that." But *Diet for a
New America*'s arguments concerning the environment and animal
rights struck a chord. The hunting of animals, for Yankovic, became
fundamentally objectionable.

Concerns about guns have only grown more pressing in the years
since. The United States has an ever-expanding list of mass shootings: at
the University of Texas, Columbine, Virginia Tech, Fort Hood, Aurora,
Sandy Hook, San Bernardino, Pulse nightclub in Orlando, Las Vegas,
Pittsburgh, and so on. And so on. Yankovic recalled to me the dilemma
this posed for the band: "[On one tour] we were going to play 'Trigger
Happy' . . . and then like the first night we were going to play it, there
was a mass shooting. And my bass player said, 'Al, we're not playing
that, right?' And I said, 'I guess not. We're not going to play it.' And
then we did wind up not playing it for the whole tour just because there
was a mass shooting every five minutes." I countered, "Why that
choice?" Perhaps the context demanded Yankovic push the song, take a
stand, and make his point. Yankovic reflected: "It does make a point. I
don't think there's anything wrong with playing it, but it's just such a
hot-button topic and people feel so fragile about it, and I just didn't . . .
want hurt feelings or controversy swirling around it. I have strong feelings about it, but I don't put myself out there politically just because . . .
I don't know. I guess I'm a coward. I don't know."

The issue of gun ownership is indeed fraught with emotion—and
one at times divorced from rational thought. As Kevin Yuill and Joe
Street observed in a 2018 study of gun control, "The issue of gun control is not only enmeshed in an increasingly bitter partisan divide between Red and Blue, but it has also transcended politics, and perhaps
even rational thought, to become a core issue of American identity."[19]
Even if Yankovic had ventured into the fray, performing his song in the
aftermath of a mass shooting, some listeners may not have recognized
the message. As with "Party in the CIA," "Trigger Happy" is based in
irony. Yankovic enjoys the approach, but there is one hitch, he told me:
"I tend not to do it too much because there's always going to be a small
percentage of people that don't understand the concept of irony." Yankovic has witnessed misunderstanding of "Trigger Happy" in this regard. He told me, "I had a number of people saying, 'Oh, I'm so glad

you wrote that song because I love guns.'" In the *Permanent Record* liner notes, Yankovic disclosed a specific incident: "[O]ne day I was doing an interview in Canada on a call-in talk show, and somebody called in and said 'Oh, I think it's great that you wrote this song, because I love guns, I got a lot of guns and I think it's great that you'd write a song like that.' Not wanting to explain the irony to someone who's heavily armed I simply said 'Thank you very much!'"

Of course, plenty of other listeners don't seem to miss a thing. One young fan, jilly7902, wrote in a 2005 discussion of "Trigger Happy" on the World of Weird Al Yankovic website: "I love how political it is. And how sarcastic, especially that line 'well you can't take my guns away I've got a constitutional right . . . I've gotta be ready if the Commies attack us tonight.' I did a project on gun control and when I listen to the song it seems to reinforce every good pro-gun control point . . . in a hilarious way."

Politics in Yankovic's work, then, is best described as overt and not. He has joked that his song "Eat It" is so beloved that he "could stand in the middle of Fifth Avenue and shoot somebody and not lose a single fan." The humor lies in his mimicking of Trump's bragging at a rally: "I could stand in the middle of Fifth Avenue and shoot somebody and I wouldn't lose voters." With his outlandish behavior, Trump has provided constant fodder for comedians. Yankovic is not alone in taking the bait. But Yankovic also reveals a certain truth, while again referencing the issue of gun violence. Yankovic's "Eat It" reputation overshadows his sometimes serious musical messages. Joe Blevins, writing for *Vulture*, confirmed this, including "Trigger Happy" in a 2015 listing of "The Surprisingly Weighty Songs of 'Weird Al' Yankovic." *Surprisingly.* Parody and collaboration contribute to the surprise of Yankovic's weighty work. His work with others and the humor, subject to individual interpretation, muddies any message. With recourse to surf music, he in this way took on gun ownership without making waves. For listeners, his funny, nice-guy rep also softens the political edge. On top of that, Yankovic has been reluctant to address politics directly, instead favoring diplomatic engagement.

Music itself is complicit, a political wolf in sheep's clothing. Music, after all, has unique connections to politics, connections beyond Yankovic's control. Music can reflect and contribute to meanings assigned class, ethnicity, and gender—all fundamental to decisions of government. Music can also foster cooperation in the collective activity of making music, while heightening "our understanding of how others might think and feel."[20] The latter effect relies on the emotion encoded in music, which can impact our capacity to empathize. Both cooperation and such emotional maturity inform a healthy operation of government.

As a voice for change, music can participate directly in democratic engagement as well. Protest song, in particular, has promoted social issues and ideals. In some cases, music allows for and invites protest. There is a poetic license in music, a seeming safe space for political comment. Music is a supposed mask. Interpretive ambiguities in performance offer plausible deniability, as does the collaborative process behind music. Who deserves the credit or blame for any one song or its message? Adding comedy to the mix can both heighten the message and further obscure it. The jokester has an out—that he was only kidding. In that muddy space, Yankovic has included politics in his music, despite his pronouncements to the contrary. Yankovic's politics therefore function in a gray zone, shielded somewhat by the complications of music, collaboration, and comedy.

Even if he did attempt explicit engagement in politics, Yankovic does not believe he could effect change. With characteristic self-deprecation, he claimed in our first interview, "I'm not one of those kind," whose opinion "is going to change anybody's mind." In fact, Yankovic joked, the opposite might occur: "It might just sway the other way. . . . Oh, if Weird Al says this. . . ." It's another funny self-insult, but in that joke there is a kernel of truth. Celebrity endorsement has a long history, dating back to the Chicago Cubs's support of Warren G. Harding during the 1920 election and the Rat Pack's support of John F. Kennedy. Later candidates have used the playing of music to imply celebrity endorsement (Trump is notorious for doing so without the musicians' permission). But voters may trust political information shared by friends more than messages from stars. Celebrities do have some powers of persuasion, but that potential has limits. It only works, according to Nives Zubcevic-Basic, writing for *The Conversation* in 2016, when the star is perceived as attractive, credible, and somehow related to the brand or political candidate. The limits of celebrity endorsement are seen clearly in Hillary Clinton's electoral college loss to Donald Trump,

despite the active campaigning of high-profile artists, like Jay Z, Beyoncé, Lady Gaga, and Bruce Springsteen, among others.

But Yankovic's more implicit approach to politics still has value.
Diplomatic engagement, rather than more pointed political intervention, has pressing relevance today, with the country divided as never
before. Then again, Yankovic still has time to take that public stand.
Though consistent in his approach to politics, on August 27, 2018, Yankovic threatened to up his game. After he asked people not to destroy
his star during his speech accepting his Hollywood Walk of Fame star,
he noted the media in attendance that day. He had a significant platform, he observed. With that opportunity, he felt the need, he said, to
"use my voice to say something really important." The audience grew
quiet and he seemed solemn, even serious, as he prepared for his
"statement." Was this moment *the* moment? Would Yankovic make a
clear political case? Had he had a change of heart? He then announced,
"I'm selling a used credenza on Craigslist." Cash only, he added. Almost
a month later, in a phone interview, I brought up this mischievous
turnaround. I told Yankovic, "I should have known." Yankovic let out a
gleeful laugh.

7

THE WOKE JOKE

Yankovic's flirtation with the political and support of the outsider overlap in his songs referencing race and religion. Like his political songs, these songs—"White & Nerdy," "Pretty Fly for a Rabbi," and "Amish Paradise," in particular—could alienate some listeners. And yet somehow Yankovic riffs on two sensitive topics without significant repercussion. As Nathan Rabin writes in his blog, "[H]e's an extremely white man who has managed to do a fair amount of ethnic material through the years yet has remained beloved." These songs focus on Yankovic's own identity as a white male, but they also incorporate markers of minority group identities—black, Jewish, and Amish—all in flux. Through the intertextual possibilities of parody, Yankovic draws on these characters, often at the same time. In so doing, he does not shy away from controversial issues of race and religion, even stereotypes and prejudice.

In 1992 Yankovic was not so brash. He ostensibly planned to dull the racial tension in Michael Jackson's 1991˙ message song "Black or White," one made more intense by Jackson's changing skin color: "It don't matter if you're black or white." Yankovic wanted to record a parody entitled "Snack All Night," completing a trilogy of Jackson parodies: "I'm never satisfied with three meals a day / While the world is sleeping I'll be munching away." He has said Jackson, whom he found "very nice" and "soft-spoken," did him a "huge favor" by refusing permission. In 2014 he told *Rolling Stone* that the song "would have been desperate and horrible." Though initially disappointed, Yankovic decided to parody Nirvana instead, which turned out to be one of the biggest hits of his career: "I realized that Michael Jackson turning me down was the greatest thing that ever happened to me."[1]

In "White & Nerdy," "Pretty Fly for a Rabbi," and "Amish Paradise," snacks are gone and race is front and center. The juxtaposition of different races and religions provides a foundation for comedy in the songs, given the incongruities. But it also invites commonality and comment. Yankovic repeats racial stereotypes but at the same time offers shared ground, in part by referencing his nerd identity. With his own outsider status, Yankovic complicates our understanding of racial and religious identity. Stereotypes exist alongside a process of equalization and acceptance. A woke joke? Not always. But there is nonetheless something fairly progressive in Yankovic's treatment of race and religion.

"WHITE & NERDY"

The 2006 song "White & Nerdy" begins by throwing us off-center with a wobbling, electronic effect and prominent keyboard dissonance. Yankovic's voice enters, but it is magnified, overdubbed. The effect drops away as Yankovic raps, outlining his nerd bona fides: "First in my class there at MIT" and a champ at D&D.

Yankovic's choice to rap poses interesting cultural questions. As author Imani Perry says in *Prophets of the Hood*, hip-hop is defined by blackness, though rap has multiracial connections. Rapping evokes black identity, no matter what the topic or who the rapper is. But there is some overlap with nerd culture in the genre of rap known as nerdcore, coined in 2000. Nerdcore is not a parody genre but proudly centers on classic nerd culture like video games, sci-fi, and science. It intersects with traditional rap as an expression of marginalization—and rebellion against that marginalization. Jessica Elizabeth Ronald alludes to this when she argues that traditional rap and nerdcore both expose "the oppressed experiences of today's youth."[2]

That correlation of the two groups' oppression is problematic. Nerdcore artists have a claim to marginalization, as mc chris notes when he reminisces about his teenage years: "I was made fun of a lot because I was different."[3] But equating the stakes of prejudice for black people and nerds too closely is dicey. In a trailer for the documentary *Nerdcore for Life*, white nerdcore rapper Monzy says: "Ladies and gentlemen, it's hard out there for a pimp. But it's even harder out there for a nerd. Us nerds are the oppressed and the downtrodden." This kind of statement is tone-deaf at best and ignorant and offensive at worst, ignoring both the vast historical subjugation of black people through slavery, political disenfranchisement, poverty, economic discrimination, and white violence as well as the relative privilege of the traditionally white male nerd. Lori Kendall notes that Monzy's statement "demonstrates a lack of sympathy with members of those [other oppressed] groups."[4] As Richard Dyer writes in his book *White*, "white people don't see their white privilege."[5] White, he insists, is instead the default blank slate.

Traditionally, rap has addressed racial oppression directly. Chamillionaire's "Ridin'" (2005), which Yankovic parodies in "White & Nerdy," refers to police surveillance of black men, racial profiling, and the disproportionate effort to punish minorities: "Tryna catch me ridin' dirty." In *Pulse of the People*, Lakeyta M. Bonnette connects "Ridin'" to rap's long history of exposing police prejudice in songs like NWA's famous "F*** tha Police" (1988). She writes, "Rap music provides information, in addition to making issues salient that otherwise may not have garnered much attention outside minority communities."

On the website Nerdcore Rising, it is clear that Yankovic as a parodist is not considered a nerdcore artist, "but is revered by nerdcorites everywhere." Not all nerdcore artists are like Monzy in their attitudes, but the very act of using a perceived black genre—rap—to celebrate and defend a traditionally white subculture is fraught with risks. On the other hand, the nerdcore community is multiracial, and many black nerdcore artists talk about a freedom in the genre. They can express their blackness and their nerdiness, and break free of stereotypes around being black. Yankovic's "White & Nerdy" also expresses a desire to move beyond type with a white nerd who really, really wants to "roll with the gangstas," testing the limits of what a white-as-sour-cream guy with a pocket protector is supposed to do and be. In the video, two black men, played by comedy duo Jordan Peele and Keegan-Michael Key, slowly cruise by Yankovic, who is waving at them from his suburban front yard. The duo lock him out because "so far they all think I'm too white and nerdy." The so-called gangstas appear afraid of the nerd, but the concern, as Kendall insists, is misplaced. The scene ignores white people's advantage in this situation. And the fear of Yankovic's nerd is funny but misplaced (or misplaced and thus funny), overlooking the actual danger two young black men might experience driving through this suburban, white neighborhood. Then again, maybe it's a nice bit of turnaround—the white guy gets to see what it's like to be unnecessarily feared.

In static shots in the video, Yankovic appears in clothes similar to Chamillionaire's in the original video, an oversized black sweatshirt emblazoned in red font with his own name. Chamillionaire's grill has become plain old braces, and Chamillionaire's graphic of a chameleon on fire has become a graphic of Pac-Man and the Schrödinger equation. While Chamillionaire is accompanied by rapper Krayzie Bone, Yankovic is hanging out with singer and teen idol Donny Osmond, who enthusiastically dances behind him with awkward conviction. Yankovic goes full nerd in the video, wearing a polo shirt with sweater tied over his shoulders and naturally curly locks replaced by a straight bowl cut. Kendall sees these changes as reinforcing the identification of nerdiness with whiteness: Curly hair is apparently too "ethnic," she writes. But of course this is the point of the parody: a lament for a particular nerdiness, the "hyperwhite."

One way that hyperwhiteness manifests is through language. Many kids in high school adopt aspects of black culture, including slang, as markers of coolness. But the nerd opts instead for superstandard English, with "hypercorrect" pronunciation. The move is related to the nerd valuation of intelligence, but it is also a refusal to conform. Linguist Mary Bucholtz confirms: "In short, for nerds the practice of avoiding casual pronunciation in favor of a literate-based speech style reflected a language ideology that ties formal speech register to intelligence. And intelligence in turn was associated, at least by nerds, with independent thought: a refusal to go along with the crowd whether in fashion or in phonetics."[6] The hyperwhiteness of the nerd differs from the invisible whiteness Dyer writes about. Far from being a universal standard in their own minds, nerds are aware of their differences and aware of the power imbalance with other, un-nerdy whites. While this "otherness" isn't as severe as someone like Monzy might assert, it does add nuance to our conception of white privilege. There is more than one way to be white. There is more than one response to white.

The marker of hypercorrect language appears throughout "White & Nerdy." In the song, Yankovic uses slang when he describes his MyS-

"White & Nerdy" Live. *Courtesy of Fred Olderr*

pace page as "pimped out." Otherwise, the song for the most part displays the language of nerdy hyperwhiteness—wordplay common to Yankovic's musical world more generally. Yankovic's title matches the original's "ridin' dirty," in rhyme and syllabic count. And his listing of nerd credentials boasts an impressive variety of rhymes with "contrary": "All of my action figures are cherry / Stephen Hawking's in my library."

Ironically, while the WASP-y academic vocabulary Yankovic uses in the song is meant to differentiate his character from the black rap culture he seeks to be a part of, it also signals a joint value—the ability to invent and play with language creatively.

But language is just one element Yankovic uses to contrast the less powerful, hyperwhite nerd and the cool black man. He also plays up the incongruity by relying on stereotypes of the nerd, with little sexual appeal, and the black man, who appears powerful and hypersexual. Cool is linked with hardness, a "defiant masculinity" that has long been valued in American culture. While there are white examples, like John Wayne, the tough male is a regular feature in gangsta rap, a projected and performed black identity. The identity, in black culture, has inter-disciplinary historical roots—from sports to dancing. As Anthony J. Le-melle Jr., in his study of black identity, writes, "Historians of black masculinity have highlighted stereotyping of black males as runners, dancers, jive talkers, and sexing bucks that are 'good for nothing' but primitive sex."[7] This version of black has been particularly popular among white consumers. The dangerous black man sells. But any posi-tive connotations in the black man's supposed strength, talent, and sex appeal may be erased by an associated criminality and deviance. Any positive ascription in the stereotype gives way to another means of persecution.

Nonetheless, Yankovic's "White & Nerdy" twists this tendency in white culture to pathologize black culture. In the video, again, it's the white weirdo who is frightening to the more "normal" black men driv-ing through the neighborhood. And, as Yankovic told me, white was used at the time "sort of like a derogatory term. I mean, it wasn't . . . meant to be empowering for white people. It was more meant to say, white in terms of bland, mayonnaise-eating dweebs." This angle is simi-lar to the work of the musical group the Lonely Island, made up of Andy Samberg, Akiva Schaffer, and Jorma Taccone (often compared to Yankovic, who appeared with them on a 2018 episode of Carpool Ka-raoke). Their digital shorts for Saturday Night Live regularly mocked the sensibilities of white people: cheesy player-types offer their "Dick in the Box" to their girlfriends as a supposedly seductive Christmas present, and two white guys, rapping with aggressive attitude, discuss their plans to get cupcakes and watch The Lion, the Witch and the Wardrobe on a "Lazy Sunday." Penny Spirou writes about how the group flips white masculinity upside down: "Race is linked to the mun-dane and monotonous, turning something that could be very masculine and controlling . . . into something awkward and embarrassing."[8] In "White & Nerdy," Yankovic, like the Lonely Island, relies on certain stereotypes. But he mixes and muddles them with his portrayal of the goofy, hyperwhite nerd.

When "White & Nerdy" was released, Chamillionaire loved the song. Despite the seriousness of his original song's message, Chamillionaire found Yankovic's nerd parody an honor, a sign of the rapper's fame, and he even praised Yankovic's rapping ability: "I remember when he redid Michael Jackson's 'Bad.' Weird Al is not gonna do a parody of your song if you're not doing it big. You gotta be a big dog."[9] While most artists have felt the same, there was one big exception: Coolio's infamous rancor at Yankovic's parody of the rapper's masterpiece "Gangsta's Paradise." Yankovic's parody again plays with notions of black and white, this time through portrayal of—that's right—the Amish.

"AMISH PARADISE"

"Gangsta's Paradise" was a single from Coolio's second album, which had the same name. The song's infectious synthetic, string riff reincarnated the song "Pastime Paradise" (1976), set off by Stevie Wonder's early adoption of the Yamaha GX-1 keyboard and the instrument's singular string sound. When Coolio requested permission to sample the part, Wonder initially hesitated. But Wonder agreed after Coolio cut from his song a few planned obscenities.[10] Coolio's song maintained its number two spot on the *Billboard* Hot 100 for twelve weeks, a distinct achievement for a rap song at the time.

In 1995 the song sounded everywhere, and in 1996 "Gangsta Paradise" won the Grammy Award for Best Rap Performance. The song's video promoted and was tied to the 1985 film *Dangerous Minds*, featuring clips from the movie as well as a face-off between the movie's star, Michelle Pfeiffer, and Coolio. All of this did much to distinguish Coolio. Soren Baker, a hip-hop journalist, observed in an oral history of "Gangsta's Paradise" published in *Rolling Stone*: "'Gangsta's Paradise' proved that Coolio wasn't a one-hit wonder, and that he didn't have to deliver a prototypical radio record in order to enjoy success. The song also showed that gangster rappers could work with Hollywood's elite, and promote a film starring a white actress."

The song itself is about the cycle of violence in the ghetto, hardly a paradise. The violent threat is everywhere: "You better watch how you talkin' and where you walkin' / Or you and your homies might be lined in chalk." To survive, a man must become hard and violent, the song avers—and that front in turn becomes the model: "Fool, I'm the kinda G the little homies wanna be like." In the video, Coolio explains this reality to Pfeiffer, who stares forward impassively. He appears with sunglasses on, smoke around him, mysterious and cool. He exudes the masculine power associated with rap. At the end of the video, the cycle outlined is realized, with a child dressed like Coolio, the next gangsta.

Remembering the song twenty years later in *Rolling Stone*, Coolio talked about the composition of his song with reverence:

> I sat down and I started writing. Hearing the bass line, the chorus line and the hook, it just opened up my mind. "As I walk through the valley of the shadow of death / I take a look at my life and I see there's nothing left"—I freestyled that; that came off the top of the dome and I wrote that down. I thought about it for a minute, and then I wrote the whole rest of the song without stopping, from the first verse to the third verse. You know, I like to believe that it was divine intervention. "Gangsta's Paradise" wanted to be born; it wanted to come to life, and it chose me as the vessel.

The song seemed like a perfect choice for a Yankovic makeover. He told *Rolling Stone* in the oral history that he liked "the fact that it was a rap song—which means more words, which generally allows for more jokes—with a melodic chorus for the hook." And Yankovic, during his career, has often rapped, even appearing on *Epic Rap Battles of History*, June 16, 2014, as Isaac Newton (his opponent, Bill Nye). But rap also has very specific expectations about who is involved in the music and why. Those assumptions are easy targets, making rap, according to Charles Hiroshi Garrett, "an especially ripe target for parody." Yankovic is not alone in capitalizing on that comedic potential.[11] For "Gangsta's Paradise," all he needed was his signature spin. Speaking to me, Yankovic outlined the origin story of "Amish Paradise": "Well, the song came about because Coolio's hit 'Gangsta's Paradise' had been number one on the charts for a few weeks. And I was thinking, what could I do with 'Gangsta's Paradise'? 'Gangasta's Paradise,' what rhymes with gangsta? How could I twist this? And then, when I thought of 'Amish

Paradise,' it was this weird epiphany. . . . I don't remember ever having a feeling like this before but immediately I got depressed, in a way, because I thought, 'Oh no, I have to do this. It's just too perfect and it's going to be a big hit and the rest of my life is going to change, right now.'" He reflected further, "Maybe I wasn't right to say depressed . . . it was just a feeling of gravitas" and an awareness of the work to come.

In "Amish Paradise," Yankovic once again substitutes the minority subject with an outsider: in this case, the Amish. The valley is no longer a biblical reference to death, but a place to harvest grain: "As I walk through the valley where I harvest my grain." It was "the comedy of opposites," Yankovic explained to me, "and there's nothing more diametrically opposed to the gangster lifestyle than the Amish lifestyle." He continued, "I just thought it would be hilarious to basically have this Amish person just rapping about life on the mean streets of Lancaster, Pennsylvania." The same repeating string ostinato in the original unifies the song. But Yankovic didn't want to sample the thin string hook; instead, his keyboardist found a way to re-create it using a Korg 01/W, a keyboard unveiled in 1991—a Yankovic-approved substitute for Wonder's expensive Yamaha GX-1. Yankovic appears in the supporting video dressed in Amish garb, topped off with beard and hat. Florence Henderson, complete with bonnet, replaces Michelle Pfeiffer. Yankovic raps about the Amish way of life as she replicates Pfeiffer's indifferent stare.

But, unlike Pfeiffer, Henderson is ostensibly a part of this paradise. Yankovic's explanation thereby focuses on aspects of Amish life specific to males: "I'm a man of the land" with "a Bible in my hand and a beard on my chin." Like Coolio's character, children look up to the Amish Yankovic: "I'm the pious guy the little Amlettes wanna be like." Rather than a problem, though, his status as a role model becomes the basis for a joke, framed by pseudo-biblical language: "Well, I know I'm a million times as humble as thou art." In the chorus, a full choir supports Yankovic with repeated block harmonies as he sings, voice newly amplified, about his life in an Amish paradise.

After an iconic scene of Yankovic walking among farm animals, played backward, he appears within the choir, all singers holding candles. Candles feature in Coolio's video, too, surrounding him as he raps. At one point Coolio holds a candle, creating an atmosphere of piety and mourning. But in Yankovic's video, the candles have practical purpose as the Amish "shun fancy things, like electricity," underscored in the video by an Amish trio stomping on a collection of quasi-modern technology—landline phones and a vinyl record. A joke within a joke, the technology is hardly up to date. Another link between the original and Yankovic's version is a surprising use of the word "fool," a brazen "fool" as exclamation. In "Gangsta's Paradise," Coolio emphasizes his plight with the insult: "[T]hat's why I know my life is out of luck, fool!" Yankovic inserts the word similarly, but as a means to brag about his new look: "And my homies agree, I really look good in black, fool."

In addition to references to the original, Yankovic smuggles into "Amish Paradise" an allusion to Prince. Yankovic attempted multiple times to get permission from the singer for parodies of his songs, among them "1999," in which Prince sings, "So tonight I'm gonna party like it's nineteen ninety-nine." But Yankovic never had any success. In 2014 Yankovic shared with *Access Hollywood*, "The only person who's consistently said no has been Prince. . . . He just wasn't into parody." In "Amish Paradise," Yankovic sings, "But if I finish all of my chores, and you finish thine / Then tonight we're gonna party like it's 1699." It was something.

Far more extensive are the song's references to the 1985 movie *Witness*. In 1993, representations of the Amish were appearing in mainstream culture. "The Great Plain" was the theme in the summer edition of *Vogue*, which preached a "minimalist" aesthetic, and David Letterman referenced the religious group in his "Top Ten Amish Pick-Up Lines": "Are thee at barn raisings often?" Other parody groups took notice: The Electric Amish released the album *Barn to Be Wild*. The Amish, a religious group related to Swiss German Anabaptists, have variants in practice—the Old Order Amish, New Order Amish, and Old Beachy Amish, for example. And yet, as a whole, the Amish in popular representation have been associated with the conservative practices of the Old Order Amish, with a rural way of life devoid of modern technology. In popular culture they are sometimes represented as religious tyrants and sometimes as a mysterious minority, with authentic ambassadors of a noble, simplistic life, an antidote to the corruption of the capitalist majority.[12]

It was this idealized vision that director Peter Weir drew on for his film, which starred Harrison Ford and Kelly McGillis. The movie opens on a field before an Amish black buggy with a single horse comes into frame. After an Amish boy witnesses a crime while traveling, Ford's character, police officer John Book, goes undercover in an Amish community to protect both the boy and himself. He assumes the traditional dress, with no buttons, though the pants are a little short. He asks McGillis, playing the Amish woman Rachel, "How do I look—do I look Amish?" She responds, "You look plain"—evidently a yes. Ford's character soon learns that the Amish get to work early; he must wake up at 4:30 in the morning to milk the cows. Later, when the Amish are harassed in town, Ford's character reacts violently. The others are disappointed—that's not the Amish way.

Many of these images and ideas appear in the "Amish Paradise" video. Yankovic's protagonist wears the same suit, with short pants. He describes his wife as "very plain": high praise. And his chores start early, milking cows at 4:30 in the morning. Unlike Ford's character, however, he successfully turns "the other cheek," when a local boy kicks him. But he takes pleasure in the knowledge of his revenge in the afterlife.

Once again, Yankovic's character represents a subculture of whiteness, an outlier from the general white culture Dyer described. He is subject to local bullying, he lacks many of the privileges conferred on other whites, and, with his biblical vocabulary, he displays a linguistic nonconformity. As with "White & Nerdy," the musical style links the song to black culture and the lyrics describe a collision between two cultures perceived as very different—rural versus urban, plain versus bling, invisible whiteness versus self-conscious difference. Yankovic brings together these various characters—nerd, black, Amish, white. Identity is fluid, unique and overlapping.

When the song was released, Coolio was not happy. The song's unique place in the history of rap, the subject matter, and Coolio's special connection to the song made him feel like the parody was disrespectful, trivializing a great artistic achievement. But years later in *Rolling Stone*, Coolio admitted that his feelings about the song had changed: "I have to say, that was probably one of the least smart things I've done over the years. I should have never been upset about that; I should have embraced it like everybody else did. Michael Jackson never got mad at him. . . . Who the fuck was *I* to take the position that I took?" Still, he couldn't resist one more jab, disparaging the parody's quality. In 2017 he told Geoff Edgers, writing for the *Washington Post*, "Okay, damn, if you're going to make a parody of my song, can't you do a better job? . . . He killed 'Beat It' when he did 'Eat It.'"

"PRETTY FLY FOR A RABBI"

If all this sounds complicated, get ready for "Pretty Fly for a Rabbi" (1999), a direct parody of the Offspring's 1998 song "Pretty Fly (for a White Guy)." Unlike "Amish Paradise" and "White & Nerdy," "Pretty Fly for a Rabbi" does not rely on rap. Instead, Yankovic manipulates a song with its own complex version of whiteness, and one that targets a particular white response to black culture, lampooning wannabes. Through parody, Yankovic layers upon that wannabe another outsider, a Jewish character. The Jewish identity—to which Yankovic himself is tied (with and without reason)—is white and not. In *Audiotopia*, Josh Kun writes, "Before World War II and the racial genocide of the Holocaust, the American Jew was commonly viewed as a racial subject, often 'Negro' or 'Oriental,' often 'less than white' or 'off-white,' yet always significantly inferior to and categorically different from the whiteness of the naturalized American citizen."[13] But after the war, in the United States, Jews became integrated, assimilation's success story.

To Emma Green, writing in the *Atlantic*, professor of history Eric Goldstein explained that "there's a lot of dissonance between those two positions."[14] For many, the question of the Jews' acceptance revolves around the question of the Jews' whiteness. For Jews, white identity has to do with power and status rather than skin color. With a recent uptick in highly visible anti-Semitic incidents, including the violent attack on a Pittsburgh synagogue in 2018, some Jews feel vulnerable, their white identity and thus mainstream acceptance in doubt. With the Jews' complicated relationship to white identity and Yankovic's perceived personal connection to the song as a supposed Jew, his "Pretty Fly for a Rabbi" is a convoluted identity mash-up, resurrecting and complicating stereotypes in a layering of Jewish, black, white, and Weird Al.

In a 1993 article in the *Independent*, writer David Usborne identified the topic of the Offspring song: "They are the 'wiggers,' the new class of white blacks, and they may be the pop culture trend of the Nineties." The character was often a young white man heavily invested in black culture—music, language, and dress. Brian Willwerth saw the identity—in this case a self-identity—as a bridge, a stance against racism. But for others at the time, the character was another example of white appropriation of black culture. Erica Fite of Los Angeles explained to Usborne, "They're perpetrating a fraud by being something they're not." In the video for "Pretty Fly (for a White Guy)," the Offspring portray the wigger as a poseur. He's skinny and white, wearing an oversized blue jersey and gold chain: "Our subject isn't cool / But he fakes it anyway." With passion, this young man attempts to fit in, but is dismissed by black men and physically removed when he attempts to join in group break dancing. His exuberant dance moves are admittedly a visual mismatch, but his fervor is almost admirable. Like the nerd, he's an outsider. But the wigger both conforms and doesn't: He attempts to assimilate into black culture and thereby find acceptance, seemingly unaware that he has no hope of doing so. The Offspring mock him, positioning themselves as cool white men in contrast. But the group at the same time celebrates him, in a way: "The world needs wannabes / So do that brand new thing."

"Pretty Fly (for a White Guy)" was immensely popular, especially in the UK. Catchy and upbeat, it was an easy parody choice for Yankovic. In Yankovic's version, "Pretty Fly for a Rabbi," he re-creates the original song's sound, complete with its high vocal register. Yankovic at times sounds like he's straining to match pitch. But there is one notable instrumental change—a clarinet lick after the early line, "And all the goyim say I'm pretty fly for a rabbi." The rapid, chromatic figuration in the clarinet is a klezmer call-out. It's a clear sonic signal of the context switch. More subtly, Yankovic replaces the initial count. The Offspring uses German nonsense, from Def Leppard's "Rock of Ages," instead of the more traditional "1, 2, 3, 4": "Gunter glieben glauten globen." Yankovic substitutes Yiddish—"Veren zol fun dir a blintze"—which sounds similar but actually has meaning: "You should turn into a blintz." The sheer amount of Yiddish that follows is rather astounding—words like *ferklempt*, *kvell*, *macher*, *meshugga*, *moyl*, *nudnicks*, *plotz*, *schlemiel*, *shalom*, *shmeer*, and *shul*, among others. In addition to his research (a common part of his parody preparation), Yankovic credits exposure to *Mad* magazine for his knowledge of Yiddish. Jewish predecessors in comedy and musical comedy informed the song as well. He told me, "If you're in comedy, you're exposed to Jewish catchphrases all the time."

In contrast to the Offspring's wannabe, this rabbi is the real deal. Some of his defining traits, according to Yankovic, are his reading of the Torah, his work ethic, his diet (kosher), his teaching, his praying, his chutzpah, and his approval among the ladies—*yentas* and *shiksas*. But Yankovic also spends time outlining the rabbi's accounting acumen and his ability to haggle: "He shops at discount stores, not just any will suffice / He has to find a bargain, 'cause he won't pay retail price." This particular prejudice has a long history. In 1843 Karl Marx connected his critique of capitalism to the Jew: "Money is the jealous god of Israel before whom no other god may stand." The prejudice confounded Jews who were artists, soon dismissed as inauthentic. In "Judaism in Music" (1850), one of the earliest texts to address Jewish music, German composer Richard Wagner disparaged Jewish composers as unoriginal, motivated by commerce rather than true art. In writings during the Nazi era, writers continued to condemn Jewish music as commercial. Yankovic's recourse to this common stereotype is meant as an inoffensive joke—and one hardly unique to Yankovic. Ethnic jokes, after all, generally thrive in comedy—both as a negative reaction to a perceived threat and a positive means to relieve a certain tension in difference.[15] And no ethnicity or nationality is immune. In comedy, any group stereotype can be a necessary shorthand. As Ruth R. Wisse writes in *No Joke: Making Jewish Humor*, "[S]tereotypes are a regular feature of joking, which depends for its effect on brevity."[16] In this light, it can be hard to castigate a joke as obnoxious. If a person tries, he or she may experience some blowback, shamed or scorned as humorless. In his book *Jokes: Philosophical Thoughts on Joking Matters*, Ted Cohen writes, "The offended person who takes issue with a joke finds himself doubly assaulted, first by the offensive portrayal in the joke, and then again by the implicit accusation that he is humorless." Still, with anti-Semitism more visible today, Yankovic's repetition of this particular stereotype stings. I will admit that upon a recent hearing, I had a visceral reaction, though I clearly continue to admire Yankovic and his art.

In his consideration of the song on his blog, Rabin notes the stereotype: "'Pretty Fly for a Rabbi' doubles as a makeshift encyclopedia of the most commonly employed Yiddish phrases, but it's also a collection of Jewish stereotypes, most notably the one involving Jews being cheap and bargain-hungry." And yet he praises Yankovic's use of Yiddish. After listing the specific prejudicial passages, Rabin writes, "Those are a lot of jokes about Jews loving to haggle and chase bargains but they're done with such affection and care that they cease to be offensive. This faithful recycling of hoary old stereotypes made less of an impression on me than both Al's extensive and impressive use of Yiddish slang and his mastery of not just the themes of Jewish comedy, but the specific rhythms and inflections as well." Ultimately, he concludes, "As a Jew, I'm flattered and charmed by 'Pretty Fly for a Rabbi' rather than insulted. It's not just kosher; it's worth kvelling about!" Somehow Yankovic's recourse to a Jewish language gives him some insider status. Related to the idea that only Jews can tell Jewish jokes, Rabin seems to excuse Yankovic's use of the stereotype. Yankovic, as an honorary Jew, has a free pass.

To others, the status, of course, isn't just honorary—it's authentic. Yankovic's nerd credentials, highlighted in his music, only support the assumption that Yankovic is Jewish. One stereotype supports another. Benjamin Nugent, for example, observes overlapping notions of Jewish and nerd identities. There is, for both, a comparable cultural value invested in reading and learning.[17] Jews, like nerds, have also been associated with a lack of physical prowess. Neither is thought to live up to notions of a stereotypical masculine athleticism or sexuality.[18] Still, Kevb01987, on the World of Weird Al Yankovic website, credited the misconception that Yankovic is Jewish to three other stereotypes: Yankovic is smart, he is a comedian, and he "has a hard-to-spell Eastern European surname."

In "Pretty Fly for a Rabbi," Yankovic seems to confirm his perceived Jewish connection. While he often assumes the characters central to his song—"I'm white and nerdy," "I'm tacky"—Yankovic does not pretend in "Pretty Fly for a Rabbi" to be a rabbi. He describes the rabbi in the third person: "He's such a macher." Still, Yankovic infers his Jewish membership, singing, "Our temple's had a fair share of rabbis in the past."

Responding to Rabin's blog write-up, one poster, Roc Kit, summed up his initial response to Yankovic's song: "It's a good thing a Gentile didn't try to do this." But some only learned of Yankovic's true background from Rabin's post: "A lot of people think Al is Jewish. 'Pretty Fly for a Rabbi' will do nothing to discourage that incorrect belief." A poster called Dude responded, "Weird Al . . . ISN'T Jewish?! I now question everything I thought I knew about the world." The discussion of "Pretty Fly for a Rabbi" on the World of Weird Al Yankovic website similarly clarified the issue for Kayy911, who had asked on June 16, 2004, "Has Al been Bar-Mitzvahed?" Algonacchick replied, "No, because Al is not Jewish." Kayy911 wrote back seconds later, "HE'S NOT??????? Prove it." There have, of course, been clues. With his curly mane replaced by a short, straight hairdo, Yankovic played Hitler on the season-two premiere of *Drunk History* in 2014. His agent had cautioned him, according to Martin Bierly in *Entertainment*, "Are you sure you wanna do this, Al?" But Yankovic viewed the Hitler appearance as in part promotional, with *Mandatory Fun* out that year and Yankovic pictured on the cover playing a dictator: "It tied into the whole totalitarian theme on the album cover."[19] He would also play Adolf Eichmann in a 2018 episode, actress Rachel Bloom's account of the Mossad operation to capture the rogue Nazi. Of course, Jews have a history of Hollywood performance as Nazis, with the German accent an asset in casting for several German Jewish actors who escaped Nazi Germany. Still, Amy Spiro, writing in the *Jerusalem Post*, wasn't buying it. She observed of the 2018 episode, "Eichmann is portrayed, jarringly, by Weird Al Yankovic."

I had to ask Yankovic about the stereotyping. And Yankovic, I learned, was well aware of the issue: "Maybe it's not the most kind of woke jokes to make." He continued, "I'm not proud of some of those jokes, but it's just part of the whole Jewish joke book."

The parody group 2 Live Jews, made up of MC Moisha (Eric Lambert) and Easy Irving (Joe Stone), salvaged the same stereotype. In their music, they played on the power of rap, much as Yankovic did, to support the Jew. Like "Pretty Fly for a Rabbi," the duo outlined Jewish attributes, what Johnny Loftus called in his write-up on the group for *All Music* an "ethnic joke with a beat." In the song "As Kosher as They Wanna Be," the group references 2 Live Crew's 1989 album *As Nasty as They Wanna Be* in a description of Jewish eating habits. But the stereotype of Jewish frugality was also part of the schtick in songs like "Beggin' for a Bargain" and "Accountant Suckers."

The group's music aligns with Jewish efforts during the 1990s to assert a coherent Jewish identity, a reaction to a notion at the time that Jewish identity in the United States was increasingly fragmented and even fast disappearing. In that climate, the Jewish joke was a plus. When in perceived need, stereotypes can become more than an abbreviated joke. In a Jewish voice, they can function as an easy identity marker and means of community cohesion. Yankovic's song, too, belongs to this time period—a period of Jewish rebuilding rather than today's pervasive fear of the resurrection of anti-Semitism. Just as the 1990s context in part explains his song, our current situation helps explain my reaction. Today's anxiety can change perceptions of Jewish jokes. In Germany, during a time of heightened anti-Semitism between 1925 and 1927, the reception of Jewish comedians similarly transformed. Critics then increasingly criticized Jewish comedians who riffed on stereotypes, accusing them of supporting radical anti-Semitism.[20] Then again, though similar in context, construction, and topic, Jewish stereotypes in the voice of 2 Live Jews are inherently different. Yankovic's non-Jewish voice matters. For 2 Live Jews, stereotypes can be empowering self-insult or even communal determination. And the group took pains to make their joke in-group only. In the song "Jokin' Jews," they maintain, "[I]f you're not Jewish, it's not funny." Perhaps I didn't laugh because I knew Yankovic isn't Jewish. Others only learned later that Yankovic is, in fact, gentile. But after their initial investment in the idea that Yankovic is Jewish, the turnaround didn't just negate the joke; they felt somehow wronged.

Yankovic acknowledges people's surprise when they find out he isn't Jewish. He has even experienced a certain backlash. He shared with me, "A lot of people were upset to find out that I wasn't Jewish." After playing "Pretty Fly for a Rabbi" at their Bar Mitzvahs, with the revelation of Yankovic's true identity, some felt betrayed. But others see "Pretty Fly for a Rabbi" in a different light. In response to a question on the website quora.com, "What do Jews think of 'Pretty Fly for a Rabbi' By Weird Al?" Shraga Weissmann posted, "It's Weird Al so right off the bat you knew it was going to be fun, and it's always nice to be represented." Though there were outspoken Jewish comedians in the 1960s and 1970s, Jewish characters were slow to appear in mainstream television sitcoms—with increasing examples in the 1990s. Given the influence of early Jewish musical comedians on Yankovic, I wondered if this history was in any way inspiration for "Pretty Fly for a Rabbi." Referencing Jewish parody artists, I asked Yankovic, "Was [the song] in any way an homage to Jewish parody or this history?" I was certainly leading the witness—so much so that Yankovic laughed. But he liked the idea.

"Let's say, sure," he said, adding, "That wasn't the intention, but I'd like to think it is."

With "Pretty Fly for a Rabbi," Yankovic built on the complicated character of the wannabe in the Offspring's original song. He layered upon the wigger reference to yet another complicated character: the rabbi, white to some, some of the time. The Jewish character overlaps many of the outsiders Yankovic conjures: the nerd and even the Amish, the latter similarly exotic in their religious fervor. In the song, as well as in "White & Nerdy" and "Amish Paradise," he depends on the racial and ethnic contrasts between characters in the original song and in his parody. But there is also correspondence between all of the characters, including real and imagined assumptions of his own persona. In this way, Yankovic reproduces stereotypes but also complicates representation of each identity, nuancing in different ways our understanding of whiteness.

When asked about "Pretty Fly for a Rabbi," Offspring guitarist Kevin Wasserman (known as Noodles), responded, "I thought it was great. Yeah, it was funny."[21] He, like Chamillionaire, seemed to appreciate the parody. Still, Yankovic's play with racial identity gives some explanation for Coolio's rejection of "Amish Paradise." Issues of identity similarly help explain a related half-refusal, Eminem's rejection of Yankovic's proposed music video "Couch Potato," a parody of the rapper's "Lose Yourself." Eminem could not avoid the effect of his whiteness on his career as a rapper. To overcome notions that rap is only part of black culture and allied charges that he himself is a wigger, Eminem relied on realness and honesty, his lower-class background crucial to his efforts to counter his perceived privileged white status. When Yankovic did a direct parody of Eminem's "Lose Yourself," inverting the energy of the song to create an ode to the couch potato, Eminem gave Yankovic permission for the song but refused to allow Yankovic to produce the video. Yankovic told the website launch.com, "Eminem was fine with me having the parody on my album but said he was afraid that a Weird Al video might detract from his legacy, that it would somehow make people take him less seriously as an important hip-hop artist." Interscope Records spokesman Dennis Dennehy tried to clarify, offering Eminem's perspective: "It's an important personal piece of music for him, a piece of art. He doesn't mind him doing the song, but he didn't want to change kids' visual perception on what that image was. He wanted to make sure the image would remain intact."[22]

His account does not make the racial issue explicit, but with Eminem already navigating a problematic white identity in hip-hop, the visual association with Yankovic was clearly a problem. In hip-hop, whiteness was never Dyer's default blank slate; rather, it is and has been highly visible in different ways. In Eminem's music, whiteness stands out as angry, frustrated, and ugly.[23] Yankovic highlighted the wigger as well as other white outsiders related to the nerd: the Jew and the Amish. Eminem granted permission for the song "Couch Potato," and his music was included in Yankovic's medley "Angry White Boy Polka" (2003). But he couldn't afford further association, he decided, with a visual image hard to erase.

SINGLE WHITE MALE

In all of these examples, Yankovic's play with identity concerns men— or, in the case of his Eminem-inclusive medley, white boys. In this chapter, I sidelined the issue of gender, but it too complicates these songs. In them, Yankovic often breaks with traditional masculinity. In "Amish Paradise" and "White & Nerdy," Yankovic's music plays on a genre defined in part by a problematic hypermasculinity. Yankovic, through the parody, creates a clash and dialogue—with his Amish character averse to fighting and his nerdy character romantically involved with bubble wrap.

This attention to gender is not atypical in Yankovic's work. While the topic of food in Yankovic's oeuvre is widely cited as the norm, another issue of identity—gender—may actually be a more definitive theme. In the next chapter, I take out the trash with discussion of Yankovic's song "Trash Day," among other songs that mess with ideas of both masculinity and femininity. These songs turn fixed notions of gender into, well, garbage.

8

JUNKING GENDER

We've seen Yankovic's (mostly) deft hand when he tackles racial and religious topics. He relies, at times, on stereotypes but often defies them as well—bringing different characters, his own and those in the original, together in a single song. The same is true of his treatment of gender.

Songs like "Couch Potato," the "Theme from Rocky XIII," "Eat It," and "Fat" all soften the masculine aggression of the original songs. The latter two parodies, in their reliance on Michael Jackson's music, wrangle with an already thorny presentation of masculinity. Comedian Eddie Murphy expressed the common opinion when he observed that Jackson "can sing, and is a good-looking guy, but ain't the most masculine fellow in the world."[1] Especially after his 1982 album *Thriller*, he appeared shy, sensitive, and slight in public appearances, a far cry from the model hypersexual, masculine black man.

Two other parodies, "Trapped in the Drive-Thru" (a parody of R. Kelly's "Trapped in the Closet") and "Word Crimes" (a take on Robin Thicke's "Blurred Lines"), play with masculine norms in a different way. Both originals glory in a kind of illicit eroticism, hypersexuality, and even deviance. That aberrant sexuality became a factor in personal controversies for both singers. Kelly has been repeatedly accused of sexual misconduct, including child pornography and sexual abuse. Thicke's song was seen as an attack on consent standards, and his personal reputation as a player didn't help. For Yankovic to take original songs that are so fraught with sexual issues and strip them of that content is subtle criticism, a mockery of the original songs and their high-stakes sexual drama. Even Yankovic's early hit "My Bologna" muddles cultural standards of gender, flipping the heteronormative search for love by turning a longing for Sharona into a quest for lunch meat.

This chapter focuses on "Taco Grande"; several other Yankovic compositions that subvert gender conventions, including parodies of songs featuring female singers; the original composition "Truck Drivin' Song"; and the medley "Polka Face." In these examples, Yankovic's treatment of the original material advances a certain ambiguity, and he performs gender in ways that do not correspond completely to either feminine or masculine ideals.[2] In so doing, he arguably avoids the pitfalls of an essentialist understanding of gender or a dismissal of gender difference in its entirety. Despite Yankovic's perceived and self-professed lighter intentions, these songs contribute to a conversation of particular significance today. By listening, we join that conversation.

"TACO GRANDE" AND "TRASH DAY"

"Rico Suave," a song by Ecuadorian singer Gerardo Mejía, appeared in 1990. Though the song was unique in its popularity as well as its mix of Spanish and English, it was also undeniably ridiculous in its over-the-top machismo. In the music video, Mejía announces himself with a sultry smirk, black leather coat, and no shirt: Rico Suave, rich and smooth. His defining trait, he sings: "My only addiction has to do with the female species / I eat 'em raw like sushi." And he makes it clear that monogamy is not an option: "There's not a woman that can handle / A man like me / That's why I juggle two or three." The song was hugely popular but also a bit of a joke, mocked on MTV and Mejía dubbed a one-hit wonder.

Offstage, Mejía was living up to his showy boast—taking advantage of more than five hundred women while he was—yes—married. He has said, "I knew I was a dirtbag."[3] But he has also excused his misconduct, telling journalist Shawn Paul Wood in 2014, "In my culture, as a Latin man, it's expected." As Aída Hurtado and Mrinal Sinha write in their study of macho posturing, "One of the most persistent social narratives in our society is the notion of machismo, with its inherent sexism, as a defining feature of all Latino cultures."[4] Mejía exploited the cultural expectation, relying on the stereotype to normalize male chauvinism and his own bad behavior. Wood was not overly concerned: "Culture aside, few people 'expected' Gerardo to be a respectable guy, so most weren't too disappointed."

Yankovic released his parody "Taco Grande" two years later, in 1992. In it, he sings in Spanglish, like Mejía, backed by the same percussive track. But his addiction isn't to women; it's to Mexican food, which he describes with an affected accent, including excessively rolled r's. Yankovic boasts of his manliness, but the brag is based on his enormous appetite for Mexican food: "Well, there's not a taco big enough for a man like me / That's why I order two or three."

Yankovic's focus on Mexican food is a simplistic stand-in for Latino culture, one that subsumes difference under a single bean-filled banner. This simplification was problematic but also affectionate. In *Taco USA*, Gustavo Arellano claims, "Mexican food has entranced Americans even while Mexicans have perplexed Americans."[5] And the specifics— that Mejía is from Ecuador, for example—mattered little. That basic approach is comical, arguably adding to the song's humor. Yankovic replaced one stereotype with another—machismo for Mexican food— and the incongruity between the two is funny: "Let me give you a tip, just try a nacho chip / It's really good with bean dip." His wordplay, as usual, is humorous and smart, with dexterous rhythmic and rhymed patter and a pun that approaches a literal rendering of the phrase "whole enchilada." The idiom, like "whole nine yards," colorfully expresses an entirety. In the parody, Yankovic sings, "That's right, I want the whole enchilada."

The humorous description of food is a welcome upending of an offensive song. Yankovic's recourse to food undermines Mejía's sensual intention, much as Yankovic did with "Word Crimes" and "Trapped in the Drive-Thru." It is cathartic to laugh at Yankovic, who is laughing at Mejía. Fan Avesjohn on the World of Weird Al Yankovic website noted how "Word Crimes" could make an "intolerable song tolerable." In anticipation of the parody, the poster declared, on July 3, 2014, "Al will finally save us from the nightmare that is 'Blurred Lines,' and I for one am looking forward to it." Yankovic performed the same service with "Taco Grande," at least for me.

Yankovic provides similar relief in "Trash Day" (2003). In the song, he shreds rapper Nelly's "Hot in Herre," an inescapable hit in the summer of 2002. The song was produced by Pharrell Williams's the Neptunes and includes samples from "Bustin' Loose," a 1979 Chuck Brown song, and Nancy Sinatra's "As Tears Go By" (1966). But Nelly takes credit for the lyrics, despite the significant role of Pharrell as a producer. He clarified in a 2017 interview with Jake Lauer for *Maxim*, "Beat makers just make the beat, and producers try to create more of a vision. But the lyrics are all me." Are you sure you want all the credit, Nelly?

In his song's headline lyric, the singer's a man in charge: "It's gettin' hot in here, so take off all your clothes." The overt sexuality of the song aligns with the hypersexual expectation of the black male. In the video, Nelly gazes at a woman, her mouth parted, "ass bodacious." When he sings the main line, "so take off all your clothes," a female singer breathlessly responds, rhythmic and almost robotic, "I am gettin' so hot, I wanna take my clothes off." It's a deviant male fantasy. "Give that man what he askin' for," Nelly commands. The only explanation is his need: "'Cause I feel like bustin' loose / and I feel like touchin' you." In his own life, Nelly allegedly made similar demands: In 2017 he was accused of rape.

In "Trash Day," Yankovic sings against the original song's mellow instrumental track—a warm, electronic keyboard sound that signals the 1970s tone of the Fender Rhodes. A series of descending chords surround the initial setup: "It's rotten, so rotten here." (I couldn't agree more.) The declaration, in Yankovic's voice, echoes before the percussion picks up and the first verse begins: "It was like, the last day before trash day / My place was getting kinda nasty." Yankovic's parody features a girl gagging, but it's from the disgusting, leaky trash bag, and she's his wife. Nelly's sleek, seductive dance tune becomes a detailed description of garbage—its smell and contents, including birthday cake and greasy bacon. Yankovic explodes the power structure as well. Gone is the masculine dominance. Rather than succumbing to the man's sexual demands, the man in Yankovic's story is subject to his wife's wrath. He sings, urging her to hold her nose to avoid the smell. A female singer responds, in a sexy, breathless voice, "Hey you disgusting slob, you better take the trash out." Nice try. It's the perfect substitute for Nelly's line, also sung by a woman, "I am gettin' so hot, I wanna take my clothes off." It's a syllabic and thus rhythmic match, with some similar sounds—slob / hot, out / off. And the contrast in power dynamics is both hilarious and empowering. After the second chorus, Yankovic succumbs to the smelly situation: "It makes you wanna (barf sound)." He replaces the suggestive sound effect in Nelly's original with rhythmic vomiting.

Referencing "White & Nerdy" and "Taco Grande," I asked Yankovic, "How do you see . . . masculinity in your music?" "Well, that's a question I've never been asked," Yankovic laughed. I am pleased, aware of the many, sometimes repetitive interviews he has done during his long career, but honestly surprised given the rampant gender play in his music. He continued, "It's nothing that I'm really aware of when I'm writing. I mean, again, there's probably always an extension of me that finds its way into song lyrics. And sometimes I make fun of toxic masculinity."

"Toxic masculinity" is a term that's gotten a lot of play in recent years. In *Teaching Tolerance*, Colleen Clemens defines toxic masculinity as "a form of *gendered behavior* that results when expectations of 'what it means to be a man' go wrong." Toxic masculinity is the result of assumptions around masculine norms, expectations that encourage men to prove their manliness through violence, selfishness, and mistreatment, including the abuse of women and children. As our culture begins to make public the high toll of such behavior, Clemens observes, "The stakes of this conversation couldn't be higher." It is important that women require more of men and that men know there is not only one right way to be a man. Ryan Douglass asks, "How can we hope to stop violent sexual behavior if violence and sexuality are still considered primary virtues of manhood?"[6]

Yankovic, in my reading of much of his repertoire, is part of this conversation. In a follow-up interview, I revisited his initial mention of "toxic masculinity": "Why do you make fun of toxic masculinity?" He easily quipped, "Because it deserves to be mocked." His answer was bright, and he downplayed the weight of his focus, adding, "It's worth taking a few shots at." Yankovic uses parody's potential as social criticism to call out problematic notions of manhood. Nonetheless, he does not announce that serious intention, and, as in the political realm, he obscures his activism in interview. The humor of his music cloaks its message as well. But activism can be funny. And comedy can be enormously successful in making a principled point, padding an argument with emotional and human interest. The serious and humorous can coexist—the weighty light and the light weighty. Listening to "Taco Grande" and "Trash Day," I laugh, but I also appreciate the way both songs undermine the original songs' accepted notion of male need and dominance, played out in some ways in the personal lives of the original artists. I mentioned to Yankovic the connection between these artists— both Nelly and R. Kelly accused of sexual abuse: "You seem to undermine male deviance before we even know the full extent of it." Again, he was cautious: "It just happened to work out that way."

"TRUCK DRIVIN' SONG"

In "Taco Grande" and "Trash Day," Yankovic targets toxic masculinity with silliness, converting the over-the-top theatrics of male dominance into a more realistic look at ordinary people—their everyday and ultimately healthy dynamic. But this isn't the only weapon in his attack against toxic masculinity. Songs like "Truck Drivin' Song" (1999), a Yankovic original, show him playing out various versions of masculinity—and thereby denying the universality of the masculine norms put out by artists like Nelly or Robin Thicke.

One such version of masculinity is the stereotype of the truck driver—a tough, even heroic figure who masters a big rig and drives through the night, a kind of lonely soldier enduring the hardships of the road. This mythology is driven home, so to speak, by dozens of truck commercials. In a commercial for the GMC Sierra, the male driver rescues other men from a fire. In an ad for the Chevrolet Silverado, he is able to play superman in a snowstorm, using his powerful truck to pull another truck and a car from a ditch. It also gave birth to the truck driving song, a subcategory of country music which emerged in the 1960s that catered to drivers in need of music during long hours on the road, offering music that mirrored their own lives and experiences on the road. A list of the ten best includes Merle Haggard's "White Line Fever" and Alabama's "Roll On (Eighteen Wheeler)." Harry Chapin's "30,000 Pounds of Bananas" is both tragic and funny—a song about a truck driving accident, the family left behind, and mashed bananas.

In "Truck Drivin' Song," Yankovic doesn't parody a single song but the genre in general, including its representation of masculinity. With pedal steel guitar accompaniment, he runs through typical themes like cops, coffee, and functional breaks: "Smokey's on my tail / and my accelerator's stuck." But the lyrics are just the beginning. Yankovic's portrayal of masculinity in "Truck Drivin' Song" continues in his vocal style. He assumes a pronounced vocal type, a far deeper voice than his own in its regular register. Yankovic is no stranger to vocal change. His voice is bound up with his persona. For listeners, his voice is the sign of a Yankovic song. But at the same time, he often changes his timbre to assume different identities. His voice signals himself as he signals others. He explained to me, "I do tend to change my voice when the occasion demands it"—especially, he continued, "when the original singer has some kind of vocal affectation." In this way, he can depict musically multiple characters—as if in cabaret—expanding his ability to complicate identity.

Yankovic noted the "very deep baritone voice" in many truck driving songs. In keeping with the genre as well as its purported founding father, Dave Dudley, who had a booming, deep, velvety voice, Yankovic pushed his voice to its limits by setting his song in the lowest possible register. "In fact, I remember it was so low that I literally had to sing it first thing in the morning," he recalled. "I would wake up, drive to the studio, not say a word to anybody, and the first thing out of my mouth would be me singing the song." He had found a natural way to alter his voice, his identity, if only for the morning. Still, the timbre of his voice makes it clear that the low range is "inside" his most comfortable range, a significant sign of musical masculinity.[7] That sound is a signature part of truck driving songs as well as the core masculine identity of country music more generally, from honky-tonk to the Nashville sound, in various ways.[8] It's not essential, as musicologist Nina Eidsheim maintains of sound in general in *The Race of Sound*, but it's expected.

The early lyrics and heavy masculine vocal stylings, however, are setting us up for a twist. Just as we're settling in, Yankovic springs the surprise: "Rollin' down the highway until the break of dawn / Drivin' a truck with my high heels on." Right along with references to gears, freight, and the interstate are the things that make this particular truck driver's haul extra tough. There's a lot to balance in a big rig: Wearing a pink angora sweater, the driver worries, "[g]ot a load to carry and some eyebrows left to pluck."

Yankovic's song depends on standardized masculine practice for a laugh. Wearing feather boas, his truck driver collides with the expected manly norm. The joke exploits that perceived incongruity but creates a space for us to consider our reaction to it. That reaction may be one of humor or surprise—or, for some, something far worse. Either way, we're made aware that there's more than one version of the truck driver, more than one possible way to be a "real man."

"I LOVE ROCKY ROAD"

Yankovic expands the gender dialogue by sometimes parodying songs by women, and young women to boot. In his 2011 interview, Nathan Rabin referred to Yankovic's Miley Cyrus parody, asking, "Does it feel weird to be parodying the songs by teenage girls?" Yankovic responded: "It is kind of odd, you know? Assuming the roles of people who don't share common life experiences with me. But that's what my whole life is." In these songs, Yankovic does not impersonate a female voice by opting for a higher register. He sings in his own voice, though he does adopt aspects of the vocal style of the original songs. His parody references the original female sound while mapping onto it his own male voice, yet another exchange between the masculine and the feminine that muddies norms of male identity. But in so doing, Yankovic also riffs on female identity and the great sexpecations reserved for women alone.

Yankovic's "I Love Rocky Road" (1983) takes on the iconic Joan Jett, part of the legendary all-girl group the Runaways before she became a solo artist. She has been described as "Rock's Toughest Woman." But, as she recalls, she had to be. Especially in the early days she confronted hateful pushback—her mere presence in the rock genre the cause. During a show in Europe in 1984, she remembers a male audience making its collective displeasure clear by spitting at her and yelling, "You fucking cunt!" But she refused to leave the stage.[9] Like country music, rock has been presumed a male space, somehow naturally expressing a male sexuality—either the aggressive, masculine sexuality of cock rock, designed for men, or the romantic, masculine sexuality of teenybop, predominantly meant for girls.[10] Jett didn't fit either category, and she experienced the ire of those invested in and thereby offended by her defiance of rock norms.

Joan Jett's song "I Love Rock 'n Roll," released in 1981, was itself a new version of an original by the Arrows. In that version, the song is from a more traditional male perspective, with a man aggressively trying to pick up a woman, hoping to score. In Jett's version, the gender dynamic flips. As her band, the Blackhearts, sets the mood with crashing guitar chords, her own punk style frames her as the aggressor. And in the song, she details her intention to take a young man home for the night: "Said can I take you home where we can be alone?" Her voice is raw and deep. She appears confident and self-assured: "[H]e was with me, yeah me." In production, producer and sound engineer Glen Kolotkin was careful to protect the roughness of her sound. He also didn't edit out specific mistakes, mistakes he felt gave the song a certain realness and energy. In 2010 he told Richard Buskin of *Sound on Sound*, "My entire goal was for it to sound live and for it to sound real."

Typical of parody songs in his early career, Yankovic's version is unabashedly different, especially in instrumentation. For one, he features the accordion, a squeezebox solo replacing the more customary rock guitar break. The switch was a subversion of rock's cool, but it also may have gendered significance. In *The Accordion in the Americas*, Helena Simonett offers some evidence that accordion playing is viewed as a masculine activity.[11] Yankovic incorporated hand percussion as well, a sound akin to a fart, created by specialist Mike Kieffer. For our purposes, however, Yankovic restores the song's initial male perspective, but in his masculine voice, Yankovic is able to explode the heteronormative search for love in both preceding versions. His desired conquest is rocky road ice cream instead of a one-night stand. In Jett's song, she begins, "I saw him dancin' there by the record machine." Yankovic replaces the line with his own fixation: "I hear those ice cream bells and I start to drool," mimicking Jett's aggressive delivery. In the accompanying music video, Yankovic extends that energy by arguably playing one of his most traditionally masculine leads, an ice cream–loving man clad in leather. He enters the ice cream parlor with confidence, two women at his side. With his chest visibly puffed out, he swaggers through the room. He takes off his glasses in one quick movement and confronts the camera, snarling as he insists there's only "one flavor good enough for me, yeah me."

Yankovic recalls wanting to bring Jett's toughness to his character, but on the day of his video's filming, it was a challenge. He explained to me: "That particular video was just done in a very quick one-day shoot. It was anarchy from what I remember." But the effect nonetheless does some justice to the raw verve of Jett's performance and the song itself. Yankovic creates a traditionally masculine character who nonetheless pursues ice cream. At the same time, his lead relies on the hard persona of Jett, who herself challenged feminine norms. Yankovic's song, then, confuses notions of masculinity and femininity as well as the gender divide itself. Gender itself becomes a . . . (ahem) rocky road.

"LIKE A SURGEON" AND "HANDY"

Two years later, in 1985, Yankovic parodied the music of another larger-than-life female singer, Madonna, who burst into the cultural landscape in the early 1980s. Her first hit was "Like a Virgin" (1984), from her early best-selling album of the same name. The song hit number one and remained there for six weeks. It generated attention before it was even released when Madonna sang it at the first MTV Video Music Awards. In a wedding dress draped with crucifixes, she sensationalized the sexuality of the song, writhing on the stage floor. The songwriter, Billy Steinberg, wrote the song with serious intentions after a bad breakup, hoping to highlight the chance for a new, pure beginning with another person. But Madonna took a campy approach that changed the song's meaning, heckling brides who wear virginal white, attempting to radiate a purity that doesn't exist.[12] Steinberg's fresh start was then subject to Madonna's mockery, even before Yankovic's. With her "Like a Virgin" video, Madonna exaggerated the effect. The video, one of the most expensive to date, was set in Italy, with gondolas and a lion. Madonna spends much of the video peering seductively at the camera, sometimes through a white wedding veil.

Yankovic does not take parody suggestions. Though many have tried, he in fact typically dislikes outside counsel on musical topics. In 2013 Yankovic confided to Blaire R. Fischer of the *Island Packet*, "Well, that's sort of the bane of my existence. I can't go anywhere in public without someone coming up to me with an idea." But he made one big exception for Madonna. Yankovic was sufficiently famous at the time that Madonna, aware of his musical strategy, said to a friend, "I wonder when 'Weird Al' is going to do 'Like a Surgeon.'" Yankovic told the *New*

York Post that Madonna's friend contacted his manager with the recommendation and Yankovic thought, "Good, idea, Madonna. Thanks!"

In his version of the song, he enlists in a traditionally male-dominated profession as a surgeon, but he clearly lacks confidence—and for good reason. Tone altered, Yankovic sings, "I'm just an intern / I still make a mistake or two." Medical school replaces the "wilderness," the overwhelming and wild world of dating in Madonna's version. The next phase of medical practice is far less exciting. The titillation of Madonna's original chorus—"Like a virgin / Touched for the very first time"— gives way to Yankovic's substitute—"Like a surgeon / Cuttin' for the very first time." Yankovic's touch is not arousing, like Madonna's, but sharp and potentially deadly. As he later admits in the song, "I'm a quack." Madonna's song is intimate, a heart to heart, ending, "Can't you hear my heart beat / For the very first time?" That beginning is an end in Yankovic's parody: "I can hear your heartbeat / For the very last time." Another patient dies, a victim of Yankovic's incompetent surgery.

Yankovic's interpretation plays with the sexual character of Madonna's original. He incorporates some sounds similar to Madonna's orgasmic noise—"heys" and "ohs"—expanding on the song's sexuality in his own video, set in a hospital, complete with his own lion roaming the halls. In one scene, his arms are back and mouth open in seeming ecstasy. He also riffs on Madonna's infamous MTV performance, suggestively sprawling on the floor, but this time at a hospital in his scrubs. These moves obviously do not translate well in the new context, nor do they play the same way when performed by a man. Masculine sexuality is typically portrayed differently, with pelvic thrusts rather than a receptive open mouth and closed eyes.

Madonna pushed the limits of accepted public sexuality, challenging puritanical expectations placed on women. But unlike Jett, she did so in traditionally feminine ways. Her character fit the archetype, the sexy woman, remaining true to a long history of sexualized imaginings around female performers, regardless of their appearance or intention. In the nineteenth century, even widow Clara Schumann couldn't avoid the charge, her concertizing on the piano viewed as "immodest."[13] Musicologist Susan McClary, however, argued that Madonna reproduces the feminine norm with a wink. She is "the woman who knows too much," and she thereby "brings this hypocrisy to the surface and problematizes it."[14] Whatever the motivation behind the performance or its effect, Madonna's overt feminine sexuality conflicts with Yankovic's similar enactment of sexuality. Yankovic highlights the different norms we hold for masculine and feminine sexuality—and the shock we feel when they are reversed—a gender-bending that brings both into dialogue.

In 2014 Yankovic released another song in this vein: "Handy." In it, Yankovic again assumes a profession typically seen as masculine—the handyman—in a parody of Iggy Azalea's "Fancy," a number one song in early 2014 that was aided in its climb up the charts by a wildly popular video. But Yankovic also seizes on Azalea's self-professed toughness: "You should want a bad bitch like this," she raps, against a punchy ostinato, punctuated by rhythmic, male "heys." The proclamation seems defiant, a rebellion against her controversial relationship to rap as a white woman from New South Wales. Early in the song, she declares, "First things first: I'm the realest." Writing for *Slate* in 2014, Christ Molanphy maintained, "Azalea's peacocking and overcompensation make a kind of sense, inasmuch as very few female rappers of any race have ever topped *Billboard*'s premier song chart." As the hook sung by Charli XCX attests, she's "so fancy," "in the fast lane," ready for fame, no matter her race, no matter her gender.

There's nothing fancy about Yankovic's handyman. As he sings in the chorus, "I'll fix your plumbing when your toilets overflow." With the same sparse accompaniment, a synthetic rubber-band bounce, produced for Azalea by the Invisible Men with coproducer Kurtis "The Arcade" McKenzie, Yankovic details his skills in his own rap. Referencing Jay Z's 2003 classic "99 Problems," he boasts about his wiring proficiency: "I got 99 problems but a switch ain't one." There is humor in the juxtaposition of Azalea's glamorous life and Yankovic's handy work. There is also a comedy in the clash between lyrical content and the sensuous style of the music, with its smooth, simplistic sound.

Yankovic plays up that clash in his video. Wearing a ridiculous blond wig—a nod to Azalea's own blonde hair—he appears in a white T-shirt, vest, and blue jeans. A carpenter's belt completes the look. The masculine ensemble assumes new heights when Yankovic flies as superman, in costume, rapping, "There's nothing in the world I can't fix." At the same time, Yankovic shows off a signature flexibility, dancing languid and lithe to the chorus. In a 2018 interview with Dan Ozzi of *Noisey*, he explained, "I'm very flexible, I think I might be hyperextended [. . .] or something. I can flip and flop every which way, and do high kicks and everything else." With two male backup dancers in overalls, Yankovic showcases this aspect of his art. His whole body rolls suggestively, movement like butter. For a moment, he rubs his torso, singing, "Let me be your stripper," before he returns to business, "Taking off lacquer, no one does it quicker."

Just as with "Like a Surgeon," Yankovic displays a stereotyped feminine sexuality in his role as a male repairman. The effect is funny, given the perceived incongruity, but it also again offers the opportunity to have a conversation concerning norms of sexuality and femininity—one that operates sonically as well as visually. He's on a roll—and I'm not just talking about his body movement.

GOING GAGA

In the songs discussed thus far, and their accompanying videos, Yankovic remains a male character despite his play with gender norms through sound and movement in performance. He is various versions of *himself*. His song "Perform This Way" (2011), from *Alpocalypse*, therefore deserves special mention. It's a parody of Lady Gaga's "Born This Way," from her 2011 album *Born This Way*, which debuted at number eight, just above Yankovic's *Alpocalypse* at number nine. In the parody video, Yankovic performs as a woman, with thick makeup—or at least, his head does. The video creates a true gender hybrid—with Yankovic's face on a woman's body. Through the use of CGI effects, dancer Vlada Gorbaneva and contortionist Marissa Heart provide Yankovic with that female body.

The parody, like "Amish Paradise," was controversial from the start, even before the mixed-gender spotlight. Though Lady Gaga eventually gave him permission, Yankovic initially received a firm denial in response to his parody request. Like Coolio, Lady Gaga and her team were initially protective of "Born This Way." Also like Coolio, Lady Gaga described the creation of the *Born This Way* album in hallowed terms: "[T]he gates just opened, and the songs kept coming. It was like an immaculate conception."[15] Elsewhere, she described "Born This Way" as "a completely magical message song."[16] In it, she sings against a dance track, the beat thumping, "I'm beautiful in my way / 'Cause God makes no mistakes." With that premise, she makes her case: We are all perfect, just as we were born, whether black, white, disabled, bullied, outcast, gay, straight, or bisexual. She exhorts her fans, "Rejoice and love yourself today." The song fits firmly within her activist campaigns, including queer rights and anti-bullying. She voiced her support of gay rights early in her career, calling Ellen DeGeneres, during an appearance on her show in May 2009, "such an inspiration for women and for the gay community." She also made known her opposition to the "don't ask, don't tell" (DADT) policy, which barred people from serving in the military if they were openly gay. On September 12, 2010, a year before the policy was repealed by Barack Obama, Lady Gaga appeared on the red carpet at the Video Music Awards with four ex-military personnel by her side—all discharged due to DADT. Her infamous meat dress, which she wore that night, was commentary on the urgency of gay rights and equality for all. If we don't stand up, she insisted, "pretty soon we're going to have as much rights as the meat on our bones."[17]

To Lady Gaga's manager, Yankovic outlined his parody of "Born This Way" as follows:

> I'd like to do a parody of Lady Gaga's "Born this Way" called "I Perform this Way." The basic concept is that I, as a Lady Gaga doppelganger of sorts, describe the incredibly extravagant ways in which I perform on stage. Meat dresses and giant eggs would most likely be referenced, but also much more ridiculous made-up examples of bizarre wardrobe and stage production. As with all my parodies, it would be respectful of the artist, while having a bit of fun with her larger-than-life image.

Yankovic posted his pitch, verbatim, on his blog, explaining in full "The Gaga Saga." When he initially approached Lady Gaga's camp, he had only the basic concept, but her team countered asking to hear it in full. Yankovic quickly worked out the lyrics and sent them along, thinking knowledge of the existing music and his new text would be enough. But Lady Gaga wanted a complete recording. Yankovic cut a family vacation short and fulfilled the request, recording the parody before permission. Yankovic explained, again on his blog, "Now, I never do that—*never*. But because I was really excited about this parody, I decided I would faithfully jump through as many hoops as Gaga deemed necessary." But the ultimate answer was a firm rebuff. "*silent scream*," Yankovic posted. There was no explanation, even with proceeds already destined for the Human Rights Campaign—"good karma," as Yankovic explained, but also a nod to Lady Gaga's activism in the area. The Human Rights Campaign, Yankovic wrote, is "an organization which I have to assume Gaga supports." In a 2011 interview about the dustup, Dave Itzkoff, writing for the *New York Times*, seemed to get at the issue of motive, asking Yankovic: "You wrote to Lady Gaga and her management that in 'Perform this Way,' you are assuming the persona of 'a Lady Gaga doppelganger of sorts.' But aren't you really pretending to be her, and mocking her?" Yankovic responded, "I certainly don't think that my humor was mean-spirited. I was making fun of her style and the over-the-top way that she performs and appears in public."

Without permission, Yankovic planned, out of respect, to drop the song from his upcoming album and abandon his vision for a promotional video, but he decided to release the song online. Shortly thereafter, there was a reversal on Lady Gaga's side. As Yankovic understood it: "Gaga's manager has now admitted that he never forwarded my parody to Gaga—she had no idea at all." Yankovic had believed Lady Gaga was behind the refusal, Itzkoff reported, but, supposedly, she had played no part. "And Gaga loves the song," Yankovic added.

In "Perform This Way," Yankovic connects Lady Gaga's complex outfits to her status as a celebrity, intimating a connection between dressing like a star and being a star: "Save your allowance, buy a bubble dress / And someday you will go far." Once successful, however, Yankovic focuses on the critics, who might view such displays as "grotesque." In Yankovic's version, Lady Gaga's original defense of minorities and outcasts is her own shield: "I might be wearing Swiss Cheese or may be covered in bees / It doesn't mean I'm crazy—I perform this way." In the second verse, Yankovic, singing as Lady Gaga, further credits the extraordinary ensembles to originality. But the song casts some doubt on the proclamation, underscored in the accompanying video with the surfacing of a Madonna look-alike, a reference to a controversy summed up in the *Atlantic* headline "Is Lady Gaga's 'Born This Way' a Rip-Off of Madonna's 'Express Yourself'?" In the video, Yankovic appears throughout as Lady Gaga, with his heavily made-up head on a woman's body. In the first sequence, the body, dressed in the same black bikini Lady Gaga herself dons in her own video, appears at first from behind. The body turns and the camera surveys its flesh, the shot moving up toward the head, which is then revealed to be Yankovic's. It's a jarring moment. When the Madonna stand-in appears, Yankovic (as Gaga) pushes her out of frame. He sings of Lady Gaga's monstrous appearance—"I'm Frankenstein! I'm Avatar!" But the description better fits his own appearance in the video—a character similarly stitched together and given life.

Lady Gaga's choice of extraordinary dress during her career has much to do with her vision of fame—a performance art totality or contemporary *Gesamtkunstwerk*. At times, particular outfits, like the meat dress Yankovic references and replicates, have a specific purpose or point. But in her appearance and music, she also subverts a traditional feminine sexiness. She has claimed, "I'm not sexy in the way that Britney Spears is sexy." Gaga's dress, she has explained, is instead "weird." "It's not what is sexy. It's graphic and it's art," she clarified. She herself attempts to portray instead "androgyny" and has even appeared as a man, her alter ego Jo Calderone.[18] In her "Born This Way" video, she wears the black bikini, revealing her feminine form as so many women do in music videos. But she upends that femininity, too, at one point grabbing her crotch, a move that might have intentionally mocked rumors that she's intersex. The humor of Yankovic's play on Lady Gaga's appearance is, then, both here and gone. Yes, her many intricate costumes seem at times ridiculous, but they also have greater significance. And alongside his comedic intention, Yankovic himself at times skews toward that significance, in his Gaga portrayal and in his music more generally. Yankovic is Lady Gaga's doppelgänger in ways he may not have intended. Both are chameleons who play with gender in different ways. Both have a history of attention to those bullied and outcast. And both have devoted fans: Little Monsters and Al-oholics.

In "Perform this Way," Yankovic takes Lady Gaga's own gender nonconformity to new heights, giving form and voice to a female-male hybrid. The performance is ostensibly an ode to Lady Gaga, but it also fits within Yankovic's personal history of gender play in music. Lady Gaga had reason to protect the serious message of "Born this Way," especially based on Yankovic's initial description of his parody—"a bit of fun with her larger-than-life image." But in light of Yankovic's record of gender dialogue, Lady Gaga had nothing to fear. "Perform This Way," with Yankovic's visual mash-up, male-female fusion, is no threat to Lady Gaga's legacy or agenda. Instead, it's a player in the same conversation for a cause.

On *Alpocalypse,* Yankovic includes a second tribute to Lady Gaga's music, his medley "Polka Face" (2011). In it, Yankovic again broadens the conversation, combining Gaga's song "Poker Face" with other songs focusing on sexuality and gender. In the same tempo and voice, with brass accompaniment and vocal harmonization, he unites these various perspectives in a generic polka. After an instrumental introduction that establishes the genre, Yankovic sings an excerpt of "Poker Face," changing only the word "poker" to "polka." The tempo is faster than the original as Yankovic sings, "No, he can't read my polka face." The section cadences with an emphatic "Hey," and the next reference begins: Britney Spears's 2008 song "Womanizer." The arrangement highlights the similarities between the two pop songs. Both play with the initial sound of the titular word—"P-p-p-poker face" and "Womanizer-wom-an-womanizer." Despite Lady Gaga's conscious differentiation from pop stars like Spears, opting for a less traditional sexuality in presentation, the songs have in common an element of female empowerment. "Womanizer," which Spears called an anthem, is about a reclamation of power in knowledge: "Boy don't try to front / I know just what you are." While the woman comprehends all in Spears's song, the man knows nothing in Lady Gaga's. The woman has a secret all her own. While she is with a man, her poker face hides her thoughts of another—a woman. The song's bisexuality is underscored later in the medley with a citation of Katy Perry's 2008 hit "I Kissed a Girl."

The last line of Yankovic's "Womanizer" excerpt culminates with "You! Womanizer!" The "You" is the point of transition to the next song, Flo Rida's "Right Round" (2009): "You spin my head right round, right round." Yankovic sings the next lyric, a reference to oral sex, "When you go down, when you go down." It's a short section, with another energetic "Hey" capping the segment as segue to the next reference. But the juxtaposition of "Right Round" after Lady Gaga and Spears, is nonetheless jarring—women first portrayed as in control now come down to their knees. Still all three sections, treated in the same way musically, become part of one continuum. And Yankovic upsets any sexual charge through his upbeat, old-world, polka homage. Once again, we are left with ambiguity.

BEING SUE

In parodies of songs by male and female singers, as well as an original composition and medley, Yankovic finds ways to complicate gender identity. He undermines masculine aggression and hypersexuality; he riffs on feminine sexuality and identity; and he defies expectations of real men. To do so, he uses his voice as well as his body, often in video. Yankovic does not take explicit ownership of his attention to gender identity or any related activist fallout. In our first interview, he insisted that, though he was aware of his attention to toxic male characters, the focus was secondary: "I'm just kind of just making fun of that kind of person." Despite his attempt to play down the interest, with a double qualification of "just," I responded, "And thank you for doing that." He did not accept the recognition or even claim it, adding another proviso, "But it's just done under the guise of comedy. Again, it's nothing that I'm consciously doing." His goal, as always, is humor above all. The medium of parody, its layering of meaning, allows him to privilege one effect over another. But multiple voices nonetheless remain in his music—one of which is this expression of gender play. It's music to my ears. The defiance of gender conventions is timely, even ahead of its time, something especially necessary today.

In recent years, there has been constant media coverage of male dominance and sexual assault, a toxic masculinity that writer Jennifer Wright connects to mass shootings, writing in *Harper's Bazaar* in 2018, "So let's start talking about the culture of toxic masculinity that makes men believe they should get a gun and shoot people with it." The gender complication in Yankovic's music is a healthy alternative to that culture, offering needed nuance to our conceptions of masculinity as well as femininity. Boys do not have to be stereotypical boys, and in the age of #MeToo and mass murder, some men must learn that domination and power do not define worth. With emotions assigned a feminine realm, men are traditionally expected to act tough, hiding emotions in need of expression. That unhealthy expectation confounds the problem, with the result that violence may appear as an acceptable outlet.

To me, the role of gender in Yankovic's music also represents a brilliant reaction to traditional masculine valuations of music itself. Masculinity is, after all, a central feature in various genres of music—gangsta rap, country music, and heavy metal, in particular—and has been part of the very language of popular music, especially rock. In rock criticism, for example, there has been a specific correlation between "masculine" traits and "good" rock. Kembrew McLeod, examining the language of rock, notes the preponderance of critical praise citing music as "forceful and powerful." In a *Rolling Stone* review of the song "Zanz Kant Danz," from John Fogerty's *Centerfield*, Kurt Loder celebrated "a sense of personal vengeance that seems near-Biblical in its relentless intensity." And Dave Marsh described Neil Young's *Tonight's the Night* as "tough and powerful, with a metallic guitar sound more akin to the abrasiveness of the Rolling Stones than the placid harmonies of CSNY."[19] The same critics have disparaged music with "feminine" descriptors: "soft," "weak," "light," "wimpy." Female musicians themselves have been dismissed or mocked as "girl groups," if they are discussed at all.[20] With this gendered valuation of popular music, where does Yankovic's music fit? His music's play with norms of masculinity and femininity defies popular music's critical framework. Perhaps that rebellion, that inconvenience, is part of the reason Yankovic's success is still met with incredulity and described as a surprise. Perhaps writers don't know what else to say. They can't write about his music according to accepted masculine ideals of popular music, so they don't write much of anything at all.

In view of his attention to gender in music, I asked Yankovic about the effect of raising a daughter: "Has your view changed of gender or been affected by raising your daughter?" He admitted, "I've been exposed to a lot more than I have been in the past." He added, "I like to think I was always pretty woke, but . . . I think that I have evolved in a way that hopefully is positive." Another influence, even earlier, may have been early inspiration Shel Silverstein. Silverstein penned the song "A Boy Named Sue," made famous in a 1969 recording by Johnny Cash. In the song, Silverstein describes a boy left by his father. Before he's abandoned, his father named him Sue—a name that makes him a target, a name that defines his course in life. Later, the boy searches for his father, bent on revenge. When he finds him he says, "My name is Sue! How do you do!? / Now you gonna die!" But after a vicious fight, his father justifies the name as a means to make sure his son grew up tough, even without his dad: "Son, this world is rough / And if a man's gonna make it, he's gotta be tough." With Sue as a name, "I knew you'd have to get tough or die." The song makes clear how a fixed, "tough" masculinity is forced upon boys—with no room for anything deemed feminine. Toxic masculinity takes root early, with an artificial divide between conventions of femininity and masculinity set up from the start. The name Sue is an obvious signal of a forbidden femininity. But many men could relate in various ways to a boy named Sue—men bent on breaking out of a suffocating circumscription of their own identities and who they were allowed to be.

Yankovic, a self-identified nerd and outsider, understands the limits of conformity. In his music, he consistently displays a sensitivity to the complexities of category—expectations of race and gender. The results are funny and substantial; they make you laugh but also have the potential to engage listeners in a conversation that matters—maybe even more so today.

9

AL-MOST FAMOUS

In a 2013 video on Funny or Die, an online site devoted to all things humorous, singer Huey Lewis and Yankovic spoof a scene from the 2000 movie *American Psycho*. Lewis takes on the role of the murderer, originally played by Christian Bale, and kills Yankovic, who had parodied Lewis's 1983 song "I Want A New Drug," turning it into "I Want a New Duck" (1985). After Yankovic plays dead, with fake blood everywhere, Lewis comments, "Try parodying one of my songs now." The video is a joke, but we know that—as in the case of "Amish Paradise"—some artists may take umbrage at Yankovic for mocking their work. Most artists, however, view Yankovic's parodies in a wholly positive light. Chamillionaire saw his parody as the ultimate testament to his success, telling the *Houston Chronicle* in 2006, "It's one thing to go platinum. Where do you go from there? Then Weird Al calls." As reported by Michael Hogan in the *Telegraph*, he even credited a Grammy win to Yankovic: "That parody was the reason I won the Grammy, because it made the record so big it was undeniable." Lady Gaga, after the initial refusal by her management, expressed appreciation for Yankovic's parody of her song "Born This Way." Flattered, she called the parody a "rite of passage."[1] Greg Kihn, the musician behind the 1983 song "Jeopardy" (the basis of Yankovic's song "I Lost on Jeopardy") dubbed Yankovic's parody "a vote of confidence." He told Geoff Edgers of the *Washington Post*, "If you're not well-enough known to be parodied, well, you're just not well-enough known."

An episode of the television series *30 Rock* tackled these dueling reactions for laughs. In a 2012 episode called "Kidnapped by Danger," the character Jenna (played by Jane Krakowski), creates a mawkish song about a kidnapping. She sings alone, in a red dress, blonde hair blowing in the wind. While viewing the video, a coworker laughs, "I didn't realize your song was the original." He shows her a Yankovic parody, "Knapsack," written especially for the episode. It's a fictional take on a real-life phenomenon, dubbed by the website TV Tropes the "'Weird Al' Effect": "when a parody of a particular work is more popular than the original work." In the video, Yankovic wears full makeup, a blonde wig, and even the red dress, mimicking Jenna's look, but with a backpack in hand. Jenna is outraged. Liz (Tina Fey's character) tries to soothe Jenna, declaring, "It's a huge honor." But Jenna doesn't agree. Yankovic, she says, "corrupted something beautiful." She decides to compose another song—this one so absurd that it is parody-proof. She sings, "I eat pizza." The chorus: "Farts so loud." But Yankovic responds in another video, singing about the safe return of American soldiers fighting overseas, in front of the American flag. In jeans and an unbuttoned plaid shirt, his hair pulled back, he alters Jenna's chorus: "Farts so loud" becomes "Hearts so proud." Jenna cries: "He reversed the parody. He normal Al'd us." But she's not mad. The Yankovic parody, this time, is an honor.

The discomfort or celebration of the parody by the original artist is itself a part of the parody process—it becomes part of the story. But though he mocks aspects of the original performance, Yankovic generally chooses songs he genuinely admires. By phone, he confirmed, "I tend to gravitate towards the songs that I actually like." There is both homage and derision—a blurry mix for listeners and artists. Yankovic flags a level of fame by choosing songs popular enough to work as parody. But he creates his own hit—with the attendant riches and fame—while playing on the popularity of another artist or song.

Another 2013 Funny or Die video, "Like a Version," riffs on this conflict. In it, a young boy sings "Like a Sturgeon," offering a fishy take on Yankovic's "Like a Surgeon." Yankovic, walking past, is alarmed: That's "my song!" He barters with the boy—twinkies and cash if he'll stop singing "Like a Sturgeon." But when Madonna seems to pull up, both the boy and Yankovic run. Whose song is it really? While all music has multiple authors and influences, the group ownership of a Yankovic song is arguably more obvious. And Yankovic is indebted to the existing fame of the original song while spotlighting and even cementing its existing success.

In 2011 Yankovic clarified in this regard his decision to parody the work of Lady Gaga, telling Gary Graff in *Billboard*: "I've come to learn over the course of my career that my albums are more successful if they are released concurrently with a single that's very topical and maybe celebrates a pop culture event of serious magnitude. I thought Lady Gaga, and specifically her new album and single, was a sufficiently large event. I thought Gaga had sufficiently rocked the zeitgeist enough for me to make that choice." Part of his job, he explained to Dan Rather, is keeping his "finger on the pulse," staying abreast of new cultural fads and fashions. That job has become more difficult as culture has become more segmented. In an *Ear to Ear* interview with Roy Zimmerman in 2010, Yankovic recalled how he originally responded to a seemingly common culture, often reflected in the *Billboard* Top 10 or on MTV, but culture since has splintered. To gauge popularity, he had to evolve, following various genres and various platforms simultaneously. Still, the focus remained the same. As Sam Anderson wrote in *Slate* in 2006, Yankovic's "real medium wasn't music, it was fame."

Through his parodies, Yankovic has become famous in his own right. And the sheer number of television guest appearances is partly proof, most recently on *Crazy Ex-Girlfriend*, *Happy!*, *Adam Ruins Every-thing*, *The Adventures of Rocky & Bullwinkle*, and *Scooby-Doo and Guess Who?* Such cameos are typically both a means to attract new audiences and also a way to honor or acknowledge another artist. Yankovic has had to fight for this recognition. In our first interview, he recalled, "Yeah, I've ebbed and flowed quite a bit, and I'm putting out albums at a much more leisurely pace these days. In the '80s, I was putting out an album virtually every year, mostly based on fear—that if I didn't, people would soon forget about me." He has adopted a philosophy to cope with these ups and downs, the natural cycle of fame: "I try not to get too full of myself when I'm on a peak and try not to get too depressed when I'm in a valley. My wife and I were inspired by something that Neil DeGrasse Tyson said on an episode of *Cosmos*. He was explaining what climate was, and basically, that weather cycles go up and down, and up and down, but the climate, it stays in the middle. And our mantra here is, 'Be the climate, not the weather.'"

His fame—with its peaks and valleys—has depended on his outsider status, his ability to mock other celebrities with the credibility of an informed observer. Matthew R. Turner has credited Yankovic's maintenance of that status, despite his fame, to his abstinence from many of the typical Hollywood vices, including alcohol: "He has avoided many of the pitfalls that come with fame and money and thus is simultaneously a part of that world *and* separated from that world."[2] In this way, he is both inside and outside the fame bubble. That precarious position is hardly stable. To me, Yankovic commented,

> Certainly, when I started out, I was completely an outsider. But after a few years, I was getting invited to the same award shows and the same parties, and I was rubbing elbows with people that I was ostensibly mocking. So it was an odd position to be in. And now I do feel— I'd like to think I still am an outsider because I'm still poking fun at people, the elite, and other pop cultural icons, but at the same time, I guess I have to count myself among their number because I've been doing this for a long time.

He laughs, adding, "And people do seem to know who I am."

Yankovic's career has a unique relationship to fame and the music industry. In many ways, fame has shaped his course in music—recognition of other musicians' fame, the music he chooses to parody, and his own related fame. But in his work, he has also targeted fame and celebrity as a theme and musical topic. *The Authorized AL* begins: "This book is dedicated to all the little people I had to step on to get where I am today." Elsewhere in the mock tome, Yankovic lampoons the traditional trajectory of fame, with its happy high and lowly low, the trappings of fame taking their toll. In *The Authorized AL*, Yankovic's supposed low leads to a moment of inward reflection: "This introspective period of Al's life spawned the highly personal and emotionally charged album entitled Me, Myself and I." I had to ask Yankovic if there was any truth to the joke, a real time of "Me, Myself and I." He laughed, "I have to remind you, that was all a joke." Indeed, even VH1 came up short, forced to invent some drama to fulfill the customary arc in the episode of *Behind the Music* dedicated to Yankovic. In the segment, the best it could do at the time was to emphasize his single status, his lonely search for love. To the *Washington Post*'s David Segal, Yankovic shared, "They keep playing that special over and over and my wife says, 'Can you please get them to change that?'" But it could have been worse. In the Funny or Die video "Weird: The Al Yankovic Story," an Al impersonator fulfills the expected celebrity narrative by drinking and making out with a would-be Madonna. The video is hilarious in part because the moody look-Al-like is so far from the truth.

In his music, Yankovic offers various perspectives on fame, including the sources and side effects of fame—the commercialism of the music industry, popular music's repetition and standardization, as well as a certain over-seriousness in the pop realm more generally. By phone, I called these latter issues his "musical pet peeves." But Yankovic cautioned me, insisting that these themes are not necessarily "pet peeves" or aspects of the music industry that bother him personally. The word is "maybe too negative," he said. For what he does, the topics are instead "fair game," practical fodder for parody and his informed perspective as both insider and outsider.

A STAR IS TORN

In "Skipper Dan" (2009), a style parody of the music of the band Weezer, Yankovic fails to achieve fame. He's an actor who had a promising start: "I starred in every high school play / Blew every drama teacher away." After Julliard, he was sure Quentin Tarantino and Annie Leibovitz would be in his fame-filled future. But instead, "I'm a tour guide on the Jungle Cruise ride / Skipper Dan is the name / And I'm doin' 34 shows every day / And every time it's the same." Sadly, Skipper Dan admits, "Now my hopes have all vanished and my dreams have all died." Yankovic observed in a 2011 interview with Nathan Rabin, "'Skipper Dan' is a bit more poignant than what I usually write." He sees it as a "kind of a character study," inspired by his own experience riding the Jungle Cruise ride at Disneyland. But his own quest for fame surely inspired the song in part. "Skipper Dan" is not a one-off among aspiring celebrities. More often than not, "Skipper Dan" is the norm for Hollywood hopefuls. Despite his own fame, in this song Yankovic remains sensitive to this reality, perhaps drawing on the memory of his early attempts to break into the music industry. In his interview with Segal, he remembered, "Right after college, in the early '80s, those were the scary years." He warded off total fear thanks to his optimistic outlook as he sought out work anywhere, "to pay for my mac and cheese."

Two years after "Skipper Dan," he adopted the opposite perspective, depicting the reverse: extreme success. In his song "TMZ" (2011), a parody of Taylor Swift's 2008 song "You Belong with Me," his character is megafamous. But the song spotlights the pitfalls of such high-profile celebrity. In the original song, Swift plays her own version of a nerd, in thick, black-rimmed glasses. In the video, she sits on a bench, reading; appears outfitted in band regalia; and later makes it clear that she has to study. But she longs for the boy next door, who is romantically linked with the clichéd cheerleader, a cool girl played by Swift's alter ego, with black hair, thick makeup, and no glasses. The song stresses these differences: "But she wears short skirts / I wear T-shirts / She's cheer captain / And I'm on the bleachers." Eventually, Swift, as her nerd protagonist, transforms into a swan, ditching her glasses and showing up to the dance in virginal white. Her double, in a sexy red dress with side cut-outs, is hardly pleased. But Swift, without her glasses, finally lands her man: "You belong with me."

Yankovic takes the song and turns it into a consideration of the world of celebrity fixation. He sings, to the same plucked banjo accompaniment, "You're sort of famous / A minor celebrity." The celebrity foil is unclear. In an animated video, the song focuses on a Swift lookalike. But Swift, at the time, was more than "sort of famous." Still, the next line fits: The world is obsessed with everything "you do."

Devoted to entertainment news, TMZ is a stand-in for paparazzi in general: "camcorders in the night." They're "praying" for a "big melt-down," a "drunken spree," a controversial romp with a transvestite, a Vegas wedding, or a quickie divorce. Many of these latter aims seem to target not Swift, but another teen star—Britney Spears: "A star decides to shave their head / Or ram their car into a tree," then they're on TMZ. Spears famously shaved her head in 2007, and several days later, beat the car of a photographer with an umbrella. The downward spiral inspired the affirmation: "If Britney can make it through 2007, then I can make it through today."[3]

Swift has been viewed as a respite in a storm of such bad behavior. In 2011 Lizzie Widdicombe wrote in the *New Yorker*, "In a world of Lohans and Winehouses, Swift is often cited as a role model, a designation she takes seriously." And she supports that distinction in her music, opting to avoid the overt sexuality of other teen princesses. She is not her alter ego in the red dress, but the girl in white, giving way to the countercriticism, according to Widdicombe, that she "promotes a noxious, fifties-style ideal of virginal, submissive femininity." Sorry, Taylor—it's a no win.

In a 2011 interview with Evan Sawdey for *PopMatters*, Yankovic insisted his parody "TMZ" was not attacking TMZ or even a particular star. Instead, he said, "It's making fun mostly about everyone's obsession with celebrity culture and how ridiculous it is and why do we even care about any of this." He has, in his career, experienced some degree of fan obsession. And TMZ even found it necessary to cover Yankovic's arrival at JFK airport in early 2011, announcing: "Looking like pals, Lisa Kudrow arrived at JFK airport on Monday with Weird Al Yankovic walking right behind her." As he sings in "TMZ," "everything celebrities do is fascinating."

Yankovic's "Perform This Way" blends the two perspectives on fame—"Skipper Dan" and "TMZ"—playing up the lengths to which musicians go to gain attention while acknowledging the resulting unwanted fixation. There is a tension in that relationship—the longing and its effect, part of the plight of fame. In the song, Yankovic, as Lady Gaga, sings, "I'll poke your eye out with a dress like this." Lady Gaga's elaborate outfit is both attention seeking and threat, part of a contradictory desire for both star standing and space. She's a siren waiting to strike. *A Star Is Born*? More like: A star is torn.

According to Milly Williamson, in her 2016 book *Celebrity: Capitalism and the Making of Fame*, celebrities are defined by their relationship to commerce: "All celebrities have a value in common—to sell products, media and otherwise." Though there are different types of celebrity, some view fame today as aligned more closely with appearance than with any special talent. Star power depends on personality rather than substance. And yet fame is generally seen as a positive, a status to covet as the new American Dream. It hasn't always been this way. At one time, fame was related to ill repute, something shameful. But even fame at its best is subject to dismissal as "social nonsense," a pathological obsession with no justification. In "The Celebrity Illusion," Timothy Caulfield singles out the dangers, including a fantasy of easy success—one that distracts from real-world methods to gain actual "mobility, such as education and advocacy for social change."[4] Lady Gaga, who pursued celebrity with a unique attention to fame itself, details the mania in her song "Paparazzi" (2008): "I'm your biggest fan / I'll follow you until you love me." Fitting, then, that in a parody of Lady Gaga, Yankovic exposes the same unhealthy obsession. The criticism, as in "TMZ," tempers the hysteria around star standing, a reckoning with our cultural obsession with celebrity.

Yankovic took on this theme again, three years later, in his song "Lame Claim to Fame" (2014), in the style of Southern Culture on the Skids. The band, which hails from North Carolina, plays with multiple genres—rock, soul, and country—often with a humorous streak, as in the zany 1995 song "Camel Walk." The lead singer nearly speaks the main line, with a heavy southern accent, over a funky guitar riff, accenting the first word with a higher pitch, "You make me wanna walk like a camel." Against a similar guitar sound, Yankovic's song features the same sort of pitched speech. In it, he has become the fan and the song chronicles his minor brushes with fame: "I swear Jack Nicholson / Looked right at me at a Lakers game." To close, "Paul Giamatti's plumber knows me by name." He also references "six degrees of Kevin Bacon," a game based on the premise that everyone is somehow connected to the actor: "I know a guy who knows a guy who knows a guy . . . who knows / Kevin Bacon." The attempt to assert importance through these "lame" claims to fame overlaps with his lesson in the song "Tacky," on the same album. In the latter song, an individual also tries to achieve significance in lame or tacky ways—for example, publicizing each meal on Instagram and name dropping. At least, Yankovic sings, "That's what Kanye West keeps telling me."

"TMZ" adopts the perspective of the star as he or she navigates celebrity obsession; with "Lame Claim to Fame," and to a lesser degree "Tacky," Yankovic poses as the one obsessed. That obsession manifests as excitement in minor celebrity connections as well as bad online behavior, both staples today of the fame game. Anyone, after all, can seek fame through social media. In his musical explorations of fame from these different standpoints, Yankovic also examines the sources and substance of fame. In several songs, Yankovic points to criticism of pop music as commercial, crediting lazy songwriting to an overriding pursuit of cash. That lazy approach gives way to a perceived standard form in music, another critique. There is and can be no originality when the endgame is only money. Yankovic's polka medleys, in particular, respond to that notion, but they lack a clear verdict. And Lin-Manuel Miranda, of all people, only adds to the confusion.

YANKILTON

The most overt example, in song, of Yankovic's comment on the connection between money and bad form is "(This Song's Just) Six Words Long." It's a parody of a George Harrison hit from 1987 called "Got My Mind Set on You." The ballad was a sweet courting song with, let's say, very limited lyrical content. In the parody, Yankovic highlights the repetition in Harrison's version. It's unlikely that Yankovic considers Harrison a money-grubbing hack, but he uses the parody to critique music that is formulaic, part of Simon Frith's definition in "What Is Bad Music?" Money, in this supposedly inferior music, trumps art. Yankovic sings, "This song's got nothing to say / But I'm recording it anyway." The justification, there is money to be made: "They're payin' me plenty of money / To sing this song, child."

The choice between art and commerce was also central in Yankovic's unreleased song "It's Still Billy Joel to Me." The song comments on Joel's bid for relevance: "Don't you know about the record business, honey / You gotta be trendy if you wanna make some money." Yankovic repeated what was becoming a common sentiment about Joel. In 2009 Ron Rosenbaum tried to unpack the Billy Joel hate in "The Worst Pop Singer Ever: Why, Exactly, Is Billy Joel So Bad?" In his write-up, published in the *Spectator*, he singled out "It's Still Rock and Roll to Me," the basis of Yankovic's parody, as the worst of Joel's output. In the song, Joel observes new trends but insists that it's still just rock and roll. To Rosenbaum, the song "shows how completely, totally clueless Billy Joel is."

In Yankovic's own career, money has, of course, been a necessary concern. He was fiscally responsible in his early pursuit of fame, maintaining a job in the mailroom at mass media company Westwood One after graduating college. He remained there even as his musical career gained momentum. One day, Yankovic saw Frank Zappa in the building. Excited, he pulled out an old copy of *Freak Out!* and asked Zappa for an autograph. In a 2015 interview with Marah Eakin for *AV Music*, Yankovic recalled, "And it kind of blew my mind, because he was like,

'Oh, you're the 'Another One Rides The Bus' guy! My son Dweezil likes that song. Can I get an autograph for him?'" (Yankovic would later have Dweezil play guitar on his Zappa-style parody "Genius in France.") Once he became truly famous with the seeming overnight success of "Eat It," Yankovic continued to be careful with his money—even cheap—avoiding the indulgence and flash of other music stars. Before Yankovic had a family, David Segal reported in the *Washington Post*, "He used to live so modestly that reporters who visited him for interviews thought he was putting them on, and would ask to see where he really lived."[5] His restraint seems to inform his parody of TI's "Whatever You Like" (2011). While TI promises his baby a $5 million home, Bentleys, and "Patrón on ice," Yankovic, in his parody "Whatever You Like" (2011), makes more moderate vows: dinner at Burger King, Top Ramen, and two-ply toilet paper: "And you can always ride the city bus / Got a stack of tokens just for us." For Yankovic, contrast is always funny, but the tight-fisted character may be rooted in his personal values. Pentiums, for Yankovic, over Benjamins.

Art, too, takes precedence. In his career, Yankovic has maintained a certain artistic integrity, privileging music at times over money. When his record label urged him to produce a Christmas song, he reacted to what he saw as a strictly commercial impetus, producing his disturbing "Christmas at Ground Zero" in response. Yankovic's 1985 song "Girls Just Wanna Have Lunch," a parody of Cyndi Lauper's "Girls Just Wanna Have Fun," is understood to be a similar kind of protest. The song happened at the urging of his record label, which recognized the potential sales in a reference to Lauper's huge hit. On his blog, Nathan Rabin described the result, "Girls Just Wanna Have Lunch," as an inferior parody. Another writer, Will Hodge, hears Yankovic's dissent in the parody's "surly vocal take."[6] Indeed, Yankovic's vocal delivery is flat, at times almost a snort, with no justification in imitation; Lauper's sound, in contrast, is bubbly and clear. Thinking of money above all, Yankovic's label attempted to influence his art, and he lodged his complaint in music.

At the same time, money is inextricably connected with the music industry. In "Don't Download this Song" (2006), a style parody of charity songs like "Do They Know It's Christmas," Yankovic shows some concern about fair compensation: "Don't take away money / From artists just like me." But he also plays up celebrity excess, nullifying the request: "How else can I afford another solid-gold Humvee / And diamond-studded swimming pools." In the early 2000s, Napster enabled the illegal downloading of music online. Since its debut, music sales have plummeted, dropping 47 percent according to the Recording Industry Association of America. Yankovic plays the issue for laughs, building on an existing tension in charity songs, which typically feature rich stars attempting to speak for the poor and downtrodden. With the star assuming the position of charity case, Yankovic's music for a cause moves from obtuse to absurd. But the issue was a real one for the music industry in 2006, with 30 billion songs downloaded between 2004 and 2009. In his song, Yankovic may admit the significance of financial payout in the music industry, but only in part. He needs money, but not really. Yankovic again is part of the music industry and not—insider and outsider. And he made his song, in the end, available as a free download.

Yankovic highlights concerns about the music industry in a different way in his polka medleys. But again, the message is unclear. Of Yankovic's medleys, David John Ferrandino makes a big claim in a study of American popular music: "These pieces expose the underlying inanity of pop lyrics and the sameness of pop song structure by stripping them of their unique vocal and instrumental qualities."[7] Theodor Adorno, a musicologist and philosopher, famously condemned popular music as music designed for the masses—a music standardized to sell in bulk. According to Adorno, part of that standardization had to do with form. Parts are interchangeable. In his polka medleys, Yankovic does substitute parts, giving credence to Adorno's claim. He creates an acceptable whole by stitching together excerpts of multiple songs, and his medleys highlight similarities between the tacked-together songs. His "Polka Face," for example, combines songs that repeat initial syllables and sounds, at times extending the effect—"p-p-p-polka face"; in the "Womanizer" section, the resounding of "you," "I," and "are"; in Jamie Foxx's "Blame It" (2008), a pronounced "a-a-a-a-a-lcohol"; and in Taio Cruz's "Break Your Heart" (2009), repetition of "break." The parallels between these songs can be seen as criticism, backing up claims of standardization—parts are similar in substitution. In the same medley, a segment of Iyaz's "Replay" (2010) seems to make the critique explicit, with the repetition of the line "stuck on replay": "It's like my iPod's stuck on replay / Stuck on replay." Pop music, too, is stuck, doomed to replay.

By reformulating these different songs in his own voice, stripping them of their original vocal sound, Yankovic further undermines popular music's hope of individualization. In "On Popular Music," Adorno claimed the system of standardization in popular music depends on an illusion, a "pseudo-individualization," which gives mass music "the halo of free choice or open market." Yes, music is all the same, but we, the listeners, do not notice. Because the performers appear different, we think the music is too. With distinct looks and personalities, bands and musicians shroud the uniformity of their supposed art, helping to deceive listeners by giving the impression that homogenous music is actually distinct. But Yankovic destroys the trickery. Without the associated original stars, the songs in Yankovic's medleys emerge in a single voice, as the songs have supposedly always been. In his medley "Angry White Boy Polka," all the associated artists—Papa Roach, the White Stripes, Rage against the Machine, Limp Bizkit, Kid Rock, and Eminem, among others—become a single angry white boy, and their music blurs into one homogenous mass. Merged as a single song, the medley supports an argument of pop music's sameness.

In a study of genre in music, Fabian Holt credits major record labels with enforcing "a high degree of standardization."[8] In the creation of popular music, among the big players there is standard practice. Country music often relies on the primacy of melody and lyrics. Other genres of popular music depend on the construction of a hook (a short, gripping melodic line created by a topliner) and a track (the instrumental backup), the domain of the producer. A compelling hook within a song recurs and should foster in the listener a sense of familiarity, which is crucial to listener engagement and enjoyment. With many specialists creating hooks and tracks for multiple artists, the resulting songs can be similar. In 2009 Beyoncé and Kelly Clarkson both had hit songs— "Halo" and "Already Gone," respectively—with tracks created by producer Ryan Tedder. Clarkson herself recognized parallels between the two songs and was concerned some listeners might assume she had copied "Halo."

Genre, as a term denoting a type of musical style, contains within its very definition the recognition of repetition and sameness. We know that a country music song is a country music song because we recognize certain established elements of the genre. But genre isn't static. There's always room for innovation, especially on independent labels, as artists' and listeners' tastes evolve and new musical practices emerge.[9] Musicologist Robert Walser maintains, "Nowhere are genre boundaries more fluid than in popular music . . . musicians are ceaselessly creating new fusions and extensions of popular genres."[10] And nowhere is that more evident, as of late, than in the work of Lin-Manuel Miranda, the creator of the wildly popular musical *Hamilton.* Miranda saw the tale of America's first treasury secretary as "a hip-hop story."[11] To give this history life, he would bring to Broadway a creative blend of time, nation, and genre. The result, *Hamilton*, mixes genre audaciously, adding rap to the traditional Broadway mix.

Amazingly, Miranda attributes his ability to mix genres in creative ways to none other than . . . Al Yankovic (plot twist!). He credits especially Yankovic's polka medleys. In 2017 he explained to Geoff Edgers of the *Washington Post*, "When you grow up with 'Weird Al,' you learn that genre is fluid."

When Miranda received a star on the Hollywood Walk of Fame, on November 30, 2018, just a month after Yankovic, Miranda had Yankovic speak at the event. Yankovic called *Hamilton* "the greatest thing of all time." Yankovic told me that he and Miranda are friends and have talked about genre a lot. In one of their conversations, Miranda explained that the polka medleys "showed him that the genre is basically just clothing that dresses up the song. A song could be any genre at all, and a song is not the genre." For Miranda, that fluidity is exciting, an energy evident in *Hamilton.* Yankovic's medleys, in this light, underscore the flexibility of genre, the possibility of artistic revolution and hybrid innovation, rather than a detrimental standardization in popular music. Yankovic's polka medleys meld various types of pop and polka, creating yet another transformative fusion.

I side somewhere between Adorno and Miranda. In Yankovic's parodies, some amount of sameness is inherent. Yankovic replicates existing sounds, and the success of his songs may rely on that repetition—a familiarity with the original song. Some listeners enjoy his parodies, at least initially, simply because they enjoy the original song. Even so, the sameness of popular music seems in his polka medleys to offer both critique and complement. In "Angry White Boy Polka," he combines songs from various genres, the last three sections blending the music of rap-rock group Limp Bizkit, Christian metal band P.O.D., and rapper Eminem. With creative segues, the songs and the genres they represent merge. But Yankovic also recontextualizes each song within a new genre, his polka stylings, with a faster pace, appropriate vocal harmonization, and prominent brass and woodwind accompaniment. Through Yankovic's voice and the varied segments' juxtaposition, the original songs in his polka medleys transform into a single composition.

This genre blending climaxed in Yankovic's medley "The Hamilton Polka." On March 2, 2018, Miranda released the medley, a five-minute mash-up of the music of *Hamilton*, as part of his Hamildrop series. Each month in 2018, the series invited other artists to engage with Miranda's work, creating "new *Hamilton* content" or an innovative riff on the musical—the next step in Miranda's genre bending. Miranda had pitched his concept to Yankovic with trepidation, hoping for the parodist's involvement. In a 2018 interview for *Rolling Stone*'s Andy Green with Miranda, Yankovic recalled Miranda's cautious approach, "Lin pitched it to me as a polka medley way more hesitantly than you should have." Miranda clarified, "Listen, as a longtime 'Weird Al' fan, that's a scary ask to make." As Miranda knew, Yankovic in his polka medleys normally linked different songs by different musicians. The only exceptions for a single group were the "Bohemian Polka" (1993) and "Hot Rocks Polka" (1989), devoted to Queen and the Rolling Stones, respectively. Both one-band polkas were rather early in Yankovic's career and both groups legendary. Miranda exclaimed, "I cannot presume to be in that rarified air as the Rolling fuckin' Stones!"

But Yankovic found Miranda worthy and accepted the challenge. The result, "The Hamilton Polka," was received with exuberance. In filmed footage, on *The Tonight Show* starring Jimmy Fallon, Miranda laughs out loud listening to Yankovic's polka for the first time, his genuine enthusiasm and excitement visible and visceral. Miranda had hoped to release the medley in February, but, busy preparing for his tour, Yankovic couldn't deliver until March 2. The two found a way around the late date, dubbing the day February 30th. One headline, by Caitlin PenzeyMoog for *AV Club*, summed it up: "How lucky we are to be alive right now: 'Weird Al' Yankovic has released a *Hamilton* polka."

WEIRD AL, TOO SERIOUSLY

During his career, Yankovic has targeted a wide variety of genres—from rap to punk, ska to country—and not just in his medleys. That move was in some ways strategic. As Yankovic explained to Roy Zimmerman, playing on more than one genre would help him catch a variety of audiences—fans of different genres. But he noodles with conventions of those genres. In his song "Good Old Days" (1988), for example, he radically departs from the perceived norms of folk music. To acoustic guitar accompaniment, he sweetly sings about arson and the abuse of rats. The humor lies somewhere in the chasm between a supposedly wholesome authenticity in folk song and the lyric content.

Still, Yankovic doesn't single out any one genre for exaggeration or distortion. In fact, any genre is potential material for a Yankovic parody, especially if a song has a prevalent note of self-serious posturing. As dissident writer Václav Havel claimed, "Anyone who takes himself too seriously always runs the risk of looking ridiculous; anyone who can consistently laugh at himself does not." Yankovic often makes this risk a reality, highlighting a final paradox of fame and the music industry. To be famous, a musician must take his or her art seriously. At the same time, if his or her music or performance appears overly serious, audiences may recoil. The musician may come off as arrogant or otherwise off-putting. The related charge of self-indulgence, Simon Frith observers in "What Is Bad Music?," is a particular description of music that's perceived as bad. In a write-up on hip-hop, for example, one writer criticizes rap along these lines: "The passion is choking it—there's a desperation for it to be taken so seriously and for it to be understood." [12] Yankovic rectifies the wrong of this desperation—his career in some ways defined by Havel's dictum. He upends in much of his music the overly serious. David Segal pronounced, "Yankovic is the only artist out there with the talent, nerve or shamelessness to point out how absurd all of this gravity is." Under apparent duress, Yankovic defines the subterfuge as his primary purpose: "If there's any point, it's that rock music takes itself too seriously." To Segal, he clarified, "I've always thought that rock music should be fun, and if I have any kind of mission it's to prick that bubble of pretentiousness a little bit."

Some of Yankovic's parodies are particularly explicit in this regard. Actor Jack Black has singled out "Smells Like Nirvana," reacting to

Yankovic's approach to Nirvana and the 1990s alternative music scene. He told Geoff Edgers of the *Washington Post*, "It was a big cultural moment, and he comes in and marble-mouths it. There's something really important about laughing at things that take themselves too seriously." This criterion also helps explain Yankovic's choice to parody Eminem's "Lose Yourself" and not another Eminem song, like "The Real Slim Shady." The latter song is already funny, a parody of popular culture and various notions of whiteness.[13] Yankovic explained, "It would have been redundant to parody 'The Real Slim Shady' because it's already a tongue-in-cheek swipe at pop culture. 'Lose Yourself' was serious enough to get the Weird Al treatment."[14]

Another serious candidate was Avril Lavigne's "Complicated," which became the parody "A Complicated Song" (2003). With the song, from her 2002 album *Let Go*, Lavigne became known for her brooding display of teen angst. For some, the front was a bit too much. In a 2002 review of her music for *Slant*, Sal Cinquemani called Lavigne's "Complicated" "more poser than punk." In the song, Lavigne begins with a big claim—"'Cause life's like this"—before she details her approach to life, with its pressure to conform. Conformity is a complicated performance, Lavigne suggests—one she hopes to avoid: "Chill out, what you yelling for? / Lay back, it's all been done before." Watching a boy act differently to impress his friends, she asks, "Why do you have to go and make things so complicated? / I see the way you're acting like you're somebody else gets me frustrated."

In "A Complicated Song," Yankovic centers his own life lesson on "extra cheese," a premise that inspires a stunning sequence of "complicated" rhymes: "Why'd you have to go and make me so constipated? / 'Cause right now I'd do anything to just get my bowels evacuated." The song inflates with increasingly ingenious completions of the rhyme—a hallmark of Yankovic's parodies: The joke progresses and develops throughout the parody. In an interview with Larry King, Yankovic explained that this approach often sets his parodies apart, despite the many YouTube parodists today. He doesn't rely on a single "punchline up front"; his joke evolves. In "A Complicated Song," he changes the chorus each time as he details distinct problems—ingesting too much cheese, accidently dating a family member, and standing on a roller coaster: "How was I supposed to know we were both related?" "Why'd I have to go and get myself decapitated?" The song offers absurdly complicated scenarios—scenarios that render Lavigne's complaint, in comparison, far less serious.

Yankovic treats the Irish rock group U2 similarly. The band is seen by some as "sanctimonious or self-righteous." For this reason, in part, Ireland has done little to honor or claim its native sons. Irishman Karl Downey tried to explain the Irish omission and even hate to Dean Van Nguyen in the *Guardian* article "Where the Streets Have No Statues: Why Do the Irish Hate U2?" Speaking personally, he said, "I think it's quite an accomplishment for Bono. He does so much for charity and the poor and yet people still do hate him. I don't really like him. Maybe it's because he's a bit sanctimonious. It might be the glasses as well. He never takes off those glasses." After his friends point out that the singer suffers from glaucoma, Downey stands by his verdict but reconsiders his glasses jab. Yankovic molds U2's "Hold Me, Thrill Me, Kiss Me, Kill Me" (1995) into his parody "Cavity Search" (1996). The foundational song is grandiose and spiritual, yet without a clear message: "You don't know how you took it / You just know what you've got." In "Cavity Search," the topic is far less transcendent, instead a terrible trip to the dentist: "Numb me, drill me, floss me, bill me." Yankovic brings the song, along with U2, down to earth. And U2's poetic mish-mash—"Oh no, don't be shy / It's a crime to cry"—becomes ordinary—"My teeth are a fright, got a huge overbite."

Yankovic's interest in taking on the overly serious also explains his ongoing attention to Prince. Though he references Prince in his music—in "Amish Paradise" and "Word Crimes"—he never parodied Prince's songs. That was, of course, not Yankovic's choice. He had some half dozen ideas—all turned down by Prince—including parodies of "Let's Go Crazy," "When Doves Cry," "Kiss," and "1999." In the 1984 song "When Doves Cry," from his *Purple Rain* album, Prince assembles a poetic sound-topia: "An ocean of violets in bloom / Animals strike curious poses / They feel the heat / The heat between me and you." The song "1999," from his 1982 album of the same name, is an invitation to party despite life's impending doom: "War is all around us, my mind says prepare to fight / So if I gotta die I'm gonna listen to my body tonight." The targets all border on the surreal and sentimental—prime territory for a Yankovic flip. For "1999," Yankovic revealed to me, "I wanted to do a song based on all those cheesy late-night infomercials . . . you know, 'You can get this incredible gadget for just $19.99!'"

In the music, Prince created a world in his image. Yankovic directly experienced the eccentricity of the man himself at an award show. In 2011 he recounted the tale to Angela Watercutter of *Wired*: "But one of the oddest things to ever happen between me and Prince was the year that he and I were at the American Music Awards at the same time. Apparently I was going to be sitting in the same row as Prince that year and I got a telegram—and I wasn't the only one—from Prince's management company saying that I was not to establish eye contact with him during the show. I just couldn't believe it." Yankovic felt the need to respond to the unusual request: "So immediately I sent back a telegram saying that he shouldn't be establishing eye contact with me either."

With the music and the man ripe for parody, what happened? In a 2019 interview on *Off Camera with Sam Jones*, Yankovic recalled Paul McCartney's rejection of the parody "Chicken Pot Pie." At least he had a reason, Yankovic explained—McCartney, as a vegetarian, hadn't wanted to support the eating of animals. Though "Tofu Pot Pie" just wouldn't work, Yankovic appreciated McCartney's honest response. Without naming Prince, Yankovic cited McCartney's handling of the parody request as far better than the alternative: "No, I don't have a sense of humor. Leave me alone." Yankovic's next topic in the same conversation was, of course, Prince. Unlike McCartney, Prince never did explain his many rebuffs of Yankovic. Perhaps he simply had no sense of humor. Still, in accounts of Prince, several writers in fact highlight Prince's humor. Ben Greenman, in *Dig If You Will the Picture: Funk, Sex, God, and Genius in the Music of Prince*, blames Prince's parody refusals instead on the musician's desire to control his music and its production: "Prince never came around to Weird Al. It wasn't that he wasn't a fan of comedy: he loved Pee-Wee Herman, for example. But he was too obsessed with controlling the movement of his work through the world." The early *Mad* parody was hardly comfort.

Later in his career, Prince was more open to humor involving his music, performing with the Muppets a version of "Rasberry Beret" titled "Rasberry Sorbet." Despite his enduring hope in the possibility, Yankovic would never get his own Prince parody. After Prince's death in 2016, Yankovic reflected, "I hadn't approached him in about 20 years because he always said no, but I had this fantasy that he'd come out with a new song, I'd have a great idea, he'd finally say yes, and it would erase decades of weirdness between us. But that's obviously not going to be the case."[15] The great white whale of the overly serious in music would remain forever out of reach.

CURLS JUST WANNA HAVE FUN

In his repertoire, Yankovic treats fame thematically. Relying on his contested relationship to fame, as insider and outsider, he shapeshifts to assume various perspectives on fame, including a special sensitivity to would-be star Skipper Dan. He also underscores issues related to fame—the balance of art and commerce, standardization, and an over-seriousness in music. His message is not always coherent: Is the fluidity of genre a strength or a sign of unoriginality and mass production? Is money necessarily connected to art, or is it a primary evil, a threat to the creative process? Instead, he explores these topics as "fair game" for parody and humor. In a certain sense, his music parodies popular music itself and its relationship to the music industry. In another sense, he parodies the famous artist.

His appearance makes a difference here. In 2003 Dan Snierson asked him, "Is your hair actually a parody of Kenny G's?" Yankovic responded, "A lot of people think it's a bad perm, but I'd like to set the record straight: It's actually bad natural hair." With his Hawaiian shirts and lustrous curly mane, but no glasses post-Lasik, Yankovic is a character playing a character. And he is aware of fan investment in his appearance. When I met him in his home, I noted the Hawaiian shirt he was wearing. He commented, "Well, I didn't want you to be disappointed." The gap he sets up between the original and the parody is often widened by the one between Yankovic himself and the original musician. Weird Al and Miley Cyrus. Weird Al and Coolio.

Then again, Weird Al, in character or not, is hardly a single, set personality—an easy contrast with other celebrities. He's so much more than curls unfurled, nerdy or nice. And that's our final story, with the book almost (Un)done.

LAST LAUGH

In interviews, Yankovic often gives the impression that his songs are simpler than we think. But there are undeniable challenges in his work, with complicated issues like identity and politics at play. His parodies take on religion, race, and gender, sometimes with an edge but mostly with a sympathetic air of independence: You can be *whoever* you are—black, white, nerd, or fly rabbi. He creates a mix of tribute and mockery in his work, and he mocks himself just as he slyly takes down the bad behavior of others, sometimes in the very same line.

The complexity of his artwork is especially evident in his recent collaboration with the band Weezer. At the end of September 2018, the internet was abuzz with a new Yankovic video. But when the video was released, it was a promo for Weezer's remake of Toto's 1983 hit "Africa." The collaboration started at Weezer's concert at the Forum in Los Angeles on August 8, where Yankovic made a surprise appearance, playing an accordion solo during the band's performance of the song. The collaboration was impromptu. The band was performing with the Pixies, friends of Yankovic's, and they had invited him to attend. Evidently, knowing Yankovic was planning to come, Weezer decided Yankovic was needed on stage. The unexpected onstage jam had special meaning for Yankovic. He explained to me, "The LA Forum is the first place that I'd ever seen a rock show." His early musical hero, Elton John, was the featured act.

But Weezer wasn't done with Yankovic. He recounted, "A few weeks later, I get another communication from Weezer and now they want me to star in their Africa video." On September 24, Weezer debuted a video for their unlikely hit, with Yankovic playing lead singer Rivers Cuomo in a parody of the band's 1994 song "Undone—The Sweater Song." In the video, Yankovic as Cuomo sings against the same dimly lit, sparse, blue stage that anchored the "Undone" video. On NPR, Stephen Thompson observed, "If you've ever wanted to see the Internet fold itself up into a burrito and consume itself hungrily over the course of four minutes, you've come to the right place." On September 24, Yankovic teased his followers on Twitter: "I make a small cameo appearance in the new @weezer video—see if you can spot it." One fan, Jeff Whitmore, responded, "Might as well cut this day short, as that was the best thing I'll see! Wrap it up, boys! See you tomorrow!" But many were confused, assuming Yankovic was in fact Cuomo. Joseph M Felicelli wrote, "I was all checking the keyboard player, and then I noticed how the lead singer was dancing, and felt kind of dumb." The dancing was the giveaway for DEEGE as well: "Is it wrong that I thought the lead singer of @Weezer looked a lot like @alyankovic . . . then he started dancing and I knew it was Al."

The video was one of the clearest examples yet of Yankovic's exploration of personhood. His lyrics as a whole tell a story of freedom in identity: the nerd, the outsider, the noncomformist. But his mimicry of the original artists in the music and the videos tell this story as well. Freedom of identity? Yankovic *becomes* everyone from Michael Jackson to Billy Ray Cyrus. A little vocal adjustment, some careful study, and voila—he can inhabit another artist's headspace. It's amazing that the same guy who mimicked R. Kelly and Nelly so transformed himself that he was legitimately mistaken for Rivers Cuomo in the "Africa" video. It's almost . . . weird.

So just how weird is Weird Al? In 2006, Sam Anderson considered Yankovic's weirdness in *Slate* under the headline "Troubadork"—a wonderful hybrid word, bringing together the nerd-adjacent word *dork* and *troubadour*, the medieval designation for a male composer and performer. Anderson wrote, "The only 'weird' thing about Weird Al Yankovic . . . is that he insists on calling himself weird." He added, "He's actually Normal Al, a common-sensical, conservative force. He's Everyman trapped on Neverland Ranch, exposing as many stylistic excesses and false profundities as he can." To Anderson, Yankovic reveals the weirdness around him and in so doing emerges as normal in comparison. And Anderson has a point. Yankovic highlights word abuse, the complications of racial and gender expectations, as well as excess and indolence in the music industry. He spotlights the foibles and imperfections of others, the vices of culture and society. He might just represent one of the more reasonable voices within music's recent past and present.

On the other hand, he also includes in his music topics regarded as weird—sci-fi fare. The focus indexes Merriam-Webster's online definition of "weird" as odd, even supernatural or magical. To this category, I must assign "Yoda" (1985), Yankovic's parody of the Kinks's 1970 song "Lola," which is turned into a description of Luke's journey in the 1980 film *The Empire Strikes Back*. There's also the song "The Saga Begins," a 1999 parody of Don McLean's classic "American Pie" (1971). McLean's children played the parody so often that the singer found himself nearly singing the parody lyrics on stage by mistake.

Plenty of other Yankovic songs boast absurd elements, including "Foil" and its reference to mind control, as well as the 1999 songs "Germs" and "Albuquerque," among others. Over eleven minutes long, "Albuquerque" is particularly surreal, complete with "sauerkraut for breakfast," ukulele-playing lepers, a donut store stocked only with weasels, and an inexplicable escape from a fiery plane crash. It's a "rock narrative," Yankovic maintained, but "a little more ridiculous." And it was never supposed to be popular. Yankovic explained his thinking to Nathan Rabin in their 2011 interview: "I'm going to make this song so long that people are only gonna want to hear it once." The song's success was the plan's failure. "Albuquerque" has become an unlikely fan favorite. On October 17, 2018, Yankovic asked via Twitter for fan help: "I'm finalizing the set list for my 2019 orchestral tour this week—which of my songs have you always wanted to hear with full symphony accompaniment?" "Albuquerque" was a popular response. Chris Gable wrote, in the spirit of Seuss, "Albuquerque with an orchestra, Albuquerque with a choir, Albuquerque acoustic . . . Every possible way."

A more overt sci-fi example is "Slime Creatures from Outer Space" (1985): "Things just haven't been the same / Since the flying saucer came." The topic, an alien invasion, fits squarely in the sci-fi genre. And Yankovic backed up the genre musically, playing the theremin. The instrument's eerie sound is created by the player's hands and their relative position to the electronic antennas. In effect, it looks as if the musician is conjuring music out of thin air. And yet Yankovic treated the sci-fi genre in a new way, downplaying the dramatic effect such an event typically evokes in the movies. In the song, an original composition, Yankovic is concerned about his rug rather than his life: "I sure hope they don't come in here / I just shampooed the rug." In some ways, the approach backs up Anderson's claim: Though it is a "weird" topic, Yankovic frames the extraordinary in terms of regular routine. The story of alien invasion is not epic but instead inconvenient, an annoyance. The slime creatures are "really getting on my nerves."

According to writer Lily Rothman, Yankovic has also become less weird over time, through no fault of his own. Social media provides a platform for self-presentation. Anyone can create wild clips to attract an audience. And so Yankovic's wacky videos have lost their weird edge. In a 2014 article in *Time* she writes, "In a world where any 'weirdo' can rack up hits on a YouTube clip, the designation begins to lose its oomph." But she doesn't think Yankovic should change his name just yet, admitting, "'Normal Al' just doesn't have the same ring to it."

Journalist Simon Sweetman dismissed Yankovic's "weird" label for another reason: not his music or new, internet-propelled competition, but instead his behavior. He wrote, "But 'Weird Al' is just 'Normal Al' Yankovic." In conversation with Yankovic, Sweetman found Yankovic to be a regular man, hardly zany or weird.[1] I noticed comparable comments elsewhere in the media and asked Yankovic about this "normal" rep: Is it "a compliment or an insult or neither?" "Most of the time, it's fact," he said. "It's almost ironic that some people say I'm one of the most normal guys in Hollywood." To Dan Rather, Yankovic said something similar. Rather asked, "Are you weird?" Yankovic called himself "chameleon-like," but said that in his personal life, he could be a "quiet, withdrawn guy." To Larry King, he compared his stage name to a common, humorous mismatch: "like when they call big people Tiny." Later in our conversation, I brought up his upcoming birthday, inquiring about his plans. His answer was entirely ordinary: "I kinda downplay birthdays. So probably not a whole lot of anything. I might go out to dinner with the family, but we don't do parties." He prefers "something very low key." I joked, that sounds "so normal Al."

Weird or not weird? How do we label Weird Al? The question is far too subjective, but I'll tell you what I do know. In our interviews, Yankovic answered my many questions thoughtfully and always with good

Serious Al. *Courtesy of Jon Schwartz*

humor. In our first interview, his body language, a lean forward, was proof of his engagement. In the many online interviews I have viewed online, Yankovic behaves similarly. Dan Rather leaned back in his chair, while Yankovic sat forward. Larry King, too, reclined as Yankovic tilted toward his host, attentive and ready. In response to questions, he is articulate while entertaining, even when queries are less than elegant. In one segment, Larry King seemed to dismiss all popular music, heralding Frank Sinatra as the pinnacle of music before its descent into garbage. Yankovic laughed, promising to parody Sinatra just for King.

In interviews, the only break in the conversational flow seems to happen when Yankovic is forced to confront solemn or grandiose questions. "What do you care about?" asked Rather. Yankovic responded, "I enjoy a good burrito." When Rather asked Yankovic about the "worst thing" to happen to him in his life, Yankovic hesitated but ultimately cited the unexpected death of his parents in 2004, an accidental carbon monoxide poisoning. "My parents were the best," Yankovic shared. Yankovic was on tour and decided to continue rather than cut his concerts short. At the time, he explained, "Going up on stage in front of thousands of supportive fans is a cathartic and somewhat therapeutic experience for me right now."[2] Yankovic was less inclined to respond when Rather asked him to name music appropriate for his memorial service. But Rather pressed, "Visualize it." Yankovic generously settled on the instrumental "Welcome to the Fun Zone" from his movie *UHF*. He also offered, with a mix of amusement and resignation, the newspaper headline he expects in the announcement of his death, "Weird Al Eats It."

Yankovic is strikingly consistent in his reaction to questions such as these, even much earlier in his career. In a 1983 interview for the *Globe and Mail*, Alan Niester asked Yankovic about his music's "social significance." An up-and-coming Al answered: "I think accordion music will change the face of Western civilization forever. Or maybe not. Can I go home now?" I was not surprised then by Yankovic's responses on the October 1, 2012, episode of "Life's Big Questions":

Q: "Why is music so powerful?"

A: ". . . it does things . . ."

Q: "What inspires you?"

A: "The *Glee* Soundtrack"

Still, I took my own shot, asking a big question—hoping Yankovic would provide some insight into his hoped-for legacy. He offered another light answer: "I just want to be known as the guy that wore nice shoes." With his vast collection of Vans, he might just get that wish.

Yankovic won't necessarily expound on the weight evident in his music or his career. He never negated my various readings of his music—big and small—but he also did not embrace my explicit political evaluations. He left the frog dissection to me. If someone was going to ruin his jokes, it wasn't going to be him. And it wasn't going to be journalist Matt Wild, either. Rejecting the various think pieces on Yankovic's work that followed the release of *Mandatory Fun*, Wild wrote, "After reading about 8,000 of these pieces, I decided that everyone was really, *really* overthinking it. Weird Al was /is funny and good because . . . he was /is funny and good." Wild might say the same of this book—another author overthinking it. At the same time, Yankovic is meticulous in the construction of his songs and acknowledges the value of his work. He also appreciates recognition of his music. By phone, he described how he felt when he finally received a star on the Hollywood Walk of Fame: "That was such an amazing day. . . . It was a lot more emotional than I thought it was going to be. I was trying to be professional and funny, but once I got there, the gravity of the whole thing kind of hit me. It was kind of like going to my own funeral." Cue "Welcome to the Fun Zone."

In the *New York Post*, Dan Aquilante observed, "Somewhere between social commentary and musical comedy lies the art of Weird Al Yankovic." Some may not believe the two strands can coexist, but Yankovic's music does not have to be one thing or the other. Serious intentions and comedy do not somehow cancel each other out. Yankovic seemingly walks a fine line: between comedic art and the serious work and engagement behind it and in it. And Yankovic himself is aware of that line. When Mark Lore, writing for the *Portland Mercury*, asked in 2013, "How important is it to you to be taken seriously as a musician?" Yankovic responded:

> Well, that's sort of a loaded question because, you know, I want to be taken seriously enough that I'm allowed to continue doing what I do. I want to be taken seriously enough that people will still want to hear my music, and allow me to record my albums and do other projects that maybe aren't musical. But when you do comedy—I mean, I'm not looking to make any kind of serious music, or any kind of serious drama, so in that sense I don't have any real need to be taken seriously.

Still, there is a seriousness in comedy and there are jokes in serious works of art. Actress Bea Arthur, in fact, discovered her comedic chops by singing seriously. Responding to the unintended audience laughter, Arthur recalled, "I was doing it from the heart, and I suddenly realized: Now I know what comedy is. It was such a revelation, it was like—comedy is being terribly serious."

Yankovic has been a part of our cultural landscape for decades, with ongoing plans for the future. In a 1996 interview for the *Philadelphia Inquirer*, Yankovic mused, "I sometimes wonder how strange it would be to be 60 and still known as 'Weird Al.'" He no longer has to wonder. Still, he's hard to define: for some "still" Weird Al and for others hardly weird at all. At one point in our first conversation, Yankovic referenced Pablo Picasso, citing his famous quote: "Every child is an artist. The problem is how to remain an artist once we grow up." For Yankovic, something of that eternal child is connected to his art, even as he evolves as a serious musician: "I think I've gotten better at what I do. I think I'm a better singer, and a better songwriter, and a better musician, but I'm still that goofy nerd making stupid jokes." There is no separation. Nor should there be.

In his latest tour, *Strings Attached*, Yankovic played in a new way with the issue of his music's import—or lack thereof—by performing on tour with a symphonic orchestra. With the tour's announcement, I thought of music comedians Victor Borge and Anna Russell, who both achieved some recognition, a kind of seriousness, given their association with classical music and an orchestra. I asked Yankovic, "Is the use of an orchestra in any way a commentary on serious music?" Quite the opposite, Yankovic responded. He had performed with the Hollywood Bowl Orchestra at the Hollywood Bowl in 2016 in a show titled "Weird Al Takes the Bowl," at the Bowl management's invitation. He told me that after the performance, he felt "It was just such an amazing experience. . . . Wouldn't it be great to do a whole tour like that?" For Yankovic, part of the fun of the *Strings Attached* tour, inspired by the Bowl appearance, would be the incongruous juxtaposition: the orchestra and "the kind of crazy stuff we do." By phone, he said, "It's just kind of an odd pairing and it amused me." He didn't expect the "orchestral sublime" to elevate his art. To the contrary—he wanted to exploit the perceived divide for laughs.

In a review of the tour's kickoff show in Clearwater, Florida, on June 5, 2019, *Tampa Bay Times* journalist Jay Cridlin claimed the orchestra actually complemented certain songs, like "Amish Paradise" and "Don't Download This Song." When I caught the show two months later at the Greek Theatre in Los Angeles, fans too seemed to respond to the new epic sound of "Don't Download This Song," created by the orchestra, waving lit-up phones like lighters. But in other songs, Yankovic played up the seeming mismatch, reveling, for instance, in the absurdity of a whole orchestra backing up his short and silly ode to a rodent pal, "Harvey the Wonder Hamster." Before the hamster tribute, he announced to the crowd, "We've been trying for 35 years, and tonight will be the first time we've played this. I didn't feel right playing this song until we had a full symphony orchestra behind us. I just thought the song deserved that, and I wanted to give it all the gravitas it needed."

While Harvey made the cut, Yankovic's Michael Jackson parodies did not. With new accusations in HBO's *Leaving Neverland* documentary, Yankovic did not want to cause any inadvertent offense with his Jackson tributes. In light of Jackson's alleged crimes, "Eat It" and "Fat" had potentially changed in meaning. He told *Billboard*: "I don't know if that's going to be permanent or not, but we just felt that with what's happened recently with the HBO documentaries, we didn't want anybody to feel uncomfortable." An official change on Twitter, the "Eat-It Guy" became "the weird one." The one and only.

Fans and critics might enjoy plumbing the implications of Yankovic's songs, the ideas they inspire, the conversations they might open up—I know I have. But the laughs are really the point for Yankovic. That doesn't mean we have to choose—laughs or meaningful dialogue. All of these things are part of Yankovic's music. And all of these things are part of Yankovic's legacy—the humor and play, the commentary and criticism, as well as, of course, the nice shoes.

NOTES

INTRODUCTION

1. Roland Barthes, "Toward a Psychosociology of Contemporary Food Consumption," in *Food and Culture: A Reader*, ed. Carole Counihan and Penny van Esterik (New York: Routledge, 2013), 25.

2. "Study Reveals the Age You Officially Become Really Boring," *Esquire*, September 1, 2017. https://www.esquire.com/uk/life/news/a16986/age-peak-boring/.

3. Iain Ellis, *Rebels Wit Attitude: Subversive Rock Humorists* (Berkeley: Soft Skull Press, 2008), 1.

4. Dan Rather, interview with "Weird Al" Yankovic, *The Big Interview with Dan Rather*, AXS TV, February 3, 2015.

5. Charles Hiroshi Garrett, "The Humor of Jazz," in *Jazz/Not Jazz: The Music and Its Boundaries*, ed. David Ake, Charles Hiroshi Garrett, and Daniel Goldmark (Berkeley: University of California Press, 2012), 50.

6. Charles Hiroshi Garrett, "'Shooting the Keys': Musical Horseplay and High Culture," in *The Oxford Handbook of the New Cultural History of Music*, ed. Jane F. Fulcher (Oxford: Oxford University Press, 2011), 253.

7. Marcia Morgado and Andrew Reilly, "Funny Kine Clothes: The Hawaiian Shirt as Popular Culture," *Paideusis* 6 (2012): D1–D24.

8. Marah Eakin, "'Weird Al' Yankovic Answers Our 11 Questions," *AV Music*, July 18, 2014, https://music.avclub.com/weird-al-yankovic-answers-our-11-questions-1798270432.

9. John Thomerson, "Parody as a Borrowing Practice in American Music, 1965–2015" (PhD diss., University of Cincinnati, 2017), 19, 26.

10. Linda Hutcheon, *A Theory of Parody: The Teachings of Twentieth-Century Art Forms* (New York: Methuen, 1985), 3–4.

11. Garrett, "The Humor of Jazz," 53.

12. Thomerson, "Parody as a Borrowing Practice in American Music, 1965–2015," 1.

13. Sander L. Gilman, *Nietzschean Parody: An Introduction to Reading Nietzsche* (Aurora, CO: Davies Group, 2001), 37.

14. See Tyler T. Ochoa, "Dr. Seuss, The Juice and Fair Use: How the Grinch Silenced a Parody," *Santa Clara University School of Law*, January 1, 1997, https://digitalcommons.law.scu.edu/facpubs/599/.

15. "Make the Rock Hall 'Weird,'" http://www.dohtem.com/al/rockhall/.

16. Quoted in David Segal, "'Weird Al': Confessions of a Parody Animal," *Washington Post*, August 17, 2003.

17. Quoted in Geoff Edgers, "Was 'Weird Al' the Real Star All Along?" *Washington Post*, February 16, 2017.

18. Quoted in Lydia Goehr, "'Music Has no Meaning to Speak Of': On the Politics of Musical Interpretation," in *The Interpretation of Music,* ed. Michael Krausz (Oxford: Clarendon Press, 1993), 177.

I. THIS IS THE LIFE

1. Nathan Rabin, *Weird Al: The Book* (New York: Abrams, 2012), 12.

2. Quoted in Harold Conrad, "The Glamorous Life of Al Yankovic," *Spin*, April 14, 1997.

3. See Marion Jacobson, "Searching for Rockordion: The Changing Image of the Accordion in America," *American Music* 25, no. 2 (summer 2007): 218. See also "'Looks Like a Cash Register and Sounds Worse': The Deiro Brothers and the Rise of the Piano Accordion in American Culture 1908–1930," *Free-Reed Journal* 3 (2001): 55–79, 227.

4. Quoted in Jacobson, "Searching for Rockordion," 237.

5. Helena Simonett, "Introduction," in *The Accordion in the Americas: Klezmer, Polka, Tango, Zydeco, and More!* ed. Helena Simonett (Urbana: University of Illinois Press, 2012), 2.

6. Quoted in Marion Jacobson, *Squeeze This! A Cultural History of the Accordion in America* (Urbana: University of Illinois Press, 2012), 109.

7. David Segal, "'Weird Al': Confessions of a Parody Animal," *Washington Post*, August 17, 2003.

8. Marah Eakin, "'Weird Al' Yankovic Answers Our 11 Questions," *AV Music*, July 18, 2014, https://music.avclub.com/weird-al-yankovic-answers-our-11-questions-1798270432.

9. John Lekich, "Weird Al 'Just Never Grew out of It,'" *Globe and Mail*, July 20, 1989.

10. Segal, "'Weird Al': Confessions of a Parody Animal."

11. Dr. Demento, foreword to *The Golden Age of Novelty Song*, by Steve Otfinoski (New York: Billboard Books, 2000). See also "Dr. Demento: Off the Air, But Still Happily Deranged," NPR Music, June 22, 2010.

12. Harold Conrad, "The Glamorous Life of Al Yankovic," *Spin*, April 14, 1997.

13. Segal, "'Weird Al': Confessions of a Parody Animal."

14. Quoted in Gerald Nachman, *Seriously Funny: The Rebel Comedians of the 1950s and 1960s* (New York: Pantheon Books, 2003), 124–27.

15. Ibid., 137.

16. Quoted in ibid., 194.

17. Mark Cohen, *Overweight Sensation: The Life and Comedy of Allan Sherman* (Waltham, MA: Brandeis University Press, 2013), 135.

18. Ibid., 138.

19. David G. Roskies, "Major Trends in Yiddish Parody," *Jewish Quarterly Review* 94, no. 1 (winter 2004): 111.

20. "6 Celebrities Everyone Thinks are Jewish," Virtual Jerusalem, March 10, 2014, http://virtualjerusalem.com/culture.php?Itemid=12332.

21. Quoted in Randy Lewis, "Parody Master Yankovic Stays a Step ahead with New, Seriously Silly Moves," *Star Advertiser*, February 28, 2017.

22. Quoted in Louis Pattison, "Spoofer Who Won't Quit—the Long, Strange Career of 'Weird Al' Jankovic [*sic*]," *Guardian*, November 25, 2010.

23. "Weird Al" Yankovic, *Permanent Record: Al In the Box*, liner notes.

24. "'Weird Al's' Advice: Follow Your Muse to 'Grow Up,'" NPR, February 26, 2011.

25. Letter from Dr. Demento to "Weird Al" Yankovic, September 27, 1979, in the private collection of Jon "Bermuda" Schwartz.

26. "The Woman behind 'My Sharona,'" *All Things Considered*, NPR, March 6, 2012.

27. Interview on "Off Camera with Sam Jones," 2019.

28. Kyle Anderson, "'Weird Al' Yankovic: The Stories behind the Songs," *EW*, July 3, 2014.

29. Adrian Chamberlain, "Weird Al Raises Ire with Canadian Idiot," *Times-Colonist*, September 6, 2007.

30. Caseen Gaines, "'The Weird Al Show': The Complete Oral History," *Rolling Stone*, September 13, 2017.

31. Rabin, *Weird Al*, 139.

32. Zack O'Malley Greenburg, "Weird Al Yankovic's Business Plan: No More Albums," *Forbes*, February 26, 2015.

33. Eric Althoff, "'Weird Al' Will Stop Recording Albums, Start Releasing Music Digitally After Tour," *Washington Post*, September 6, 2016.

2. THE PRINCE OF POP PARODY

1. Patricia Shehan Campbell, *Songs in Their Heads: Music and Its Meaning in Children's Lives* (Oxford: Oxford University Press, 2010), 58.

2. Robert Chambers, *Parody: The Art That Plays with Art* (New York: Peter Lang, 2010), 4.

3. Quoted in "Interviewing the Men Who Scold Me for Not Liking Weird Al."

4. Austin Roelofs, interview with the author, April 4, 2019.

5. Ray Padgett, *Cover Me: The Stories Behind the Greatest Cover Songs of All Time* (New York: Sterling, 2017), 143.

6. Ibid., 145.

7. See Mark Savage, "The History of Allegations against R Kelly," BBC News, May 23, 2018.

8. Kevin Coffey, "Q&A: 'Weird Al' Yankovic on Parody, Pastiche and becoming a Singles Artist," *Omaha World-Herald*, July 24, 2013, https://www.omaha.com/go/music/rock_candy/q-a-weird-al-yankovic-on-parody-pastiche-and-becoming/article_fda5f0ac-e6b0-5885-8757-45b31fa7dc57.html.

9. Anne Erickson, "The Gibson Interview: 'Weird Al' Yankovic," Gibson.com, June 20, 2011.

10. See Padgett, *Cover Me*, 142.

11. Sharon Hochhauser, "Take Me Down to the Parodies City," *Journal of Popular Music Studies* 30, no. 1–2 (2018): 62.

12. Quoted in Bob Dolgan, *America's Polka King: The Real History of Frankie Yankovic and His Music* (Cleveland: Gray & Company, 2006), preface.

13. Ragnhild Brovig-Hanssen and Paul Harkins, "Contextual Incongruity and Musical Congruity: The Aesthetics and Humour of Mash-ups," *Popular Music* 31, no. 1 (January 2012): 99.

14. See Jordan R. Young, *Spike Jones Off the Record: The Man Who Murdered Music* (Beverly Hills: Past Times, 1984), 19.

15. Thomerson, "Parody as a Borrowing Practice in American Music, 1965–2015," 83.

16. Padgett, *Cover Me*, 143.

17. Christopher R. Weingarten, "Weird Al Yankovic Looks Back at 20 Years of 'Smells Like Nirvana," *Spin*, October 11, 2012.

18. Coffey, "Q&A: 'Weird Al' Yankovic on Parody, Pastiche and becoming a Singles Artist."

19. Thomerson, "Parody as a Borrowing Practice in American Music, 1965–2015," 93.

20. Lisa Popeil, "Singers on Singing: 'Weird Al' Yankovic," *Voice Council*, August 31, 2014.

21. See Kate Heidemann, "A System for Describing Vocal Timbre in Popular Song," *A Journal of the Society for Music Theory* 22, no. 1 (March 2016).

22. Sue Shellenbarger, "Is This How You Really Talk?" *Wall Street Journal*, April 23, 2013.

23. Jesse David Fox, "How Weird Al Yankovic Removed the Misogyny of 'Blurred Lines' by Adding Grammar Lessons," *Vulture*, March 10, 2017, http://www.vulture.com/2017/03/weird-al-on-word-crimes-his-blurred-lines-parody.html.

24. Simon Frith, *Taking Popular Music Seriously: Selected Essays* (England: Ashgate, 2007), 229.

25. See Dai Griffiths, "From Lyric to Anti-lyric: Analyzing the Words in Pop Songs," in *Analyzing Popular Music*, ed. Allan F. Moore (Cambridge: Cambridge University Press, 2003), 40.

3. POLICING AND PLAYING WITH LANGUAGE

1. See John Keane, "On Tools and Language: Habermas on Work and Interaction," *New German Critique* 6 (autumn, 1975): 82–100.

2. See Jacob M. Held, ed., *Dr. Seuss and Philosophy: Oh, the Thinks You Can Think* (Lanham, MD: Rowman & Littlefield, 2011).

3. Lisa Rogak, *A Boy Named Shel: The Life and Times of Shel Silverstein* (New York: St. Martin's Press, 2007), xi, 92–93.

4. Quoted in Greg Prato, *MTV Ruled the World: The Early Years of Music Video* (N.p.: Author, 2010), 330.

5. Quoted in Christopher R. Weingarten, "'Weird Al' Yankovic Looks Back at 20 Years of 'Smells Like Nirvana," *Spin*, October 11, 2012, https://www.spin.com/2012/10/weird-al-yankovic-looks-back-at-20-years-of-smells-like-nirvana/.

6. Ibid.

7. Maria Reidelbach, *Completely MAD: A History of the Comic Book and Magazine* (Boston: Little, Brown, 1991), 20–23.

8. Ibid., 60, 65–67.

9. Ben Greenman, *Dig If You Will the Picture: Funk, Sex, God, and Genius in the Music of Prince* (New York: Holt, 2017), 58.

10. Reidelbach, *Completely MAD*, 56.

11. Ibid., 58.

12. See Lawrence J. Epstein, *The Haunted Smile: The Story of Jewish Comedians in America* (Cambridge, MA: Perseus Books, 2001).

13. Bryan Kirschen, "Multilingual Manipulation and Humor in 'I Love Lucy,'" *Hispania* 96, no. 4 (December 2013).

14. Rabin, *Weird Al: The Book*, 42.

15. Adrienne Gibbs, "Marvin Gaye's Family Wins 'Blurred Lines' Appeal; Pharrel, Robin Thicke Must Pay," *Forbes*, March 21, 2018; see also Austin Siegemund-Broka, "How Similar is 'Blurred Lines' to a 1977 Marvin Gaye Hit?" *Hollywood Reporter*, March 3, 2015.

16. Quoted in Jon Blistein, "Weird Al Shows Off Big Dictionary in Robin Thicke Parody 'Word Crimes,'" *Rolling Stone*, July 15, 2014.

17. See John Pollack, *The Pun Also Rises* (New York: Penguin, 2011), 11.

18. Ibid., 63.

19. Gordon C. F. Bearn, "The Possibility of Puns: A Defense of Derrida," *Philosophy and Literature* 19, no., 2 (October 1995).

20. "Capitol, 'Weird Al' Yankovic, 'My Bologna,'" December 24, 1979, in the Private Collection of Jon "Bermuda" Schwarz.

21. Quoted in Craig Marks and Rob Tannenbaum, *I Want My MTV: The Uncensored Story of The Music Video Revolution* (New York: Dutton, 2011), 181.

22. Ibid., 182.

23. Mathias Bonde Korsgaard, *Music Video after MTV: Audiovisual Studies, New Media, and Popular Music* (London: Routledge, 2017), 4.

24. Ben Grant, *The Aphorism and Other Short Forms* (London: Routledge, 2016), 7.

25. Petula Dvorak, "No, Those Weren't the Good Old Days," *Washington Post*, May 24, 2018.

26. William Cheng, "Taking Back the Laugh: Comedic Alibis, Funny Fails," *Critical Theory* 43 (winter 2017): 532.

4. SUGAR AND SPICE AND
EVERYTHING ALMOST NICE

1. Michael Hogan, "'Weird Al' Yancovic: Why Pop's Parody King is No Joke," *The Telegraph* (February 9, 2015).

2. Prato, *MTV Ruled the World: The Early Years of Music Video*, 327.

3. John Katsilometes, "In Five Minutes, Barry Manilow Turns Out Another Catchy Tune," *Las Vegas Sun*, August 20, 2010, https://lasvegassun.com/vegasdeluxe/2010/aug/20/five-minutes-barry-manilow-turns-out-another-catch/.

4. Quoted in Angela Watercutter, "Alpocalypse Now: 'Weird Al' Yankovic Says 'Twitter Saved My Album,'" *Wired*, June 20, 2011.

5. Rose Eveleth, "Let 'Weird' Al Yankovic Teach You How to Make a Good Parody," *Smithsonian*, October 30, 2012.

6. Linda Hutcheon, *A Theory of Parody: The Teachings of Twentieth-Century Art Forms* (New York: Methuen, 1985), 16.

7. Ibid., 44.

8. Neil Strauss, "Kurt Cobain's Downward Spiral: The Last Days of Nirvana's Leader," *Rolling Stone*, June 2, 1994.

9. "Weird Al's 'Word Crime' Accused of Being Offensive," *Talk Music to Me*, July 21, 2014, https://talkmusictome.wordpress.com/2014/07/21/weird-als-word-crime-accused-of-being-offensive/.

10. John Allison, "The Borodin Quartet: 'We Are Not Here to Perform Nice Music,'" *Telegraph*, August 29, 2018, https://www.telegraph.co.uk/culture/music/classicalmusic/11699383/The-Borodin-Quartet-We-are-not-here-to-perform-nice-music.html.

11. Joan Duncan Oliver, *The Meaning of Nice: How Compassion and Civility Can Change Your Life (and the World)* (New York: Berkley Books, 2012), xiv; and Carrie Tirado Bramen, *American Niceness: A Cultural History* (Cambridge, MA: Harvard University Press, 2017), 10.

5. THE ART OF SELF-DEPRECATION

1. Maria Reidelbach, *Completely MAD: A History of the Comic Book and Magazine* (Boston: Little, Brown, 1991), 188–89.

2. Mark Cohen, *Overweight Sensation: The Life and Comedy of Allan Sherman* (Waltham, MA: Brandeis University Press, 2013), 154.

3. See Mark E. Bleiweiss, "Self-Deprecation and the Jewish Humor of Woody Allen," in *The Films of Woody Allen: Critical Essays*, ed. Charles L. P. Silet (Lanham, MD: Scarecrow Press, 2006), 59–61; Lawrence J. Epstein, *The Haunted Smile: The Story of Jewish Comedians in America* (Cambridge, MA: Perseus Books, 2001), xiii.

4. Larry Bartleet, "50 Songs about Depression," *NME*, April 11, 2016, http://www.nme.com/list/50-songs-about-depression-1109.

5. Sarah E. Esralew, "Beating Others to the Punch: Exploring the Influence of Self-Deprecating Humor on Source Perceptions through Expectancy Violations Theory" (master's thesis, The Ohio State University, 2012), 4.

6. See Benjamin Nugent, *American Nerd: The Story of My People* (New York: Scribner, 2008), 8.

7. See Phil Ford, *Dig: Sound and Music in Hip Culture* (Oxford: Oxford University Press, 2013), 5.

8. Quoted in Nugent, *American Nerd*, 129.

9. Anastasia Salter and Bridget Blodgett, *Toxic Geek Masculinity in Media: Sexism, Trolling, and Identity Policing* (Cham, Switzerland: Palgrave Macmillan, 2017), 5.

10. Mary Bucholtz, *White Kids: Language, Race, and Styles of Youth Identity* (Cambridge: Cambridge University Press, 2011), 157–58.

11. Jessica Elizabeth Ronald, "Alternative Performances of Race and Gender in Hip-Hop Music: Nerdcore Counterculture" (master's thesis, University of Louisville, 2012), 49.

12. Ken Elpus, "Music and Theater Students Are Bullied More Than Other Students," *Medium*, August 11, 2016.

13. Mike Tunison, "The Incredibly Sad Saga of Star Wars Kid," *Daily Dot*, July 6, 2017.

14. Quoted in Kathy McCabe, "Weird Al Yankovic welcomes the Wookies and the Wonderful to his Australian polka party," News Corp Australia, October 3, 2015, https://www.news.com.au/entertainment/music/weird-al-yankovic-welcomes-the-wookies-and-the-wonderful-to-his-australian-polka-party/news-story/91cfac3a081dbd40157b15635e5b6d49.

15. Marc Silverberg, "Quest for the A Capella Major—My Friend Al," *CASA*, September 9, 2014, casa.org.

16. Tim Donnelly, "With Weird Al, Nerdy America Found Its Hero," *New York Post*, July 16, 2014.

17. Andrea Romano, "Young 'Star Wars' Fan Gets Teased at School, Weird Al Yankovic Saves the Day," *Mashable*, August 24, 2015, https://mashable.com/2015/08/24/star-wars-girl-bullied-weird-al/#LBosmGM7Csq5.

18. Todd Leopold, "Fans Backing Weird Al for Super Bowl Halftime," CNN, August 7, 2014.

19. See Henry Jenkins, "'Strangers No More, We Sing': Filking and the Social Construction of the Science Fiction," in *The Adoring Audience: Fan Culture and Popular Media*, ed. Lisa A. Lewis (London: Routledge, 1992), 214–15.

20. Quoted in Chris Dickerson, "'Weird Al' Dares to Be Stupid Live," *Charleston Daily Mail*, August 17, 2000.

21. Natalie L. Lapacek-Trout, "'Cool Buzzword' or 'Social Failure'? Examining the Nerd on Television" (master's thesis, Southern Illinois University at Edwardsville, 2014).

22. Mike Ryan, "'Weird Al' Yankovic Talks about Everything," *Screen Crush*, July 15, 2014.

6. PRESIDENT AL

1. Joseph Serna, "Man Who Says He Destroyed Trump's Walk of Fame Star Is Booked on Felony Vandalism Charge, Police Say," *Los Angeles Times*, July 25, 2018.

2. Quoted in Randall Colburn, "West Hollywood City Council Votes to Remove Trump's Walk of Fame Star," *Consequence of Sound*, August 7, 2018.

3. Michael D. Cohen and Sung Chull Kim, "A New Challenge, a New Debate," in *North Korea and Nuclear Weapons*, ed. Sung Chull Kim and Michael D. Cohen (Washington, DC: Georgetown University Press, 2017), 1.

4. Terence Roehrig, "Stability or Instability?" in *North Korea and Nuclear Weapons*, ed. Sung Chull Kim and Michael D. Cohen (Washington, DC: Georgetown University Press, 2017), 137.

5. Andrei Lankov, *The Real North Korea: Life and Politics in the Failed Stalinist Utopia* (Oxford: Oxford University Press, 2013), xiii.

6. "20 Incredible Things You Didn't Know about North Korea," *Telegraph*, May 9, 2018.

7. Danielle Fosler-Lussier, *Music in American's Cold War Diplomacy* (Berkeley: University of California Press, 2015), 11, 20.

8. Ibid., 194.

9. The Gregory Brothers and "Weird Al" Yankovic, "Bad Hombres, Nasty Women: The Presidential Debate in Song," *New York Times*, October 20, 2016.

10. Quoted in James B. Murphy, *Becoming the Beach Boys, 1961–1963* (Jefferson, NC: McFarland, 2015), 148.

11. Quoted in ibid., 149.

12. William Briggs, *How America Got its Guns: A History of the Gun Violence Crisis* (Albuquerque: University of New Mexico Press, 2017), 32.

13. Quoted in "Critics Assail Bush Veto of Waterboarding Ban," NBC News, March 8, 2008.

14. Stephen Grey, *Ghost Plane: The True Story of The CIA Torture Program* (New York: St. Martin's Press, 2006), 261–62.

15. Quoted in Ben Norton, "This Is Why They Hate Us: The Real American History neither Ted Cruz nor the New York Times Will Tell You," *Salon*, November 15, 2015.

16. Patrick J. Charles, *Armed in America: A History of Gun Rights from Colonial Militias to Concealed Carry* (Amherst, NY: Prometheus Books, 2018), 311.

17. Quoted in Briggs, *How America Got its Guns*, 127.

18. Ann Marie Kordas, *The Politics of Childhood in Cold War America* (London: Pickering & Chatto, 2013), 77.

19. Kevin Yuill and Joe Street, "Introduction," in *The Second Amendment and Gun Control: Freedom, Fear, and the American Constitution*, ed. Kevin Yuill and Joe Street (London: Routledge, 2018), 3.

20. David Hesmondhalgh, "Towards a Political Aesthetics of Music," in *The Cultural Study of Music: A Critical Introduction*, ed. Martin Clayton, Trevor Herbert, and Richard Middleton (New York: Routledge, 2012), 372.

7. THE WOKE JOKE

1. Quoted in Andy Greene, "Flashback: The Lost 'Weird Al' Song That Michael Jackson Rejected," *Rolling Stone*, November 1, 2018.

2. Jessica Elizabeth Ronald, "Alternative Performances of Race and Gender in Hip-Hop Music: Nerdcore Counterculture" (master's thesis, University of Louisville, 2012), 46.

3. Quoted in Amanda Sewell, "Nerdcore Hip-Hop," in *The Cambridge Companion to Hip-Hop*, ed. Justin A. Williams (Cambridge: Cambridge University Press, 2015), 225.

4. Lori Kendall, "'White and Nerdy': Computers, Race, and the Nerd Stereotype," *Journal of Popular Culture* 44, no. 3 (2011): 16.

5. Richard Dyer, *White* (London: Routledge, 1997), 9.

6. Mary Bucholtz, *White Kids: Language, Race, and Styles of Youth Identity* (Cambridge: Cambridge University Press, 2011), 154.

7. Anthony J. Lemelle Jr., *Black Masculinity and Sexual Politics* (New York: Routledge, 2010), 50.

8. Penny Spirou, "The Lonely Island's 'SNL Digital Short' as Music Video Parody: Building on *Saturday Night Live*'s Legacy," in *Music in Comedy Television: Notes on Laughs*, ed. Liz Giuffre and Philip Hayward (New York: Routledge, 2017), 138.

9. Quoted in "High Praise from Chamillionaire," *Yank Blog*, September 13, 2006, http://yankovic.org/blog/2006/09/13/high-praise-from-chamillionaire.

10. See Ian McCann, "From Stevie Wonder's Pastime Paradise to Coolio's Gangsta's Paradise," *Financial Times*, August 27, 2018.

11. See Charles Hiroshi Garrett, "'Pranksta Rap': Humor as Difference in Hip Hop," in *Rethinking Difference in Music Scholarship*, ed. Olivia Bloechl, Melanie Lowe, and Jeffrey Kallberg (Cambridge: Cambridge University Press, 2015), 332.

12. David Weaver-Zercher, *The Amish in the American Imagination* (Baltimore: Johns Hopkins University Press, 2001), 84, 113.

13. Josh Kun, *Audiotopia: Music, Race, and America* (Berkeley: University of California Press, 2005), 51.

14. See Emma Green, "Are Jews White?" *Atlantic*, December 5, 2016.

15. Joseph Boskin and Joseph Dorinson, "Ethnic Humor: Subversion and Survival," *American Quarterly* 37, no. 1 (spring 1985): 81.

16. Ruth R. Wisse, *No Joke: Making Jewish Humor* (Princeton, NJ: Princeton University Press, 2013), 2.

17. Benjamin Nugent, *American Nerd: The Story of My People* (New York: Scribner, 2008), 80.

18. Sarah Imhoff, *Masculinity and the Making of American Judaism* (Bloomington: Indiana University Press, 2017), 3.

19. Mike Pearl, "'Weird Al' Yankovic Sat Down with Us to Explain How He Conquered the Internet," *Vice*, July 22, 2014.

20. See Peter Jelavich, "When Are Jewish Jokes No Longer Funny? Ethnic Humour in Imperial and Republican Berlin," in *The Politics of Humour: Laughter, Inclusion, and Exclusion in the Twentieth Century*, ed. Martina Kessel and Patrick Merziger (Toronto: University of Toronto Press, 2012), 36.

21. Dave Gerrera, "A Q& A with Noodles from Offspring ahead of Vegas show," *Las Vegas Review-Journal*, July 17, 2015.

22. Rudie Obias, "9 Musicians Who Refused to Let 'Weird Al' Yankovic Parody Their Songs," Mental Floss, February 7, 2016.

23. Loren Kajikawa, "Eminem's 'My Name Is': Signifying Whiteness, Rearticulating Race," *Journal of the Society for American Music* 3, no. 3 (2009): 361.

8. JUNKING GENDER

1. Quoted in Andreana Clay, "Working Day and Night: Black Masculinity and the King of Pop," *Journal of Popular Music Studies* 23, no. 1 (2011): 10.

2. For a discussion of "ambiguity of gender," see Gavin Less, "Introduction: From Difference to Ambiguity," in *Rethinking Difference in Gender, Sexuality, and Popular Music: Theory and Politics of Ambiguity*, ed. Gavin Lee (London: Routledge, 2018), 4.

3. Quoted in Ashley Hamilton, "'Rico Suave' Singer: 'I Knew I was a Dirtbag,'" *OWN*, March 21, 2016.

4. Aída Hurtado and Mrinal Sinha, *Beyond Machismo: Intersectional Latino Masculinities* (Austin: University of Texas Press, 2016), xi.

5. Gustavo Arellano, *Taco USA: How Mexican Food Conquered America* (New York: Scribner, 2012), 17.

6. Ryan Douglass, "More Men Should Learn the Difference between Masculinity and Toxic Masculinity," *Huffington Post*, August 4, 2017, https://www.

huffpost.com/entry/the-difference-between-masculinity-and-toxic-masculinity_b_59842e3ce4b0f2c7d93f54ce.

7. See Nina Sun Eidsheim, "'The Triumph of Jimmy Scott': A Voice beyond Category," in *The Relentless Pursuit of Tone: Timbre in Popular Music*, ed. Robert Fink, Zachary Wallmark, and Melinda Latour (New York: Oxford University Press, 2018), 150–52.

8. See Diane Pecknold, "'I Wanna Play House': Configurations of Masculinity in the Nashville Sound Era," in *A Boy Named Sue: Gender and Country Music*, ed. Kristine M. McCusker and Diane Pecknold (Jackson: University Press of Mississippi, 2004), 86.

9. Quoted in Evelyn McDonald, "Joan Jett on 20 Years as Rock's Toughest Woman," *Rolling Stone*, November 13, 1997.

10. Fred Everett Maus, "Music, Gender, and Sexuality," in *The Cultural Study of Music: A Critical Introduction*, ed. Martin Clayton, Trevor Herbert, and Richard Middleton (London: Routledge, 2012), 320.

11. Helena Simonett, "Introduction," in *The Accordion in the Americas: Klezmer, Polka, Tango, Zydeco, and More!*, ed. Helena Simonett (Urbana: University of Illinois Press, 2012), 16.

12. Neda Ulaby, "'Like a Virgin' Live On," NPR, August 20, 2018.

13. See Susan McClary, *Feminine Endings: Music, Gender, and Sexuality* (Minneapolis: University of Minnesota Press, 2002), 151; and Sheila Whiteley, *Women and Popular Music: Sexuality, Identity and Subjectivity* (London: Routledge, 2000), 137.

14. Ibid., 151.

15. Quoted in Aylin Zafar, "Deconstructing Lady Gaga's 'Born This Way' Video," *Atlantic*, March 2, 2011.

16. Quoted in Mathieu Deflem, *Lady Gaga and the Sociology of Fame: The Rise of a Pop Star in an Age of Celebrity* (New York: Palgrave Macmillan, 2017), 155.

17. Quoted in ibid., 149.

18. See ibid., 173.

19. Quoted in Kembrew McLeod, "Between Rock and a Hard Place: Gender and Rock Criticism," in *Pop Music and the Press*, ed. Steve Jones (Philadelphia: Temple University Press, 2002), 97–98.

20. Brenda Johnson-Grau, "Sweet Nothings: Presentation of Women Musicians in Pop Journalism," in *Pop Music and the Press*, ed. Steve Jones (Philadelphia: Temple University Press, 2002), 205.

9. AL-MOST FAMOUS

1. Quoted in "Lady Gaga Weird Al Parody 'Empowering,'" *Rolling Stone*, May 25, 2011, https://www.rollingstone.com/music/music-news/lady-gaga-weird-al-parody-empowering-56218/.

2. Matthew R. Turner, "Performing Pop: Lady Gaga, 'Weird Al' Yankovic and Parodied Performance," in *The Performance Identities of Lady Gaga: Critical Essays*, ed. Richard J. Gray II (Jefferson, NC: McFarland, 2012), 193.

3. Stephanie Marcus, "10 Years Later, Britney Spears' Head-Shaving Moment Is Still Unforgettable," *Huffington Post*, February 17, 2017.

4. Timothy Caulfield, "The Celebrity Illusion," *Chronicle of Higher Education*, April 13, 2015.

5. David Segal, "'Weird Al': Confessions of A Parody Animal," *Washington Post*, August 17, 2003.

6. Will Hodge, "For 'Weird Al' Yankovic, 'Eat It' Was Both a Hit Song and a Creative Mantra," *Takeout*, May 23, 2018.

7. David John Ferrandino, "Irony, Mimicry, and Mockery: American Popular Music of the Late Twentieth Century" (PhD thesis, State University of New York at Buffalo), 3.

8. Fabian Holt, *Genre in Popular Music* (Chicago: University of Chicago Press, 2007), 4.

9. See David Brackett, *Categorizing Sound: Genre and Twentieth-Century Popular Music* (Berkeley: University of California Press, 2016), 2–3.

10. Quoted in Holt, *Genre in Popular Music*, 4.

11. Rebecca Mead, "All about the Hamiltons," *New Yorker*, February 2, 2015.

12. Simon Sweetman, "The Last Genre to Take Itself Too Seriously," *Off the Tracks*, June 21, 2012, http://www.stuff.co.nz/entertainment/blogs/blog-on-the-tracks/7142315/The-last-genre-to-take-itself-too-seriously.

13. See Loren Kajikawa, "Eminem's 'My Name Is': Signifying Whiteness, Rearticulating Race," *Journal of the Society for American Music* 3, no. 3 (2009): 347.

14. Quoted in Dan Aquilante, "Yanking Our Chains—Weird Al Is Serious about Silly Songs," *New York Post*, July 18, 2003.

15. Quoted in Dennis DiClaudio, "'Weird' Al Laments All the Prince Parody Songs That Will Never Exist," *AV News*, August 3, 2016.

LAST LAUGH

1. Simon Sweetman, "The 'Weird Al' Yankovic Interview," *Entertainment*, February 3, 2011.

2. Quoted in Lee Margulies, "Weird Al to Tour Despite Tragedy," *Los Angeles Times*, April 13, 2004.

INDEX

ABOUT THE AUTHOR

Lily E. Hirsch is a writer, musicologist, and visiting scholar at California State University, Bakersfield. She studied music history as an undergraduate at the University of the Pacific and earned her PhD in musicology from Duke University. She then taught as assistant professor of music at Cleveland State University. Her past books include *A Jewish Orchestra in Nazi Germany: Musical Politics and the Berlin Jewish Culture League* (2010), *Music in American Crime Prevention and Punishment* (2012), *Anneliese Landau's Life in Music: Nazi Germany to Émigré California* (2019), and, as coeditor, *Dislocated Memories: Jews, Music, and Postwar German Culture* (2014), winner of the American Musicological Society's Ruth A. Solie Award. In addition to chapters in *You Shook Me All Campaign Long*, *Rethinking Schumann*, *Sound Studies*, and the *Cambridge Companion to Jewish Music*, she has published articles in *Musical Quarterly*; *Philomusica*; the *Journal of Popular Music Studies*; *American Music*; *Music & Politics*; *Popular Music*; *Popular Music & Society*; and *Law, Culture, and the Humanities*; as well as the *Guardian*, the *Washington Post*, *A Women's Thing*, and *The Establishment*.